YO-BUB-246

LABEL INSIDE

THE
ENCYCLOPEDIA
OF DELUSIONS

A critical scrutiny of current beliefs and conventions

Complied by
RONALD DUNCAN
and
MIRANDA WESTON-SMITH

A WALLABY BOOK
Published by Simon & Schuster
NEW YORK

AZ
999
E52
1981

Copyright © 1979 this collection Pergamon Press Ltd.

All rights reserved
including the right of reproduction
in whole or in part in any form

Published by Wallaby Books
A Simon & Schuster Division of
Gulf & Western Corporation
Simon & Schuster Building
1230 Avenue of the Americas
New York, New York 10020

WALLABY and colophon are registered trademarks
of Simon & Schuster

Originally published in England in 1979
by Pergamon Press, Ltd.

First Wallaby Books Printing November 1981
10 9 8 7 6 5 4 3 2 1
Manufactured in the United States of America

Library of Congress Cataloging in Publication Data
Main entry under title:

The Encyclopedia of delusions.

   Rev. ed. of: Lying truths.
   "A Wallaby book."
   1. Errors, Popular—Addresses, essays, lectures.
I. Duncan, Ronald.   II. Weston-Smith, Miranda.
III. Lying truths.
AZ999.E52   1981   001.9'6   81-8750

ISBN 0-671-42391-6   AACR2

CALIFORNIA STATE UNIVERSITY, HAYWARD
LIBRARY

Contents

Introduction

Whereas the media spread ideas, it is the purpose of this book to disrupt them. We maintain that what we now call the climate of opinion is made up of a series of lies which are accepted without question. These beliefs are frequently called 'common sense'. They exist in education, philosophy, sociology, politics, science and art. It is easy for us to deride foolish notions that have existed in previous eras; but we do not identify or consider our own so readily.

We believe that truth exists; that it is an absolute. Knowledge is thought to be our perception of truth. Each scientific fact or observation of the universe is supposed to reveal truth, to bring its complete understanding nearer to us until eventually our discoveries will strip truth and reveal it naked before our eyes. It is possible that this fundamental concept to all our thought is completely fallacious.

Just as the horizon recedes as we approach it, and does not exist in itself, so too truth may never be unveiled, reached or apprehended.

It is not just a question that the part cannot comprehend the whole, nor the observer perceive himself observing, nor the eye see the eye. Perhaps we have erred in thinking of truth as something static, whereas it is mobile. We have considered it as an unalterable law, whereas it may consist of changeable and complementary opposites. We have tried to construct an edifice of brick out of building blocks of facts. It is possible that there are no such things as true facts, only hypotheses which are tenable for a brief time.

Could truth itself not be an image projected through the lens of our minds, with no other reality than our imagination and concepts? Has truth any home but in our minds which seek it? Though many of us no longer believe in the existence of God, we persist in our belief in truth, perhaps as a compensation or another word for the Divinity.

1

The Editors wish to stress that the contributors to this book do not necessarily share one anothers' biased opinions, nor the Editors'.

Ronald Duncan
Miranda Weston-Smith

Colin Wilson

Colin Wilson was born in Leicester in 1931, the son of a boot and shoe worker, and attended the Gateway Secondary School until the age of 16. After a year as a lab assistant, a year as a Civil Servant, and a year in the RAF, he became a tramp while working on his first novel *Ritual in the Dark* (published 1960). A period in Paris and Strasbourg was followed by a move to London, where he wrote *The Outsider* (published 1956). In 1957 he moved to Cornwall, where he has lived ever since. He has written some 40 books including 14 novels and a study called *The Occult* (1971). He is married and has four children.

Man is born free, and he is everywhere in chains

'Man is born free, and he is everywhere in chains.' The sentence has a breezy assertiveness that suggests that Rousseau would have made a fortune on Madison Avenue. He had, in fact, made a discovery that has since become the stand-by of every politician: that if you utter the word freedom with enough conviction, even in the most nonsensical context, the audience will rise to its feet and cheer.

In the case of Rousseau's most famous dictum, a moment's thought reveals the fallacy. Man is *not* born free; he is born a slave to his body, his desires, his hunger, his biological needs and his temperament—as well as to fear, illness, boredom and death. And then, for most human beings, there is a particularly irritating slavery: to the need to work for a living. This, I suspect, is what Rousseau really objected to. Like all writers—I speak from self-observation—he was a natural layabout. He objected to a social system in which there are two classes: those who can lie in bed in the morning, and those who are forced to get up to work. He objected even more to being born into the second group.

Without wishing to take up an extreme position—for there is much about Rousseau that I admire—I still feel that it is important to remember that he was basically a weak and dishonest character. This was the man who accused a maidservant of a theft that he himself had committed and caused her dismissal; who took the five children that he fathered on his mistress and dropped them in the box of the foundlings home. At the age of sixteen, he allowed himself a hypocritical conversion to Catholicism for the sake of a roof over his head and twenty francs. And in the *Confessions*, where he made a great show of frankness, he nevertheless increases his period of 'resistance' to conversion from nine days to a month.

All this is no proof that Rousseau was basically a despicable character; and in any case, there is no reason why a despicable character should be a bad philosopher. But it is as well to recognise the element of opportunism in Rousseau's thought as well as in his life. The story of his first successful literary work is a case in point. Rousseau was walking from Paris to Vincennes—to see Diderot, who was in prison—when he read in a newspaper about the prize offered by the Academy of Dijon for the best essay on the question: *Has the progress of science and art contributed to purify or corrupt morals?* He describes how he sank down under a tree, 'my head whirling in a giddiness like that of intoxication', and in two hours, worked out his famous Discourse. Inevitably, his answer was that science and art have done nothing to improve mankind—only to make it more corrupt and vicious. According to Rousseau, primitive man was innocent and happy. Then came civilisation, which spoiled everything. . . . It was not merely a silly oversimplification; it was downright untrue. Rousseau knew nothing of savages, noble or otherwise; but his own hardships and wanderings should have demonstrated to him that Nature is not a particularly kind mistress. However, Rousseau was not really concerned with facts; only with expressing his own miseries, frustrations and longings.

Let us be clear about one thing: there is no possible objection to a man of genius expressing his sense of the disparity between the ideal and the real. But the value of the exercise depends on the accuracy of his intuition of reality. Shaw pointed out that there are two types of imagination, the Romantic and the Realistic; one is the power to imagine things as they are not; the other to grasp the reality of things that are not actually present to the senses. Romantic imagination conjures up fairy-tales and ends up in bad-tempered disappointment with the real world; realistic imagination attempts to foresee realities that have not yet been experienced and strives to bring them about. Rousseau was a romantic masquerading as a realist: an opportunist, a bender of the truth, a wishful thinker with a remarkable capacity for self-deception. This weakling who found the real world too much for him used his talent for rhetoric to present romantic day-dreaming as a realistic assessment of society. His talent for day-dreaming triggered the French Revolution. And, as Lady Bracknell says, we all know what that unfortunate movement led to.

Now the real objection to romantic imagination is not so much that it creates unrealities as that it prevents us from recognising reality when we see it. It does this by blurring clear outlines, by undermining the precision of language. And this is true in the case of the famous dictum about freedom. It sounds á marvellous concept—to say that man is everywhere in chains and that he ought to be free. For there cannot be a soul on earth who would fail to agree that he is in chains of one kind or another. But what Rousseau is suggesting is that there is one simple, objective solution; overthrow 'the oppressors' and all will be well. To arms, citizens! Ecrasez l'infame! Murder the bourgeoisie and the aristocracy and the Golden Age will return. . . . And this imbecilic and poisonous simplification has produced more misery and bloodshed in two centuries than the old 'oppressors' produced in twenty.

I agree that my arguments against Rousseau have so far been negative; they have concentrated on his shortcomings.

My real objections are more positive; they are based on my sense of the true nature of freedom. And the essence of this insight is that there is no simple road to freedom, no easy way of grabbing it. Political freedom is undoubtedly a valuable ideal; but it guarantees nothing. The real destroyer of freedom is boredom and lack of purpose. Fichte put his finger on the paradox when he said: 'Frey seyn ist nichts; frey werden ist der Himmel'—'to be free is nothing; to *become* free is heavenly.' We experience the ecstasy of freedom at the moment of becoming free—when the schoolboy escapes from school, when the grown man averts danger or emergency—just as you most enjoy the warmth of the bed when you have to get up in five minutes on a freezing winter morning. On a Sunday morning, when you can stay in bed, the warmth somehow loses its charm. To appreciate freedom, we need to be *reminded* of the lack of it; the threat needs to loom above us. Remove that shadow, and the freedom quickly degenerates into a lukewarm contentment, then vanishes. Some men subject themselves to absurd dangers—climbing mountains, sailing the world in a leaky boat—to prevent the sense of freedom from falling asleep. Others are obsessively competitive, pursuing fame or sex or possessions— for the moment of triumph also brings the pure taste of freedom.

What all this amounts to is that consciousness can only be aware of freedom when it is in a peculiarly self-reflective state. Freedom can only exist in conjunction with a sense of alertness. That is to say, if you are free—physically free—but *not* aware of it, then you are not free at all.

The trouble is that there is no formula for producing this kind of awakeness. Even playing Russian roulette with a loaded revolver can become a bore, as Graham Greene discovered. I have come to believe that the answer lies in the development of a mental 'muscle' of whose existence we are hardly aware.

But one thing is clear: that anyone who thinks he has a formula for freedom is mistaken. And that the peddlers of such easy formulae are liars and crooks. If we really understood Rousseau's disservice to language and ideas, we would cease to regard him as a social reformer, and burn him in effigy every May Day. . . .

The right to work

I have the impression that the phrase 'right to work' became current at about the time the Arabs raised the price of oil and started the present trend towards mass unemployment. Every day the television newsreels seemed to be showing workers threatened with redundancy marching down Whitehall carrying placards about their 'right to work'—the same workers who, throughout the strike-bound sixties, had been equally emphatic about their right *not* to work if they felt like it. The implication seemed to be that they had some legal title or prerogative to employment, and that, if necessary, the government ought to pass laws forcing employers to offer them work. Oddly enough, no one seemed to dispute the matter; at least, as far as I know, no one stood up and made the obvious point that the 'right to work' is a grotesque piece of illogicality amounting to a confidence trick.

Nobody, of course, disputes the 'right to work' when it involves no one but yourself. We all have a perfect right to decide whether to dig the garden or go to the pub. It is when other people are concerned that the matter of my rights becomes more complicated. Chesterton mentions an anarchist who declared that, since freedom is man's inalienable right, he had a right to punch someone on the nose. Chesterton sensibly replied: 'No, your freedom ends where my nose begins.' Which is only to say that where more than one individual is concerned, the question of rights is complicated by the inconvenience they might cause one another.

We take this for granted in all matters that involve collaboration. That is, the objection of one of the partners overrules the desires of the other. If a man falls in love with a woman who finds him unattractive, then the intensity of his desire is irrelevant; she has the final say in whether they become lovers. If a businessman feels that a merger with another firm would be to their mutual advantage, then it becomes incumbent on him to

8

persuade the other man to see his point of view. The fact that he may be correct, and that a partnership may make both of them millionaires, becomes irrelevant if the other man dislikes his reasons or his face.

That is to say, that where collaboration is concerned, the right to refuse overrules all others. And since the relation between an employer and an employee *is* basically a collaboration, this seems to dispose of the notion that anyone has a right to demand work.

There have, of course, been philosophers who have suggested basic amendments to this idea of 'rights'—the most distinguished being that master of inverted logic, the Marquis de Sade. De Sade argues that since there is no God, there can be no rights either. Rights, he says in *Philosophy of the Boudoir*, were invented by the rich and powerful to protect their depredations. The poor also find it a convenient line of argument, since some of the rich are stupid enough to be taken in by it. De Sade's alternative philosophy is quite simple: a sufficiently powerful desire constitutes its own right to satisfaction. If a man wants an attractive girl, then he has a right to grab her and undress her—having first of all lured her into a position where she cannot resist. The girl's own desires are irrelevant; they would only become relevant if she had the strength to impose them on the man.

De Sade made the mistake of preaching his inverted morality instead of merely practising it; this was tantamount to public confession, so they lost no time in throwing him into jail. Later advocates of the same principle took care to camouflage it with talk of morality and altruism. De Sade had argued that there is a war between the weak and the strong, and that the weak are the natural prey of the strong. Marx also insisted there was a war, but he switched the emphasis from sex to class. If the social classes are really enemies, then the question of 'rights' vanishes; the business of the poor is to turn the tables and plunder the rich. But in case anyone should be troubled by the morality of the procedure, they should remember that the ultimate aim is the brotherhood of man and the abolition of misery. . . . So the basic principle of de Sade—that desire constitutes its own right to satisfaction—is given an air of respectability, of nonconformist piety.

De Sade and Marx would have approved the principle of the Right to Work; it would have been thoroughly in accord with their belief that only one class of society has any rights. But before socialist politicians add it to their next election manifesto, I wish they would read *The Philosophy of the Boudoir*, and see what else de Sade had in mind. . . .

Ronald Duncan

Ronald Duncan, poet and dramatist, was described by Ezra Pound as 'the lone wolf of English letters'. He is most well known for *This Way to the Tomb, The Eagle has Two Heads, Don Juan, Abelard and Heloise,* and three volumes of autobiography. He founded the Royal Court Theatre. In the last ten years he has focused his interest on science and composed the epic poem *Man.* He co-edited *The Encyclopaedia of Ignorance* with Miranda Weston-Smith.

Merit is always recognised

Only the fact that the ubiquitous editor treads on my heels, and stands on my feet, persuades me to contribute. My difficulty is to choose which hobby-horse to mount, having a whole stable of steeds rearing to charge against a contemporary fallacy.

But there is one which has angered me for forty years. It is a like a bat with nine wives. I myself have tried to shoot the bird down many times, but to no avail: the vulture still lives, flies and feeds. Not a single feather singed or fallen.

My target is the current and persistent notion that merit is inevitably, eventually recognised. This absurd belief is generally applied to creative work in the arts or sciences.

The reason why this fallacy persists is, of course, it removes any burden from the social conscience for failing to recognise and removes from people any guilt for their inability to distinguish between taste and fashion.

Of course it is true that Joseph Haydn has perforated St. Dunstans. But what happened to Michael, his father, who also wrote several dozen elegant symphonies? How many, even amongst musicians, have heard of him?

True, we kneel to Mozart now—but even he had to wait a century before London heard one of his operas and would have waited another if it hadn't been for the eccentric enthusiasm of Tommy Beecham.

And where would Schubert's Leider be had it not been for that accident when Sullivan put his hat on the top of a cupboard at a Vienna publishers and, in retrieving his bowler, brought down a sheaf of forgotten master-pieces?

'To buried merit raise the tardy bust. . . .' 'Tardy' is putting it mildly. Schubert wrote fourteen operas. Not one has yet received a professional performance in this country. Why? Would it be likely that Schubert could not write vocal music? His libretti are poor—it's true that one or two such as *Alphonso and Estrella* and *Fierabras* are little better dramatically than say *The Magic Flute*; but when in *The War of the Sexes* he used Aristophanes' story that charge is hardly valid. If a Schubert after a century and a half cannot get a toe into the Union dominated Coliseum or Royal Opera House, how many other unknown, unnamed composers endure his oblivion never to be unearthed, heard?

The myth that merit must inevitably be recognised does not bear the most casual scrutiny. Indeed the opposite is more likely to be true: mediocrity is sure of its applause and recognition while great merit will, because of its capacity to disturb, generally be overlooked.

I recall Brancusi asking me to try to get a gallery in London to show his work. I went to the Marlborough. Not interested.

In 1937 in Rapallo, Ezra Pound showed me Henri Gaudier-Brezka's notebook. It was a children's autograph album. Gaudier had kept it in the trenches in Flanders and filled it with notes and drawings. I told Pound that I thought the book should be reproduced exactly as it was. I took it to London. I showed it to Eliot. Uninterested. Still unpublished, fifty years after Gaudier's death. More interesting, to my eye, than Henry Moore's excellent Tube notebook.

Nor did my brush with Stravinsky's publishers, Boosey and Hawkes, exactly help me to believe in the recognition of merit. Stravinsky told me he would be willing to write a piece especially for a concert at the Queen's Hall. When I informed Ralph Hawkes he said: 'Stravinsky hasn't written anything interesting since *Firebird*'. This dictum of idiocy was in 1938. I then wrote to the Royal Philharmonic Orchestra. They replied. Not interested either. A question of fashion, not taste. Perhaps it is not irrelevant to recall that in Latin 'fama' means fashion or fame. Indeed, Latin identifies them.

And where would Gerard Manley Hopkins be? Still no doubt unpublished in Robert Bridge's bottom drawer if it had not been for accident rather than the Poet Laureate's recognition. The same applies to the poet, Isaac Rosenberg, still hardly known in spite of Leavis's comments. He lies beneath the rubble of Wilfred Owen and Rupert Brooke. Just as Sir Walter Raleigh, and the Earls of Rochester and Dorset were passed by.

Perhaps it takes genius alone to recognise merit in another? Certainly that was the case with Pound, when he unearthed several dozen Vivaldi concertos in a box where they had lain forgotten in the Vatican Library. Even then it took a Count Chigi to do anything about it and get this music played.

When Bach was appointed Kappelmeister at Leipzig they wrote: 'We couldn't get the composer we wanted, so we've taken on a composer called Bach'. The man they wanted, and whom Bach himself looked up to, was called Frohberger. Who plays him?

We hear of Purcell, Boyce and Morley. But Jenkins, and a dozen more Elizabethan thrushes, where are they? At the taxidermists?

I remember going round Leopold Survage's studio, or rather crawling between his thousand stacked canvasses. Survage used to share a studio with Picasso. Survage, the better painter, not draughtsman. But fashion has decreed he should remain almost totally unknown because he lacked his colleague's gift for self-publicity.

What do these bitter comments amount to? The resentment that merit goes unrecognised except by accident, circumstances little to do with the work's worth. And it is my conviction that there is more good music, or if you stake me, great music entirely unknown than there is known. My hunch is that the same applies to painting and poetry too.

How could it be otherwise when you consider the level of criticism which greets any new work? To assume that merit is recognised is the assumption that we have perceptive critics, or to give them their correct title, journalists. Turn back the pages: read their comments on *Peter Grimes*'s first performance, on *Sacre du Printemps*, on Jacob Epstein's first exhibition; on T. S. Eliot's *Waste Land*; on Verdi's *Otello*. A review of our reviews reveals that they could ignore a Rembrandt as they did a Van Gogh; that even if a 10th Beethoven Symphony were discovered they wouldn't know from the notes. To them: one criterion: the name that is known whether that is in soap flakes or contraceptives.

The fact that Brancusi and Stravinsky are now accepted does not disprove my thesis. I am concerned with the Brancusis who remain unknown, the Stravinsky who will never be heard.

One gloomy day Hermann Bondi listed the names of people to me whose scientific discoveries when submitted to the Royal Society had been ignored. They were too soon. One young man had the effrontry to describe the Heaverside Layer and its effects thirty years before it was recognised. There have been others, too many others.

Can anything be done to rectify? Possibly some sort of sieve to focus on specific eras, to re-examine some of the submitted operas, re-read some of the unpublished unperformed plays.

Mob education and mass media which lower standards and criteria perceptibly every decade only get the known names more widely known. They do nothing to assist discrimination, the ability to tell chalk from cheese. Indeed the more educated we become and the more mass media we suffer, the less chance there is of talent being recognised because the printers of textbooks, their teachers too and the compilers of T.V. programmes for the many dare not risk promoting the unknown. 'We cannot televise one of your plays', they wrote recently to an unknown dramatist, 'until you have had one televised.'

So I am sure there are still more strawberries in the hedge than ever reached a plate. We equate fashion with taste. And our worst artistic fallacy in the notion that people have any of the latter at all. Fashion is other people's bad taste.

Antony Flew

Antony Flew has been Professor of Philosophy in the University of Reading since 1973. He gained the John Locke prize (1948) and MA (1949), Oxford; D.Litt (1974), Keele. He was previously employed by the Universities of Aberdeen and Keele; and for short periods as a Visiting Professor by many universities in the USA, Canada, Australia and Malawi. He is the author of *Hume's Philosophy of Belief* (1961), *God and Philosophy* (1966), *An Introduction to Western Philosophy* (1971), *Crime or Disease?* (1973), *Thinking about Thinking* (1975), *Sociology, Equality and Education* (1976), and *A Rational Animal* (1978). Editor of *Logic and Language* (First and Second Series), *Essays in Conceptual Analysis, Body, Mind and Death*, and *Malthus on Population*. Joint Editor of *New Essays in Philosophical Theology*. Consulting editor of a forthcoming *Dictionary of Philosophy*.

He is Vice-President of the Rationalist Press Association and the Selsdon Group, Chairman of the Voluntary Euthanasia Society, and Founder Member of the Council of the National Association for Freedom.

Intended conduct and unintended consequences

But it is only for the sake of profit that any man employs a capital in the support of industry; and he will always, therefore, endeavour to employ it in the support of that industry of which the produce is likely to be of the greatest value . . . But the annual revenue of every society is always precisely equal to the exchangeable value of the whole annual produce . . . or rather is precisely the same thing with that exchangeable value. As every individual, therefore, endeavours as much as he can both to employ his capital . . . and so to direct . . . that its produce may be of the greatest value; every individual necessarily labours to render the annual revenue of the society as great as he can. He generally, indeed, neither intends to promote the public interest, nor knows how much he is promoting it . . . he is in this, as in many other cases, led by an invisible hand to promote an end which was no part of his intention. Nor is it always the worse for society that it was no part of it. By pursuing his own interest he frequently promotes that of the society more effectually than when he really intends to promote it. I have never known much good done by those who affected to trade for the public good.

Adam Smith: *The Wealth of Nations*, IV (ii)

In its most elementary and straightforward form the mistake is to assume that, if people's motives or interests point in some particular direction, then what they actually do for the fulfilment of these desires or in pursuit of these interests will in fact produce all and only those consequences which they themselves intend. What is, in the strictest sense, the fallacy here consists in moving, from propositions stating motives or interests, direct and with no further premises given, to the conclusion that these and only these motives or interests will in the event be satisfied. It is an invalid move for which you will not find in the traditional logic books any accepted name. Though common everywhere it is perhaps most frequently seen among socialists, and supporting socialist conclusions. In that context the nerve of the characteristic but invalid argument is to urge that the pursuit of private purposes can produce only private goods; whereas state institutions, established with the single-minded intention of advancing the welfare of the public, are certain, or at any rate overwhelmingly likely, so to do. Recognising that that is indeed its favourite habitat we may perhaps christen our chosen prey The Socialist Fallacy. But, if we do, then we must be on guard never to forget either that it does occur elsewhere or that there are those who contrive to reach socialist conclusions without benefit of such illicit aid.

To point, as we have done, to the most elementary and straightforward form of a mistake is always to provoke the objection that that mistake is just obvious. It is too obvious, surely, to be made by any sensible person; and hence too obvious to be practically important. For allow that some people—most people—are pursuing their own purposes and trying to secure their own interests. They are, in the jargon of the economists, 'striving to maximize their utilities'; or, in the better and one hopes immortal words of the Balzac of Broadway Mr. Damon Runyon, 'they are doing the best they can'. Yet everyone knows, of course, that sometimes what they do will be from their own standpoint counter-productive. Everyone knows too that it will have consequences, maybe very important consequences, for other people; consequences some of which were not foreseen, and therefore neither were nor could have been part of the intentions of the agent. The discovery of such counter-productive results, and the uncovering of such unintended consequences, is a large part of the work and of the charm both of the fictitious chronicler—Mr. Runyon again—and of the true historian. In another aspect it is the essential subject matter of sociology.

The fact, however, that the nerve of some fallacy becomes manifest once it has been displayed in a cool, abstract demonstration provides no sort of guarantee that everything will be equally obvious in the heat of the controversial kitchen, or when the outlines are obscured by complications. There are also other related fallacies of which it is instructive to take account at the same time.

Consider as a first concrete example our Socialist fallacy as committed in a recent exchange between Mr. Ralph Nader and Dr. Tibor Machan at Hillsdale College, Michigan. Mr. Nader had been advocating various legal controls and federal agencies, one of the stated purposes of which was, or would be, the reduction of air pollution. These policies were challenged by Dr. Machan. Mr. Nader's immediate response was the question: 'Have you ever seen anyone dying of emphysema?'

Whether or not Dr. Machan was able to answer in the affirmative, there is no doubt that Mr. Nader is at fault in simply assuming that the only possible ground for objecting to his policies must be an indifference either ignorant or callous to the incidence of emphysema. But in fact Dr. Machan dissents because he believes: either that these policies are not producing, or would not produce, the intended relief; or that, even if they are or would, that most desirable relief is being, or would be, neutralized by some more than offsetting harm. Whether or not Dr. Machan is on this particular account right, Mr. Nader is utterly wrong thus to take it as beyond dispute that his preferred policies must realize his aims; and that they could not have unforeseen, unintended and perhaps overwhelming disadvantages.

In general we all need to take to heart a great lesson Sir Karl Popper has long laboured to teach us: the lesson that the affairs of people in society are so complicated, and so impossible to predict comprehensively, that anyone genuinely wanting to do good has to proceed tentatively and piecemeal. He has to monitor progress and the lack of it every step of the way, in the never disappointed expectation that practice will reveal weaknesses and drawbacks in even the best-laid plans. And he has then to be ever ready to alter or reverse any policy, in the face of such actual failure to achieve the aims intended.

Next, consider again and now more closely that famous and never too often quoted passage serving as the text for our present sermon. Many may wish to dismiss the whole statement as unpardonably untrendy, a piece of apologetic for capitalism, and even—spare the mark!—for *laissez-faire*. All this, it can scarcely be denied, it is. But notice that and how Adam Smith (1723-1790) is completely aware that our new-labelled Socialist Fallacy is indeed a fallacy. The (private) capitalist seeking always the safest and highest return on his capital 'neither intends to promote the public interest, nor knows how much he is promoting it . . . he is in this, as in many other cases, led by an invisible hand to promote an end which was no part of his intention'. Smith adds drily: 'Nor is it always the worse for society that it was no part of it . . . I have never known much good done by those who affected to trade for the public good.'

What Smith says about the ideal capitalist in his ideal market economy applies, with appropriate alterations, equally to the ideal consumer and to the ideal seller of labour. Each in 'doing the best they can' for themselves; is led, as if 'by an invisible hand', to promote the most efficient allocation of resources for the production of whatever as consumers they all severally want and can afford. For, just as the capitalist, seeking the best return on his capital, is led to invest where there is most room for profitable investment to meet consumer demand; so the consumer, seeking the best buy for his money, is in getting it led to reward and encourage the producer doing the best overall job of satisfying such demand.

Of course, being human and therefore fallible, in real life all concerned are liable to make mistakes. From the standpoint of his own interests the actual capitalist may make a bad investment, and the actual consumer may make a bad buy. But necessarily, simply by pursuing those private interests, and without any further or public intention, they are continually being led to promote the most efficient allocation of always scarce resources; and hence the maximization of the national product. Of course, too, as the insertion of that significant phrase 'and are able to afford' will already have suggested, the observed dispersion of wealth and income within a market economy is most unlikely to correspond with anyone's ideal distribution—the distribution, that is, which it is thought ought to be enforced by the controllers of a command economy. But that raises questions which it is no business of ours here to pursue.

The prime present task is instead to underline the unsoundness of arguing: 'from propositions stating motives or interests, direct . . . to the conclusion that these and only these motives or interests will in the event be satisfied.' The Nader–Machan example emphasized the error of assuming that these will be satisfied, the Adam Smith illustration that of taking it that it will be only these. Our Socialist Fallacy can be seen in both its aspects in the following argument. Alleging that the private owners of some industry are out (only) to maximize their profits, it is concluded forthwith that it would be better both for the employees and for the customers if by nationalizing we dedicated it (wholly) to the service of the public. Like any other conclusion of a fallacious argument this may nevertheless be true, even known to be true. The fallacy lies only and precisely in the logical fact that this conclusion cannot be validly derived from that premise.[1] For we cannot infer that the private owners, however single-minded their pursuit of the greatest possible profits, are not also producing more generally valuable results. Nor can we infer that any institutions established to pursue some splendid purpose will in fact achieve what was intended.

Turn from the abstract and general to the concrete and particular: those who invest their own money, or that of the pension funds which they manage, in Marks and Spencer presumably invest in hopes of dividends and capital gains; and so far these hopes have not been disappointed. But that is no reason for refusing to recognize that that fine firm is a model employer constantly providing a remarkable proportion of the best buys for the customer. On the contrary, it is precisely this competitive achievement which alone sustains the investment record of the shares.[2] Contrast with this the story of the British consumers' cooperatives, long established for the sole purpose of serving their customers; and paying dividends to them alone. Why, we should ask, have these cooperatives, not long since, in fair and open competition, succeeded in driving all the orthodox capitalist opposition out of business?

Adam Smith says of his ideal (private) capitalist in his ideal pluralist and market economy, that 'it is only for the sake of profit that any man employs a capital in the support of industry', and that in such an economy his self-interested purposes will tend at the same time to further the public interest: 'he is in this, as in many other cases, led by an invisible hand to promote an end which was no part of his intention.' (Notice, by the way, that although Smith does not himself insert the qualification 'ideal', he is nevertheless here talking about an idealized, abstract capitalist; or, if you like, about the capitalist simply qua capitalist. Actual flesh and blood capitalists will, of course, have additional and often inhibiting purposes.[3] In the test too of his account of a pluralist and market economy Smith must be understood as developing a model for theoretical understanding— and maybe practical emulation—rather than limning a picture of any contemporary Britain.)

For saying what he did say about an invisible hand he has been subjected to a deluge of misrepresentation and uncomprehending ridicule. Above all it is suggested that he betrays social science by superstitiously postulating a divine Providence transmuting private interest into public by a miracle; that his message is that if only we *laissez-faire* God will provide. Nothing could be more wrong.

In the first place, Smith is fully persuaded that a competitive and pluralist market economy can be established and maintained only within a suitable framework of enforced laws. The state has to secure the defence of the realm, to protect the persons and property of all its citizens, to enforce contracts, to prevent the formation of monopolies, and to do well several other things which only a state can do at all.

Under these headings, by the way, Smith could consistently have allowed various measures for environmental protection and conservation. Thus, had he known what we can know about the possibilities of pollution he could, and surely would, have advocated a great extension of property rights to include more amenities, thus making polluters liable to compensate their vicitims. (Such indirect and libertarian measures might well turn out to be both more effective and less economically burdensome than direct *ad hoc* legislation enforced by ever-expanding government regulatory agencies.)

In the second place, Smith is not in fact appealing to any sort of miraculous overriding of the ordinary course of nature. On the contrary: his 'economic miracle', like others since, was to be achieved and repeated by exploiting individual self-interest for the common good. In effect Smith is insisting that, frail and fallible though we all are, there is much more chance of getting the right, wealth-creating investment if all the key decisions are made by people with strong personal interests in making these as productive as possible; and standing to suffer a correspondingly heavy personal loss if they get them wrong.

There is one fundamental, perennially ruinous trouble about having investment decisions made, not by independent capitalists or their professional agents 'in pursuit of private profit', but—as is nowadays the all too frequently preferred British alternative—'in the public interest' by civil servants, politicians and the creatures of politicians. This trouble precisely is that these last do not have—indeed are not allowed to have—any strong personal share in either the future profit or the loss. They are, however, all no less if no more inclined than other men to seek to maximize their utilities. Hence no one ought to be surprised to learn that the considerations which in practice carry most weight are advancement in the party pecking order, satisfaction of the noisiest and most easily organized pressure groups, inter-departmental rivalry, and indeed almost everything else but the maximization of the national wealth and income.[4]

Third, and most to the present point, Smith's reference here to 'an invisible hand' is no lapse into superstition. It signifies progress in social science, not betrayal. For he is contending that 'in this, as in many other cases', a social phenomenon is the unintended consequence of intended action, and he gives what could be a text-book example of how the social scientist discovers and displays the mechanisms involved. Here the social phenomenon is the institution of a capital market. The 'many other cases' to which Smith refers include, not only several further economic phenomena discussed elsewhere in *The Wealth of Nations* (1776), but also the other fundamental social institutions investigated by his own older friend the philosopher and historian Bernard Mandeville (1676-1733). Following the superficially mischievous yet ultimately sober author of *The Fable of the Bees* (1728), David Hume (1711-76), and later followed by such other Scottish founding fathers of social science as Adam Ferguson, Hume in *A Treatise of Human Nature* (1739-40) excogitated seminal arguments to show that the first origin of promising, of languages in general, and of the state itself, neither was nor could have been in either individual or collective planning. As Ferguson was later to write in *An Essay on the History of Civil Society* (1767), men 'stumble upon establishments, which are indeed the result of human action, but not the execution of any human design'.

It is one of the many paradoxes of the history of thought that developments just described occurred first in the fields of the human rather than of the natural and biological sciences. (Karl Marx, incidentally, knew and respected the work of some of these Scottish founding fathers; which is more than can be said for most of the other leading sociological thinkers of the 1800s.) What these great Scots were finding was that and how certain phenomena looking as if they must have been the products of design instead could—sometimes indeed must—have been the outcome of non-intentional processes. Just as, in the following century, Charles Darwin argued for the origin of the species by natural selection; so they too earlier—in what may perhaps be a still more sensitive area—contended for natural evolution as opposed to special creation. Those shadowy demigods and mythical culture heroes whose existence had once been postulated as single-handed inventors and wholesale creators of social institutions and political constitutions now began to be replaced by long stories of piecemeal historical development or revealing accounts of the operations of mechanisms blind and undesigned.

Lycurgus, for instance, had been postulated as the creator of the constitution of Sparta; a constitution much admired by Plato and by his laconizing contemporaries, as well as by many later generations of authoritarian élitists. We may now see this and similar postulations as instances of the converse of our Socialist Fallacy. That, it should be recalled, 'consists in moving, from propositions stating motives or interests, direct and with no further premises given, to the conclusion that these and only these motives or interests will in the event be satisfied'. This, which I now with a parallel abusiveness christen The Creationist Fallacy, involves the reverse move. It consists in inferring, from the proposition that some institution or constitution might appear to have been established in order to satisfy certain interests or to achieve certain ends, immediately to the conclusion that—to use Ferguson's word—these 'establishments' were in fact originally created with these ends in view, either by an individual planner or by a collective of planners. Because, for instance, any halfway tolerable political order can be seen as involving a measure of mutually beneficial give and take among all the participants, it is immediately inferred that every legitimate state in fact must have originated in some kind of universal social contract between all concerned—with everyone having their own several benefits and costs in mind.[5]

The Creationist Fallacy is today neither so prevalent nor so important as the Socialist. It is not so prevalent because plain unacademic people are more concerned about present and future effects than past origins. Yet it is found. For this is the nerve of the argument wherever people insist that some seemingly purposive performance not merely may but must have been intended; wherever, for instance, anyone without sufficient evidence remains invincibly persuaded that some generally anonymous 'they' are scheming to do down us, and in particular him.

That last remark is a cue for someone to say: 'Ah, the Conspiracy Theory'. It is in both cases important, and rather rare, to recognize that to utter the phrases 'Creationist Fallacy' or 'Conspiracy Theory' is not in itself to refute any conclusion previously drawn. For there actually are both creations and conspiracies. No one, therefore, has the right to dismiss unheard every suggestion that what is under consideration may in fact have been produced by one or the other. This is, once it has been clearly said, obvious. Yet many having learnt to speak of the Conspiracy Theory, like others who during the Vietnam War heard tell of the Domino Theory, have made, and made, and made again this obvious mistake. Thus in the USA during the academic year 1970/1 I must have had a dozen or more conversations with philosophical colleagues, conversations in which my observation that an American withdrawal from Vietnam would be followed by the fall of Laos and Cambodia, and increased pressure on Thailand and Malaysia, met with those comfortable words: 'Ah, the Domino Theory'. No one thereafter believed it necessary to vouchsafe anything else in rebuttal of a forecast which has, in the event, proved all too true.

What is necessarily wrong with both the Creationist and Socialist Fallacy, as with all other fallacies, is not the actual conclusion drawn, but the argument through which that conclusion is reached. The conclusion thus illegitimately recommended may just happen to be true, and we may even have sufficient independent grounds for holding this to be so. But what we cannot say is that, given only the premise or premises as offered, then that conclusion must follow. In the stricter sense in which it is a semi-technical logician's term of art, not a superfluous synonym for 'error' or 'misconception', that is what the word 'fallacy' by definition means.

The crux here can be illuminated by contemplating the most powerful and pervasive of all British social institutions, labour unions. Seeing these today to be concerned primarily to secure for their members higher pay for shorter hours, someone might infer that they must originally have been set up with that main aim in mind, presumably by some sort of contract among the founders. This argument would be unsound. It constitutes a flagrant specimen of a delinquent class, The Creationist Fallacy. Yet its conclusion is substantially true; and, by all acquainted with the brave saga of George Loveless and his companions,[6] known to be so.

Again, knowing that the British labour unions like their opposite numbers in other countries were thus originally founded with the purposes of raising wages and bettering conditions of work, and knowing too that their own spokesmen with apparent sincerity always proclaim that these are the continuing prime objects, it may be tempting immediately to infer that these intended consequences have been and are being achieved. But, as by now every reader will easily recognize, this argument would be unsound. It constitutes an equally flagrant specimen of another delinquent class, The Socialist Fallacy.

Is the conclusion, as before, substantially true nevertheless? Almost everyone seems to think so. Nor would any seeker of popularity dare to say that it is not. Certainly too it would be hard to deny that some unions are extremely successful in getting more for their members than is got by people with comparable skills belonging to other unions or to no union at all. It is enough to mention the notorious three or fourfold difference in pay between the highly unionized (and all white and all male) printers in Fleet Street and the largely ununionized (and almost all female) copy typists around and about. These last, at least given the new technology, easily could, and given a free labour market would, replace some of those male chauvinist and labour monopolist printers.

Suppose next that we emphasize the word 'British', and attempt comparisons with our more successful neighbours on the European continent. Then the affirmative answer is no longer so inevitable. For now we have to weigh the economic costs of the inordinate overmanning so triumphantly maintained by these British unions. We have to put in the scales vindictive and immensely burdensome taxes on both wealth and income, massive and malign nationalizations, vast and open-ended subsidies for inefficient and declining industries. For it is primarily unions which can and do effectively demand such 'sweeteners' from governments; and all these very bitter 'sweeteners' must surely carry some share of discredit for the shameful facts that, in the years since World War II, average real wages in Britain have been declining relative to those in almost all the other eight members of the EEC; and that, but for the free enterprise bonanza of North Sea oil, they might by now have plummeted absolutely.

We are, at last, in position to attack a third and final fallacy. This consists in arguing that, because all human social institutions have to be generated by nothing else but human activity, therefore it must be possible for us, acting collectively, to reshape any or all of these institutions so as the better to accord with whatever may be or become our hearts' desires. This is a kind of thinking which F. A. Hayek traces back to René Descartes (1596-1650), and to which Hayek now applies the hostile label 'constructivistic'.[7] To anyone who has hauled on board the several points made earlier about the unintended consequences of intended action, it will be instantly obvious that the constructivistic conclusion is not guaranteed.

The crux is that what truly is brought about by nothing else but human activity is not by that token the intended consequence of that activity; and, *a fortiori*, what is in fact brought about by what are not necessarily (and are not often in fact) the consciously coordinated activities of large numbers of people, is not by the same token the intended (and presumably therefore readily restructurable) product of collective intention and decision. That first summary statement constitutes, perhaps, an awkward mouthful. But both its meaning and its truth become manifest in application to the relatively uncontroversial and unpolitical case of language.

Beyond question every natural language is a social product, the offspring of nothing else but human activity. It is even more certain that no natural language either was or could have been the intended product of intended action. (Indeed the point of inserting the qualification 'natural' exactly is to rule out such 'artificial languages' as chess or chemical notation, by definition.) We are, therefore, by no means entitled to infer that any society which has produced its own natural language could, acting in a coordinated and collective way, create some new and vastly improved language, designed and better designed to fulfil the designs of an actual controlling élite of planners, politicians or whoever else.

In fact every natural language is an instrument of enormous richness and subtlety. Even the most careful and competent masters of these instruments would fail a challenge to provide explicit accounts of all the refinements of distinction which they themselves so regularly and so fruitfully employ. The best demonstration of this truth is that masterpiece of linguistic philosophy, John Austin's methodological manifesto 'A Plea for Excuses'.[8]

In that characteristically delightful essay Austin examines the case of *Regina* v. *Finney*, explicating a few of the many ordinarily available, almost always implicit, untechnical distinctions. These in this particular case were all being collapsed and confounded by both counsel and the learned judge; whereas 'Finney, by contrast, stands out as an evident master of the Queen's English'.[9] Austin himself draws the presently relevant moral, albeit not quite in Hayekian terms. Any natural language, like anything human, is bound to be imperfect. It is open, therefore, to change for the better; or—for that matter—for the worse. But if reform really is to improve and to enrich, then it has to begin with the most thorough and open-minded review of all existing strengths and weaknesses; and then to make sure progress piecemeal. It cannot proceed wholesale, restarting everything anew from the ground up.

To Descartes, however, it seemed that this revolutionary and Utopian approach must everywhere be best[10]; and he himself attempted—for, he claimed, himself alone—a constructivistic reconstruction of all knowledge. Thus in Part II of the *Discourse* (1637), his first shattering publication, where 'that French cavalier stepped forward with so bold a stride', he observes that things are (almost) always better when their design and construction has been from the beginning the work of a single master. So Descartes goes on to launch his own programme of systematic doubt, in order to build, on the basis of whatever this Cartesian bulldozer cannot raze, a really secure structure of unshakeable knowledge. 'My design', his modest explanation runs, 'has never extended beyond trying to reform my own opinions and to build on a foundation which is entirely my own'. Only that; and nothing more!

It was left to successors in later centuries to press this constructivistic Cartesian approach into the field of social policy. Voltaire, for instance, expressed the whole spirit of the French Enlightenment when in the article on 'Law' in the great *Encyclopaedia* he wrote: 'if you want good laws, burn those you have and make yourselves new ones'. It was in this same spirit that the men of 1789 attempted to live each day as if their first.

To some readers such phrases may recall the student *émeutes* of 1968. (It was, surely, the Prophet Marx who allowed that history did repeat itself—'only the second time as farce'.) For us there is no better way to conclude than by savouring a paradox. It is notorious that an altogether disproportionate number of the ultras of that fun revolution hailed from departments of sociology; a subject which as a science has been defined as the study of the unintended consequences of intended action. Had they really taken to heart the profounder lessons of the subject they were supposed to be studying, then they scarcely could have accepted as scientific Radical programmes for the total planned reconstruction of society, 'from the ground up'.

References

1. I think here of one outrageous argument, without which no Labour Party conference would be complete. It begins with the self-contradictory proposition that such and such an industry is dominated by three or four (private perhaps even multi-national)

monopolies. It rushes directly to the applauded conclusion that that industry is overripe for nationalization: to be made, that is, what on the speaker's own account it now both is and is not, a (state) monopoly.

2. The story is told, *ben trovato*, although surely this is too good to be true, that during the Prague Spring of 1968 and before the reconquest by the tanks of imperial 'normalization' some student demonstrators chanted the reactionary slogan: 'We want Marks and Spencers, not Marx and Engels!'

3. See, for instance, my discussion of 'The Profit Motive' in *Ethics* (Chicago) for July 1976, pp. 312-22.

4. See, for instance, Frank Broadway on *Upper Clyde Shipbuilders* and Colin Jones on *The £300,000 Job* (London: Centre for Policy Studies, 1976 and 1977, respectively).

5. British readers may need to be reminded that in the long history of this notion, stretching back at least as far as Plato and his immediate predecessors, the social contract was always construed as involving the free adherence of every full citizen or full citizen to be. It was an unlovely innovation in the unlovely corporativist Britain of the seventies to apply such a time-hallowed expression to an unwritten backstairs deal between the bosses of the main labour unions and the leaders of the particular political party which is their creature.

6. The Tolpuddle Martyrs.

7. See his *New Studies in Philosophy, Politics, Economics and the History of Ideas* (London: Routledge and Kegan Paul, 1978), Chapter I.

8. In his *Philosophical Papers* (Oxford: Clarendon, 1961).

9. Ibid., p. 145.

10. For the history of these two by now almost inseparable ideas see Melvin Lasky *Utopia and Revolution* (London: Macmillan, 1976).

Miranda Weston-Smith

Miranda Weston-Smith co-edited *The Encyclopaedia of Ignorance* with Ronald Duncan. She is the granddaughter of the great cosmologist E. A. Milne.

Mass media assist communication

To refute the fallacy that mass media assist communication it is necessary to ask what it is one wants communicated? Is it the football and cricket results? Whose baby has just been snatched from its pram? The demands of Transport House and squabbles over differentials? Or is it remotely possible that some people might be interested in the news that a new particle has been discovered or that Graham Sutherland has completed a new portrait?

The media is not dilatory in passing on gossip about the Test Matches or 'industrial action'. After all this is precisely the kind of news which the majority regards as important. Neither science nor art receives the same amount of attention. Of what consequence is this to the Shop Floor Steward? He may take advantage of technology and science when he switches on his television but there his interest ends. These topics are of interest to a minority who are persecuted by being ignored. The function of mass media is to cater for the demands of the masses or as a newspaper once aptly mis-printed 'them asses'. The notion therefore that the mass media could ever communicate news of any enduring value is directly in conflict with its function.

Civilisation has been built on the discoveries and inventions of a handful of people. The artists who have made our heritage would not fill a double decker bus. Perhaps we have come to the end of the road and it is not considered necessary to continue its construction? If that is the case then it is of no consequence that the public remains uninformed on new discoveries in science or achievements in art.

Never before has so much been communicated. Not only do the BBC radio and television and ITV television buzz with trivia but there is also a host of local radio stations pumping out pop-music and jazz interrupted by advertisements for hair shampoos.

The chance of any piece of news of enduring importance being given is therefore infinitesimally small. And if it were mentioned how could it be expected either to impinge on its audience, read with the same monotonous Anglo-American accent, or to survive the mire of trivia in which it is set? News of the inflammable condition in Angola or Rhodesia, or the death of Benjamin Britten is squeezed between the football results. The distinction in relative significance eludes the editor of the news.

Now that science and medicine are progressing so rapidly how unfortunate it must be that research teams at different universities may discover that they have both been engaged on exactly the same problem. A useful collaboration is wasted. An announcement in an improvement in treatment or new cure of some disease can go unheard by a suffering patient or a doctor. But it is not only in science but also in art that this isolation of talent occurs. How many Bachs, Haydns or Mozarts have been discovered and encouraged by the BBC? The Court of the Wittlebachs gave more opportunity for 'expression' than the mass media ever have.

Does a 'magazine' such as *Kaleidoscope* compare with or replace Addison's *Spectator*? How many new T. S. Eliots, Ezra Pounds or Wyndham Lewises can the BBC and ITV claim to have discovered? Will any of their protegés develop into a Stravinsky or a Prokofiev? The media have not one quarter of the conviction of a Diaghilev in promoting what will endure in art. The editor's concern is not to produce a programme which might possibly stimulate a handful of people creatively, but rather in securing a *large* enough audience to ensure that the programme is continued and obtains high rating.

What qualifications are required by a news editor whose purpose is to communicate matters of importance? How many times has Henry Moore or Graham Greene been asked to edit an arts programme? The interests and controversies of a creative artist are far more likely to be in line with other artists than the magazine-knowledge of a BBC or ITV editor. To decide what is communicated is to direct and develop interests and shape the future.

Brian Crozier

Brian Crozier reported situations of violence in various countries for Reuters, *The Economist* and other organizations, then pioneered the systematic study of rebellions and insurgencies with his first book, *The Rebels* (1960). In 1970, with Professor Leonard Schapiro, Sir Robert Thompson and others, he founded the Institute for the Study of Conflict, the first privately financed research centre specializing in security problems the world over. A recognized authority on Communism, he is the author of *The Future of Communist Power* (1970; in USA, *Since Stalin*), *A Theory of Conflict* and other works, including major biographies of Franco, de Gaulle and Chiang Kai-shek. His latest work, *Strategy of Survival* (1978), is a survey of the Third World War, better known as 'the Cold War'.

The Cold War is over

The Cold War is the name we have given to the contest between the two giant constellations of power, the spreading Muscovite empire and the North Atlantic coalition, which started, roughly speaking, in 1945 and ended, roughly speaking, the other day.

From the dust-jacket of
The Cold War as History,
by Louis J. Halle (London, 1967)

Peaceful co-existence does not signify the end of the struggle between the two world social systems. The struggle will continue . . . until the complete and final victory of Communism on a world scale. *Pravda*, 22 August 1973

It may seem unsatisfactory to quote from a dust-jacket rather than from the book it contains, but the book itself nowhere offers as succinct a statement of its underlying assumption, which is that the Cold War ended in the 1960s. Professor Halle, a lucid and elegant stylist and a former senior official of the US Department of State, declared in his Preface that it was his ambition to describe the Cold War, which belonged to our present, much as Thucydides described the Peloponnesian War, which belonged to his own present. The quotation from *Pravda* may well cause legitimate doubts to arise: if the struggle is to continue until Communism wins, can the Cold War really have ended in the 1960s?

Nor should the *Pravda* quotation be dismissed as mere newspaper talk or as an isolated case. *Pravda* is the daily organ of the Communist Party of the Soviet Union (CPSU), which has the monopoly of power in that country, and nothing appears in it that is not approved by the Party. I have chosen this particular quotation because it has the merit of absolute brevity and clarity, but the views it expressed represent official doctrine and are repeated several times a year in speeches by Soviet leaders or in official statements.

It is essential to deal with the terms 'Cold War' and 'peaceful co-existence' together and to grasp their *Soviet* connotations. To the Western reader, there is a glaring contradiction between the assumption that the Cold War is over and repeated statements from the Soviet side that the ideological struggle will go on until Communism has triumphed. But from the Soviet standpoint, there is no contradiction, because the terms are essentially synonymous; or, to be more accurate, 'Cold War' and 'peaceful co-existence' are obverse or complementary aspects of the same phenomenon. There has been a general failure on the part of Western politicians and commentators to grasp the ideological semantics of the great confrontation of our time. Hence the widely accepted fallacy that the Cold War is over. From the Soviet point of view, it is not over; it is merely called 'peaceful co-existence'.

The twin fallacy on the Western side is that 'peaceful co-existence' implies a spirit of 'live and let live', with the end of the ideological struggle between 'Communism' and 'Capitalism' and 'Imperialism'. Nothing could be further from the truth, and Western statesmen, such as President Giscard d'Estaing, who have publicly expressed this assumption have invariably been rudely rebuked by the Soviet leaders. The example of the French president is particularly illuminating, for it was made in the context of 'détente' (which to Western minds implies something akin to peaceful co-existence). On his visit to Moscow in October 1975, the French Head of State publicly interpreted détente as implying a relaxation of ideological tensions; his host, Leonid Brezhnev, snubbed him by cancelling part of the arranged programme. The notion that 'détente' implies any relaxation of anti-Western activities has been denounced repeatedly in Moscow. Instead, the struggle goes on: the Russians call it peaceful co-existence, and we call it (or rather, used to call it) the Cold War.

It is important to remember that 'Cold War' is a Western coinage, while 'peaceful co-existence' was coined in the USSR. It was Bernard Baruch, the American financier and presidential adviser, who first used the words 'Cold War' during a congressional debate in 1947. The 1975 *Encyclopaedia Britannica* correctly defines it as 'denoting the open yet restricted rivalry that developed after World War II between the United States and Soviet Union and their respective allies, a war fought on political and economic fronts, with limited recourse to weapons, largely because of fear of a nuclear holocaust'.

As such, 'Cold War' was a useful concept, describing the sum total of hostile words and deeds, falling short of armed hostilities, on either side of the Iron Curtain. The *Encyclopaedia Britannica* definition accurately describes the Western understanding of the term, which is seen as applying to a two-way struggle, as in normal wars. This definition of the term, however, has never been current usage in the USSR. On the Soviet side, as Sir William Hayter, a former British ambassador to Moscow explained in a symposium, *The Cold War* edited by Evan Luard (London, 1964), to which I also contributed, 'Cold War' means attacks on or. criticisms of the Soviet Union and its allies and nothing else. It is thus seen as a *one-way* process, with the West as the aggressor. What the Russians do to the West is covered, and sanctified, by 'peaceful co-existence'.

That is why the Russians have consistently called for an end to the Cold War, and for peaceful co-existence. When the West stopped systematically attacking or criticising the Soviet regime at the official level, Professor Halle and others assumed the Cold War was over, and it soon became fashionable to accept that assumption. This suited the Soviet side admirably, because it was open to the Soviet spokesmen and commentators to accuse anybody in the West who criticise shortcomings in the Soviet regime of being 'Cold War warriors', or 'hankering for a return to the Cold War'. Thus anybody who criticises the detention of Soviet dissidents in psychiatric wards or who draws attention to the excessive Soviet expenditure on armaments, is dismissed as a 'Cold War warrior'. It goes without saying that the term has repeatedly been applied to myself.

It follows that Western leaders or writers who state their belief that the Cold War is over are using the term in its Soviet not its Western connotation. For on the Soviet side, anti-Western activities have *increased* during the period of 'détente', that is, since Professor Halle attempted to write the history of the Cold War on the assumption that it was over. Examples of intensified anti-Western activity from the USSR will be given later in this article. At this point, however, it is necessary to look more closely at the concept of peaceful co-existence.

From Chicherin to Khrushchev

Lenin and his associates confidently expected that their Bolshevik Revolution would be followed in quick sequence by similar revolutions in the industrialised countries of Western Europe. When it became clear that this was not going to happen, Lenin modified the policy of the Third

International (Comintern) to one of seeking alliances of convenience (united fronts) with 'bourgeois' parties in a more or less prolonged interim period during which treaties could be signed and trade relations cultivated with the capitalist powers. He did not, in fact, expect this period to be prolonged, for as he put it, 'existence side by side' was bound to end in 'most horrible collisions' between the Soviet Republics and the 'imperialist States', with the triumph of one side or the other.

Lenin's Commissar for Foreign Affairs, Georgy Vassilievich Chicherin (1872-1936) was apparently the first to use the term 'peaceful co-existence' to describe the interim period Lenin had in mind. The point to note is that the adoption of co-existence in the 1920s did not imply that the dogma of inevitable armed conflict between the two camps was being abandoned.

Three decades later, the expected revolutions had still not broken out—at least, not in the advanced countries, as Marx and Lenin had expected. There had been brief upheavals at the end of the First World War in Germany and Hungary and some unrest elsewhere, but not on the anticipated scale. Communist regimes had been imposed on Eastern Europe, with Yugoslavia as a special case; and Communism of a different kind had come to China as a result of war and a peasant insurrection which did not conform to the Marxist-Leninist prescription. Was the dogma in need of revision?

Nikita Khrushchev, who had come out on top in the power struggle that followed Stalin's death in 1953, decided that it did. The main reason for his decision was undoubtedly the advent of nuclear weapons, which made the prospect of war one that could no longer be faced with equanimity. During the eventful 20th Congress of the CPSU in February 1956, he declared that war was 'no longer fatally inevitable' between the two camps. But he did not discard the doctrine of the two camps and made it clear that the struggle between Communism ('the Socialist camp') and the pluralist democracies ('the imperialist camp') would continue until the inevitable final victory of the former.

It should be noted that the 20th Congress also abandoned or modified other cherished Marxist-Leninist dogmas, including the inevitability of violence in achieving State power for Communist Parties, and Moscow's claim to be the one and only centre of the world Communist movement. Khrushchev laid down that in certain circumstances, the transition to socialism might be achieved by parliamentary means. It was this last doctrinal change that weakened Moscow's claim to be centre of the Communist world (which was never formally abandoned). Palmiro Togliatti, leader of the Italian Communist Party (PCI)—the largest outside the Communist countries—declared in an interview that 'the Soviet model cannot and should not any longer be obligatory' as far as Communist parties were concerned. In this famous interview, which appeared in his party's paper *L'Unità* on 17 June 1956, Togliatti went on to say that 'the whole system is becoming polycentric'. The idea of 'different roads to socialism' has been known ever since as 'polycentrism'.

Khrushchev had shattered both Stalin's reputation as an idol and the myth of the infallibility of Communist dogma. The consequences included the upheavals in Poland and especially Hungary later that year, and an increasing tendency in China to challenge the leadership of the Soviet Union in the world Communist movement. He therefore sought to restore the authority which he himself had weakened (although some weakening was inherent in the fact that history was not doing what had been expected of it). He convened a great conference of 81 Communist parties, including that of the Chinese People's Republic, which met in Moscow in November and December 1960.

This was an important, even momentous event, for it was the last time the Soviet and Chinese Communist Parties jointly endorsed a doctrinal statement. The Final Declaration of the 1960 conference, which ran to 15,000 words, had this to say about 'peaceful co-existence':

> Co-existence between States of differing social systems is a form of class struggle between socialism and capitalism. . . . (It) does not mean a reconciliation between the socialist and bourgeois ideologies . . . it implies an intensification of the struggle.

This was a far cry indeed from the 'Five Principles of Peaceful Co-existence' (also known as the Panch Sila), jointly endorsed by China and India in 1954, and which are perhaps worth recalling here, for there is no doubt that many people assimilate the peaceful co-existence of the Five Principles with Moscow's version: they have nothing in common. the Five Principles were:

1. Mutual respect for each other's territorial integrity and sovereignty.
2. Mutual non-aggression.
3. Mutual non-interference in each other's affairs.
4. Equality and mutual benefit.
5. Peaceful co-existence.

The Five Principles, incidentally, did not save India from a Chinese armed attack in 1962, but that is a different story.

The new twist given to 'peaceful co-existence' in the 1960 Declaration is crucial, for it demonstrates that to the Russians, the term means almost exactly the opposite to its normal meaning to uninitiated Western readers.

The Declaration went on to call upon Communists and their sympathisers in the newly-independent countries to work from within to make their governments adopt Communist-type policies. To this end, they were to form a 'national-democratic-front', rid themselves of foreign companies, liquidate the 'remnants and survivals of feudalism' (meaning, for instance, religious observance, tribal customs, or the power of the local chiefs), forge special links with the Communist countries and embark on the path of 'non-capitalist development'.

Before turning from the theory to the practice of peaceful co-existence, it may be appropriate to quote further Soviet authorities on the subject. One is Brezhnev, no less, who in recent years has added the titles of President and Commander-in-Chief to that of head of the Communist Party—his real power base. Welcoming Fidel Castro of Cuba at a dinner in Moscow on 27 June 1972, Brezhnev had this to say:

While pressing for the assertion of the principle of peaceful co-existence, we realise that successes in this important matter in no way signify the possibility of weakening the ideological struggle.

On the contrary, we should be prepared for an intensification of this struggle and for it becoming an increasingly acute form of the struggle between the two social systems. We have no doubt as to the outcome of this struggle, because the truth of history and the objective laws of social development are on our side.

In a book entitled *Peaceful Co-existence and the Revolutionary Process*, a less well-known Party ideologist named V. N. Egorov went further and argued that the policy of peaceful co-existence as practised by socialist countries 'promotes the development and intensification of the world revolutionary processes, and the development of both peaceful and non-peaceful forms of the struggle'.

Are these strong words just words? Unfortunately not, as the facts of recent history demonstrate.

The Third World War

In *The Cold War as History*, from which I quoted at the beginning of this article, Halle described the Cold War as, in effect, World War III, although it differed from previous world wars in that there had been no direct hostilities between the major powers. This was a correct assessment. His mistake lay in the supposition that it had ended, a conclusion drawn largely from the temporary bonhomie generated by Khrushchev's visit to the United States. 'By the middle of the 1960s,' he writes, 'both sides in the original Cold War were disposed to discontinue the contest and to seek the development of more rewarding relations between them. Although far from ready to swear friendship, the powers that had been led by Moscow and those that had been led by Washington were ready to make peace.'

Let me now recount, in brief summary, what has actually happened since those wishful words were written.

Khrushchev was overthrown by a 'palace revolution' in October 1964, and it is now clear that one of the things his colleagues held against him was the passivity of his last two years in power, after the Cuban missiles crisis of 1962. He had, for instance, discontinued aid to left-wing groups in Laos and the Congo (now Zaïre) and in general kept out of trouble. As soon as he was out of the way, the new team (Brezhnev and Kosygin) took these crucial decisions:

1. To give all-out aid to North Vietnam, especially in modern weapons.
2. To overtake the United States in strategic weapons systems.
3. To create the biggest Navy and support fleet in the world.

Eleven years later, all three of these ambitious aims had been achieved:

1. Armed overwhelmingly with Soviet weapons and equipment, the North Vietnamese forces had completed their conquest of South Vietnam, with the total defeat of the Americans and their South Vietnamese allies.
2. The Russians had caught up with the Americans in strategic weapons systems, and had even, in the view of some specialists, achieved a slight margin of superiority.
3. The Soviet Navy, which was almost negligible strategically in 1964, had become by 1975 the most powerful fleet in the world. There had been a parallel expansion of the merchant and fishing fleets, which provided a variety of auxiliary services, including electronic surveillance.

The past decade in particular has seen both increased and accelerating Soviet pressures on a world scale in what I term for convenience the 'Target Area'—that is, at any time, all countries that have not yet come under Soviet domination. During this period, the Soviet Union has also suffered reverses, some of them major. But the point is that the strategic drive goes on, regardless of setbacks. Here is a brief chronology:

1968. Czechoslovakia occupied by Warsaw Pact forces. End of Dubcek's experiment of 'Communism with a human face'. Ten years later, occupation continues. Soviet economic blockade of Cuba forces Castro into subservience. Secret agreement brings Cuban Intelligence system (DGI) under Soviet KGB's control. Satellisation of Cuba consolidated over next two years.

1971. Moscow-backed revolutionary attempt fails in Mexico. Moscow-backed *coup* in Sudan collapses. Soviet Friendship treaties with Egypt and India (a stage in attempted satellisation). Britain expels 105 Soviet spies.

1970-73. Signing and ratification of Bonn–Moscow and Bonn–Warsaw treaties, Four-Power agreement on Berlin and East–West German treaty, thereby gaining recognition for East German regime and important facilities in West Berlin.

1972. Soviet Friendship treaty with Iraq. Egypt expels 17,000 Soviet advisers.

1973. Allende regime in Chile (which had become main centre for Cuban and Soviet subversion in Latin America) overthrown.

1974. Soviet Friendship treaty with Somalia, by then a satellite. Soviet hold on South Yemen consolidated. Soviet involvement in armed forces *coup* in Portugal. Soviet-trained guerrillas take over in Angola, Mozambique and Portuguese Guinea. Soviet military aid pact with Afghanistan.

1975. Communist *coup* foiled in Portugal. Soviet-backed insurgents defeated in Oman. Soviet-backed North Vietnamese complete conquest of South Vietnam.

1976. Soviet-backed Cuban expedition conquers most of Angola. Huge Soviet arms deal with Libya.

1977. Soviet arms deal with Ethiopia. Somalia expels Russians. In subsequent war between the two countries, the USSR sides with Ethiopia: Somalia defeated.

1978. Pro-Soviet *coup* in Afghanistan.

If such events are taken in isolation, their real meaning is elusive. In conjunction, they add up to so many 'battles' in the Third World War, which Professor Halle rightly equated with the Cold War. But there is much more to it than even the events I have briefly recalled. Since the Cold War was supposed to be over, the enormous apparatus of the Soviet KGB and of the International Department of the CPSU's Central Committee has been deployed on an ever-growing scale, along with the trade union organisation's own International Department and the vast propaganda machine controlled from Moscow.

The revelations of Soviet defectors over the past few years have thrown fresh light on these activities. It is now known that the Central Committee's International Department is the direct successor to Lenin's old Comintern, which Stalin formally 'dissolved' in 1943 to reassure his wartime allies. Its head, Boris Ponomarev, was formerly a member of the Comintern's Executive Committee and is now responsible for Soviet subversion all over the world. Among other activities, the International Department recruits potential terrorists and guerrilla fighters for special training in the Soviet Union. Perhaps the best-known of the Moscow-trained terrorists is Ilich Ramírez ('Carlos'), who in fact was recruited by the KGB in his native Venezuela.

The KGB's main functions are repression at home and espionage abroad. But it also runs a 'disinformation' Department, for the systematic dissemination of false rumours and reports, the fabrication of documents and smear campaigns to discredit individuals and organisations. The expulsion of the 105 Soviet agents from Britain in 1971 drew attention to the scale of espionage activities. Up to 75 per cent of Soviet embassy staffs are actually KGB spies, and in all countries for which intelligence data are available, the KGB's presence has increased substantially since 1971. This is true, for instance, of France, West Germany and even neutral Switzerland. As for the USA, the largest of all KGB spy centres is the headquarters of the United Nations in New York, from which agents with UN accreditation may roam freely all over the United States. The KGB has also greatly increased its activities on Capitol Hill. It is worth noting that since the Watergate affair, the American counter-espionage organisation, the FBI, has been forbidden to operate both in the UN and in Congress.

The International Department of the Soviet trade union organisation (AUCCTU)—not to be confused with Ponomarev's department—plays an important role in Soviet industrial subversion. It maintains a large research staff to recruit likely helpers among West European trade union leaders and to provoke or take advantage of strikes, some of which have been internationally coordinated.

As for propaganda, the Soviet Union has continued to maintain a relentless flow of hostile comment against the West. There are occasional breaks, for instance when an American President visits Moscow. Otherwise the flow of hostility continues and has never abated in the years since the 'end' of the Cold War. For instance, Soviet reporting of the Ulster situation, both for home consumption and for abroad, is consistently anti-British, and the attempt to contain IRA terrorism is presented as ruthless imperialist repression of a legitimate nationalist liberation movement.

The American CIA, in a report made public in late July 1978 by the House Permanent Select Committee on Intelligence, disclosed that Russia spends at least $2 billion a year to spread pro-Communist and anti-US propaganda through a world-wide network that includes international front organisations controlled by the Kremlin. There are thirteen major fronts, the best known of which are the World Peace Council, the World Federation of Trade Unions and the World Federation of Democratic Youth. One of the newer ones is the Christian Peace Conference, with headquarters in Prague (where most of the fronts are situated).

The Soviet network includes short-wave broadcasts in 84 languages; the news agency Tass, and the features agency Novosti, whose services are often available gratis; some 75 Communist Parties outside the Soviet bloc, which, whatever their own differences with Moscow, do act as channels for Soviet propaganda; and similar services and agencies in Cuba and the East European satellites.

At times, this hostile network can be extraordinarily effective. In the wake of Watergate, it helped to discredit the CIA and FBI, reducing both to near impotence. Perhaps its biggest recent success, however, was in spreading hostility to America's neutron bomb as 'the ultimate capitalist weapon, one which kills people but leaves property intact'. The purpose of enhanced radiation warhead (to give the 'neutron bomb' its correct name) was in fact to destroy Soviet tank crews without damage to the environment, in the event of a Soviet aggression in central Europe. In September 1977, President Carter announced that production of the neutron bomb would not go ahead unless the European members of NATO agreed to deploy it. The Soviet effort then switched to Europe, where the neutron bomb became an emotive issue in most capitals.

No, the Cold War is not over. But let us henceforth call it the Third World War, for that is what it really is.

Further Reading:

The issues are discussed in greater detail in Brian Crozier's book, *Strategy for Survival* (Temple Smith, London, 1978). See also:

The publications of the Institute for the Study of Conflict, London, especially: *European Security and the Soviet Problem* (1972), *The Peacetime Strategy of the Soviet Union* (1973), and Conflict Studies Nos. 35 (*Soviet Pressures in the Caribbean*), 54 (*The Soviet Presence in Somalia*), 76 (*Security and the Myth of 'Peace'*), 77 (*Soviet Penetration of Africa*), 84 (*Soviet Seapower Power: The Covert Support Fleet*), and 92 (*The Surrogate Forces of the Soviet Union*); and the successive editions of the *Annual of Power and Conflict*, 1971-78.

John Barron, KGB: The Secret Work of Soviet Secret Agents (New York, 1974).

Robert Moss, *The Collapse of Democracy* (Temple Smith, 1975), and the same author's weekly column in the *Daily Telegraph*, from May 1978.

Aleksei Myagkov, *Inside the KGB: an exposé by an officer of the Third Directorate* (Foreign Affairs Publishing Company, 1976).

Colin Welch

Colin Welch was born in 1924 at Ickleton in Cambridgeshire and educated at Stowe and Peterhouse, Cambridge (major history scholar and degree). In service in the Royal Warwickshire Regiment from 1942 to 1945, he was twice wounded. He spent a year with the *Glasgow Herald* in the late '40s, and has since been writing leaders for the *Daily Telegraph* with an interval as half of Peter Simple: Deputy Editor, 1964.

Broken eggs, but no omelette: Russia before the Revolution

How many military aircraft a month was Tsarist Russia producing at the end of 1916, just before its collapse? You may know the answer. The distinguished historian Norman Stone, to whom all students of old Russia are infinitely in debt, supplies it in his 'Eastern Front, 1914-1917' (Hodder).

If on the other hand you are, like most of us, honest but uninstructed, you will suspect a catch in the question: why otherwise would I ask it or attach any importance to the answer? How many *aircraft*? Your mind may grope among vague memories of the Tsar's armies in the First World War, of hordes of heroic but bedraggled, starving and frozen peasants, armed with long-handled axes or if lucky with precious rifles seized from the dead, and hurled with little or no artillery or other support against an enemy infinitely better equipped than they. You may have recently read Solzhenitsyn's sombre masterwork 'August 1914'. Here we find generals and staff work of an incompetence which would be incredible if it were not reproduced in other armies of the period. In fact Russia's best generals were as good as any: were her worst worse than the worst of others? We also find repeated by Solzhenitsyn dark hints of treason and dirty work in high places, at court, in the circles of the German-born Empress and of the 'sinister' Chief of Staff, Sukhomlinov—hints durable yet all, so far as I know, without the slightest foundation in fact, part of a gigantic anti--Tsarist myth. Certainly nowhere in 'August 1914' do we find evidence of advanced technology applied to warfare.

How many aircraft, then? Well, precious few if any, a sort of scornful instinct tells us, and those presumably made of logs, string, furs and mud, piloted by drunken superstitious mouzhiks, blessed by verminous priests and crashing all the same on take-off.

Yet of course there is a catch: the real figure is 175 effective military air-craft a month (we at that time produced about the same number). This fact bears brooding on. Think of all the relatively sophisticated electrical and mechanical parts which go into the most primitive flying machine and ponder how precisely the word 'backward' fits an economy, an industrial system capable of manufacturing them—and that in 1916, more than 60 years ago! Nor were these aircraft just knocked together out of imported parts, though some of the machine tools used in their manufacture may indeed have been imported or designed abroad. Russia in 1916 was prac-tically cut off from her allies. It was thus from her own resources that she achieved an increase over 1914 production of 2,000 per cent more shells, 1,000 per cent more guns, 1,100 per cent more rifles, apart from adequate supplies of wireless sets, telephones, gas masks, hand grenades and all the necessities of (then) modern warfare. By January 1917, on the very eve of the revolution, the Russian army was superior to the German and Austro-Hungarian armies facing it not only in numbers but also in *materiél*—a superiority, according to Mr. Stone, akin to that of the West over the Central powers in 1918.

Remarkable achievements these, especially from the feeble and primitive Tsarist economy of legend—that economy which, according to every self-exculpating Tsarist general's memoirs, could not produce the shells he needed for the victory which eluded him, but which in fact produced shells in abundance, to be fired off by those generals senselessly into bogs. Why, even the Tsar's railways—always said to have 'broken down'—acquired in the war more track, more rolling stock, more engines. Harvests in the war, as before it, were abundant. Why then did the cities 'starve'? Katkov, in his fascinating 'February 1917' doubts whether they did: he finds evidence of food enough in or available to Petrograd in early 1917. The huge angry queues present us with a riddle—one of so many. The answer to this one lies, I suspect, not in mechanical breakdowns or 'backwardness' but rather in a thoroughly modern combination of hideous inflation (336 per cent from 1914 to the end of 1916) and idiotic price controls, two factors which can always be relied upon to produce want amidst plenty. These phenomena were by no means unique to Russia at that time (like other belligerents, she expected a short war, to be financed by unorthodox makeshifts) nor are they unknown to us today. Nor perhaps need the war have been long, had Russia adhered to her original intention of invading

East Prussia not with two armies, but with four. Her mobilisation was in fact, if chaotic, extremely rapid. Even misdeployed as they undoubtedly were, her impetuous forces badly messed up the time-scale of the Schlieffen plan—France knocked out quickly first, then Russia at leisure. They saved France but, alas, not Russia.

The pre-1914 German General Staff was simply terrified of Russia's growing might. We assume them now to have been timid superstitious men, frightened by spectres and goblins, as subsequent events appear to confirm. No one who reads or credits Mr. Stone can doubt that their fears were perfectly reasonable or even wholly justified.

My task here is in fact to draw attention to a very great lie, a lie not merely of historical importance but one powerfully affecting our judgement of the most important geo-political fact facing us today—the Soviet Union. For who can understand this baleful threat who knows not what preceded it, what it replaced?

The lie takes many forms, infests many heads, not all of them 'progressive', many of them seemingly shrewd and realistic. Mr. Stone himself in an interview mocked it in its most absurd form—a view of pre-1917 Russia as 'a howling desert over which Stalin waved a wand and turned it into Welwyn Garden City'. The lie postulates that Russia was till 1917 hopelessly and in all ways backward; that it took the Bolshevik revolution to drag her into the twentieth century; that the material, educational and social progress achieved since then is vast, and of a sort and scale which the Tsarist regime would not or could not possibly have achieved. That all this has been accomplished at a fearful cost, the lie does not always deny: it calls up subordinate lies, however, to put the cost 'into perspective'. Thus: if the Russian people have utterly lost their freedom, the lie asserts, they have in fact lost nothing, for they never had any. And thus again: if the Bolsheviks have murdered and imprisoned millions without trial or compunction, what are they doing according to the lie but re-applying the cruel and barbarous penal practices of the Tsars, if on a larger scale then perhaps for a nobler or more constructive purpose?

I submit that all of this, where not at least questionable or gravely misleading, is the most unmitigated tripe. If praise or blame are ever appropriate in human life or history, they are here absolutely and perversely maldistributed, with the Soviet regime taking credit for Tsarist achievements and the Tsars blamed for Soviet crimes.

How many aircraft? I approached the great lie first by the military route, not because I think an ability to threaten or wage war the sure or sole mark of the good society: if that were so, Stalin and his successors would certainly have the edge over the Alexanders and Nicholases. No, rather do I suggest that the startling achievements of the Tsar's war economy, thrown by the final disaster into an obscurity in which they remained till Mr. Stone's searchlight was turned on to them, may indeed be the proof and climax of the equally startling though less unfamiliar economic progress before the war.

It is not unknown, though it is often forgotten because it does not fit the lie, that Russia enjoyed a fantastic rate of growth before 1914 (Mr. Stone newly demonstrates that this continued or even accelerated after 1914, albeit in a form distorted by the demands of war). Out of the last 25 years before 1914, Russia's growth rate led the world in 18 of them. Her average rise in industrial output from 1894 to 1914 was about eight per cent per year. In the latter part of the period agricultural production rose proportionately, at an accelerating rate, stimulated by land reform. In the same period Russia's coal output went up fivefold, iron fourfold; output of oil and grain doubled, as did railway mileage and the cattle herd. In these last three fields the Soviet regime has achieved nothing comparable in 60 years!

But all this progress, some will object, was achieved from an incredibly low starting level. This is not wholly wrong: yet by 1913 Russia was the world's fifth industrial power, just ahead of Austro-Hungary and behind only the United States, Germany, Britain and France, the last of which she must have overtaken during the war, despite the loss of Polish industry. In 1913 she held second place in world oil production, third place in railway construction and cotton manufacture, fourth place in machine building.[1]

As Sir Donald Mackenzie Wallace reminds us,[2] Russian statistics should always be treated with caution—yes, but more now than then. For Tsarist statistics show a steady advance in precision and comprehensiveness; Tsarist Russia moreover, unlike its successor, was an almost completely open society, in which official statistics could be checked (as Wallace checked them) against private information and personal observation. It was not a Russian, anyway, but a Frenchman, Edmond Théry, who wrote in 1912: 'If things develop in the major European countries as they have done between 1900 and 1912, Russia will towards the middle of the present century dominate Europe politically as well as from the economic and financial points of view'. Foreign observers all tended to agree that Russia would by that time have become the world's second industrial power—and this of course without all the horrors of the revolution.

But surely all this progress must under the Tsars have been achieved at terrible cost? Indeed there are costs inseparable from industrial development, though these may of course be reduced by those who industrialise later and who can thus learn from the successes and mistakes of others. In fact the Russian standard of living rose pretty steadily throughout the period of industrialisation, reaching in 1913 a level not again attained till well after the Second World War. It was not till 1965, for instance, that Russians enjoyed again the pre-revolutionary density of 6.6 square metres of living space per head—a figure unsatisfactory in 1913, perhaps, quite shocking 50 years later, and not to be explained away by any sort of population increase. The Russian population between 1860 and 1914 actually doubled; the post-revolutionary population, for various reasons, some grim indeed, has not.

In real terms, the pre-revolutionary Russian industrial worker earned about half as much as his British counterpart; he now probably earns about a third. At least until recently, his impoverishment was absolute as well as relative. As Professor Richard Pipes put it about ten years ago, 'The Soviet citizen today is poor not only in comparison with his counterpart in other European countries, but also in comparison with his own grandfather. In terms of essentials—food, clothing and housing—the Soviet population as a whole is worse off than it was before the revolution'.

The Tsarist Government also intervened actively to protect the welfare of the worker. Its factory legislation, enforced by an inspectorate, was generally modelled on that of Germany and Britain, though in some respects it was even more advanced—for instance, in the provisions for free medical care at work. Hours of work were reduced by law in 1897 to 11½ hours a day (less for women and children) and again in 1906 to nine or 10 hours for most and eight hours for many workers. Trade unions were legalised in 1906, though they had been active for some time before. In 1903 employers were made liable for factory accidents, sickness benefits and pensions for those disabled. In 1912 this act was reinforced; workers' compensation and disability payments were raised under a scheme largely administered by the workers themselves (in old Russia there was always a lot of democracy at the lower levels, as in the village communes). Large factories outside towns (as many or most were) were bound by law to supply free schools, libraries, hospitals and bath-houses.

In all this paternal activity we can discern one great advantage the Russian grandfather had over his descendants. The State was not then, as it is now, the sole employer, the sole trade union, the sole provider of goods and services (as it is now, save for the astonishing plenty still produced by the two per cent of land still in private cultivation, which produces half Russia's meat, vegetables, milk and eggs and without which she would assuredly starve). No, the Tsar's administration stood for the most part outside and above the economic process; it did not even greatly like capitalists (nor did they like it: most were Liberals; one or two of the most prominent were Marxists and lavishly financed their own destruction); it regulated their operations if not very effectively at least with a sort of well-meaning impartiality.

This paternal activity also shows Nicholas II in an unfamiliar light, as a great reforming Tsar, or at least as one who if he did not initiate at least endorsed the vigorous reforming activities of his Ministers. Nor have we touched yet on the peasantry, who were the beneficiaries of the greatest reforms of all, the agrarian reforms launched and carried through after 1905 by Stolypin, without doubt the greatest Russian statesman of this century—that is to say, if greatness has any moral content, any connection with the public weal, rather than just expressing grovelling admiration for mere power, however wickedly and destructively used. These reforms empowered the peasants to break up the village communes and to consolidate their scattered strips into privately owned farms. By low-interest loans and grants the peasants were encouraged to buy land from the gentry, the State and the Imperial family, as also to settle in virgin Siberia. Lenin saw at once with fury what was afoot—nothing less than the consummation of the work set in hand by Alexander II with the emancipation of the serfs. Stolypin had shot his fox, and gravely jeopardised his chances of starting a revolution. Nonetheless, 'All land to the people' remained the Bolshevik slogan—another gigantic lie! For by 1916 about 89 per cent of the total cultivated area was owned by the peasantry, as was about 94 per cent of the livestock. 'All land *from* the people' would have been an apter slogan, a slogan given fearful effect by Stalin in the early thirties when, in a crime for which no Romanov offers any precedent, accompanied by mass murder, famine and brutality, he stole the land back from the peasants and in effect restored serfdom—or rather slavery, a better word for what existed before 1861 and exists again today.

Another subordinate lie, bolstering the great lie, is the Communists' claim, widely credited even by their enemies ('you've got to be fair'), to have educated the Russian people, to have found them illiterate and to have made them masters of all the arts and sciences. At first glance this lie finds some support in fact, for undoubtedly and not surprisingly more Russian people are literate now than were in 1913. Yet literacy is not in itself education; and we must be sure that those Russians who were before the revolution truly educated had got for themselves something not obtainable at all, unless in secret, in the Soviet Union. Maurice Baring, no fool nor stranger to Russia, wrote in 1914 that 'The average Russian of the educated middle-class [is] extremely well educated—so much better educated than the average educated Englishman that comparison would be silly'.[3] Mr. Baring would hardly have written so of the instructed dogma-blinkered automata which Soviet education apparently aims with some success to produce.

It was in the main from this educated class that there sprang that abundance of great novelists, poets and thinkers, of musicians, artists and scientists, which is the sublime glory of late Tsarist Russia and her imperishable legacy to a rather ungrateful world. It was also of course this class which provided the critical audience for their efforts: they did not create in a void. To attribute their fantastic achievements to the regime would be absurd, though indeed imperial and official patronage of the arts and sciences was on a heroic scale; and to say that Nicholas II was, from our knowledge of his private tastes and public benefactions, the most cultivated ruler Russia has known in this century, is (despite Lenin's narrow intellectuality) to understate rather than overstate the truth. It would be equally absurd, on the other hand, to deny to the regime such credit as must be due to it, if not actually for fostering, then at least for permitting this stupendous flowering—a flowering which continued in exotic profusion right up to 1917, after that to be part cruelly extinguished, part dispersed, part to find a brief and hectic prosperity in the twenties, part left to wither away in sad and obscure silence, in prison, poverty or in death. It would be equally absurd too (though it has happened) somehow to transfer the credit for this stupendous flowering from the epoch and conditions which actually produced it to the succeeding epoch which extinguished it. Eugene Lyons in 'Assignment in Utopia' describes how in 1928, young and still full of illusions, he arrived in the land of his dreams:

> I took in the Russian theater, ballet and opera in great draughts. Ardently if illogically, I gave the revolution credit for everything cultural that it had inherited from the tsarist era. A hundred years of classical ballet, the meticulous art of Stanislavsky's theaters, the piled-up treasures of Russian music and stagecraft were for me, as for all foreign worshippers, subtle confirmation of Karl Marx's theories. Tchaikovsky and Mussorgsky, Moskvin and Madame Geltzer have made more converts to Sovietism among visiting outsiders than the marvels of the Five Year Plan or the adroitness of the guides.

One can see how this *legerdemain* might deceive honest people. The achievements of pre-revolutionary Russian genius might be regarded by some (not by me) as the achievements of the Russian people as a whole; of this people the Soviet regime could speciously claim to be the embodiment and representative in a way that the Tsars could not have done; this regime could thus further claim to have acquired its cultural riches not by theft but by just inheritance. As well might any jackal which prowls in the ruins of Persepolis claim the lawful ownership thereof!

The contribution of Russian Jewry to this flowering is immense and unforgettable, and it would certainly be particularly perverse to give any of the credit for their achievements to a regime which on the whole, if with many exceptions, treated them so shabbily and shamefully. Not without justice did George Kennan describe the alienation of the Jews from the Tsarist regime as one of that regime's gravest sins and most fatal mistakes. For it is probably true that most of Russia's Jews *wanted* to be as loyal subjects of the Tsar as most of their fellow Jews elsewhere were conspicuously loyal to Kaisers, Kings and Presidents. If they were not allowed to be, the fault was the Tsar's rather than their own. Yet even in this painful area we must note that, had the Jews been as appallingly oppressed as is often suggested, had the laws against them been as cruel and as rigidly enforced, then they could not possibly have made the resplendent contribution which they actually did. Further we must note the continuous if slow and belated progress towards liberalisation made with the active support of the Tsar's more enlightened ministers: the Pale of Settlement, for instance, which in theory restricted most Jews to certain traditional areas, was abolished in 1915. Further again we must note that the revolution did not end the miseries of Russian Jews (except for those who fled or found themselves citizens of new successor states), though of course their miseries are less conspicuous now amidst the general misery, the extinction of their particular culture less tragic-seeming amidst the extinction of other cultures, particular and general.

Returning to education in pre-revolutionary Russia we find in this field too the reforming Tsardom busily at work.

When Nicholas II came to the throne, only about 25 per cent of his subjects were literate (though we must remember that this total included the inhabitants of newly acquired colonial territories in the East: our own educational statistics at that time would not have looked so good had India, say, been included). By 1914 the figure had doubled to nearly half. In 1908 universal primary education was introduced; by 1915 more than half the children of the relevant age were receiving it. In that year, despite the war, it was proposed to make it compulsory and to introduce compulsory secondary education up to the age of 15 by 1925, by which date also illiteracy should have been wiped out except among the very old. Progress along these lines was rapid and tangible. The effect of the revolution was not to accelerate these developments but greatly to retard them. It was not till 1930 that the Soviet regime aimed at the same targets; not till about 1950 did it actually hit them.

We tend perhaps to think of higher education under the Tsars as the preserve of the well-to-do, unavailable to the masses. Nicholas II's reign saw great changes here too. In 1880, as Mr. FitzLyon points out, university students of working-class origin accounted for only 12.4 per cent of the total student body, of peasant origin 3.3 per cent. By 1914 24.3 per cent of students were of working-class origin and 14.5 per cent of peasant origin— more than a third altogether (and also more than Soviet Russia can today produce). At other higher educational establishments workers and peasants together accounted for more than 50 per cent of the student body. Fees were low; for the poor they were waived altogether; state grants and bursaries were also available.

Disorders at these universities caused much understandable disquiet at the time (no less than three of the Tsar's Ministers were murdered by students between 1900 and 1904) and have served since to discredit the Tsarist regime, to reinforce doubts of its legitimacy and acceptibility. It was until recently perhaps too readily taken for granted that rioting and the outrages of terrorists were, whether evil or not in themselves, a sure indicator of the evil nature of the regime against which they were directed and, in particular, an expression of the fact that all other roads to freedom and justice were obviously blocked. I do not seek to deny all truth to this view,[4] though the fate for instance of President McKinley, the free choice of the American people, was even then awkward for its proponents. In recent years, moreover, we have seen student unrest and acts of terrorism persistently directed against societies which are indisputably legitimate from the democratic point of view and which offer no obstruction whatever to reforms genuinely desired by a majority of the people. With this new wisdom, with this new lack of confidence in our own standards of judgement, we may perhaps be forgiven for wondering now whether all the manifestations of discontent under the later Tsars tell us more about the nature of the regime than about the nature of its opponents (again I do not deny that these two natures were closely interlinked). Do they tell us that it was an intolerable, unalterable and irreformable tyranny? Or do they rather tell us that its opponents, whether liberals (Cadets, i.e. constitutional democrats) or extremists of various sorts, were impatient, unreasonable and irresponsible?[5]

Completely satisfactory and comprehensive answers to these questions are not possible. I will concede one major point, which might be put thus: that every revolutionary regime bears more resemblance to the regime it overthrew than to any ideal which it presumably had in mind. More than by any books or teachings, the new rulers are shaped by the old and by the attitudes and institutions which they inherited from them. If this view were to stand without reservation, it would damn the Tsars more than anything else could. Yet in mitigation it must be pleaded that the inheritance was a partial and perverse one. What was good about the old regime died with it; its crimes and atrocities, however, committed as for the most part they were even centuries before, have been resurrected in new and unprecedentedly monstrous forms. In particular we must note the amount of freedom under the law which the Russian people did enjoy in 1914, and which is quite sufficient to rebut that part of the great lie which suggests that they have never known freedom or justice in any form.

In the first place, there were irremovable judges, to whose independence, incorruptibility and zeal for the truth Kerensky, himself a revolutionary, pays touching tribute in his memoirs. There was trial by jury in all criminal cases (though this was understandably withdrawn in serious political cases, after a jury had found the terrorist Vera Zasulich not guilty of shooting General Trepov, whom she had indisputably shot). There was no death penalty, except for attempts on the lives of the Imperial family and except in times of emergency, such as after the 1905 revolution. It was also after the 1905 revolution that Tsarist Russia record-ed its highest figure of persons in custody, 184,000 in 1912 according to Robert Conquest in 'The Great Terror',[6] a figure which compares quite reasonably with modern free countries like our own and America, which normally keep in prison just under 1,000 persons per million of population (.01 per cent). Stalin by contrast held in 1952 some 15 to 18 million people in labour camps, not far off a tenth of the population, and would have held many more had not so many died in his charge.

Had not so many died. . . . It is a modest but surviving part of the great lie that at least the Bolsheviks brought peace and an end of bloodshed to a Russia war-tormented and bled white. In fact it brought first a civil war, with mortality greater than that of the First World War, terrible as that had been. During collectivisation of the land by Stalin four million peasants died; during the ensuing famine, another six million; in the Great Purge, six million more; in other purges, in exportations and deportations during and after the Second World War, three, four, five million more—we shall never know. More than 20 million dead, therefore, untried, undefended, to be presumed innocent: and this is a very conser-vative estimate—Solzhenitsyn, quoting Professor Kurganov, puts the cost of Communism to Russia at 110 million lives.[7] Nor of course can any such statistics encompass the sum total of human misery involved—the blasted hopes, the wrecked careers, the exile, the families sundered or ruined, the tears of the living who envied the dead. So many million eggs broken, if you will forgive the coarse expression, and no omelette. In all these respects here indeed is progress, vast, monstrous and indisputable, pro-gress of a kind which marks the transition from an authoritarian to a totalitarian state, which marks in one grim way the difference between an imperfect society, as all are, and a hell on earth, which all are not.

To what extent was pre-war Tsarism even an authoritarian society? To the end of his reign, Nicholas II called himself autocrat: but he was no longer so. There was freedom of religion after 1903. Foreign travel was unrestricted. The censorship had been abolished. The Press was free, even to be scurrilous. We remember the impotent fury of the poor Tsaritsa, her relationship with Rasputin grossly calumniated in the St. Petersburg papers, and her husband's patient explanations that nothing now could be done about it. Bolshevik and other revolutionary publications appeared without restriction. Bolsheviks and other revolutionaries sat in the Duma, the Russian Parliament, which from 1906 till the fall of the monarchy was neither all-powerful nor impotent, a force to be reckoned with for good and for mischief alike. Had Tsarist Russia survived until the present day with all her institutions and laws unaltered (unlikely, this, since these were in a constant state of flux, moving generally if with backslidings in a liberal direction), she would have to be numbered, as Tibor Szamuely puts it, 'compared to the 126 members of the United Nations Organisation, as one of the 15 or 20 most liberal states in the world'.

Of those moderate well-intentioned liberals who assisted in her over-throw, and who thus assisted in their own overthrow and in the overthrow of all freedom and hope for the future (of both of which there might have seemed then to a reasonable man so much), a recollection of Sir Donald Mackenzie Wallace is terribly revealing. (Please remember he is writing in 1912, with no advantage of hindsight.) 'In theory the Cadets were a moderate constitutional party, and if they had possessed a little more prudence and patience they might have led the country gradually into the paths of genuine constitutional government; but, like everyone in Russia at that time, they were in a hurry. . . . Their impatience was curiously illustrated during a friendly conversation which I had one evening with a leader of the party (at the time of the opening of the first Duma in 1906). With all due deference, I ventured to suggest that, instead of maintaining an attitude of systematic and uncompromising hostility to the Ministry, the party might co-operate with the Government and thereby create something like the English parliamentary system, for which they professed such admiration; possibly in eight or ten years this desirable result might be obtained. On hearing these last words my friend suddenly interrupted me and exclaimed: "Eight or ten years? We cannot wait as long as that!".'

Poor, vain, impatient, sad dreamers, indeed, who died by violence or in exile, with all their hopes unfulfilled. They could not wait eight or ten years. They had to wait for ever.

References

1. These figures, which are generally confirmed by other authorities, are all set out in the late Tibor Szamuely's fascinating 'Postscript' to Tufton Beamish's 'Half Marx'. He had hoped to write at length of Russia between the 1905 and 1917 revolutions, in his view the least known and most misunderstood epoch of Russian history. Of this projected work the 'Postscript' was a foretaste so vivid and fresh as to make us regret all the more bitterly that death prevented him.
2. In 'Russia' (revised edition 1912), surely the greatest survey of Tsarist Russia ever to appear originally in the English language.
3. Quoted in Kyril FitzLyon's admirable introduction to 'Before the Revolution', to which I am also greatly indebted.
4. For a full and vivid analysis of the dark interrelation between Russian tyranny and Russian terrorism, I refer my readers to the book Tibor Szamuely actually did write, *The Russian Tradition*.
5. Tibor Szamuely's daughter Helen, in an unpublished thesis, regards Edward and Constance Garnett as rather typical of British intellectuals at that time in seeing little difference between liberals, nihilists and terrorists and in approving of *all* opposition to the Tsars. Yet the Liberator Tsar, Alexander II, was murdered just as he was about to embark on further major reforms.
6. Szamuely gives a higher figure, 235,000: did he perhaps include people under restrictions or in exile (which could, according to Lenin among others, be pleasant and fruitful) but not actually in custody?
7. Dostoevsky had predicted that it would be 100 million.

Rhodes Boyson

Dr. Rhodes Boyson, Conservative Member of Parliament for Brent North and Opposition Spokesman on Education, is Chairman of the National Council for Educational Standards and was for eighteen years a headmaster of a secondary modern school, two comprehensive schools and a grammar school. He has written widely on historical, political and educational subjects.

Compulsory state education raises educational standards

What is the purpose of education? It is firstly for literacy and numeracy without which no real full life in the modern sense is possible. Secondly, it is for the dissemination of knowledge—historical, geographical, literary, scientific—which gives a person areas of information on which he can build to make his judgements and conduct his life. Thirdly, it must give him both the habits and the skills to hold down a job at a reasonable wage otherwise all his preparation for leisure will be of little use since he will have the ultimate pointless leisure of the dole queue. Fourthly, it should make him a 'whole' person with appreciation of music, art, philosophy, religion, politics and other studies and pursuits which can give him purpose.

Was a child in the 1870's before compulsory state education, and allowing for the resources of the time, more likely to have a body of general knowledge, the skills and abilities to earn a living and to take an interest in general culture than one growing up now a hundred years later?

It is important first to indicate what educational opportunities were available in the nineteenth century before the state stepped in. The myth that the mid-nineteenth century was an educational and cultural desert bears no relationship with that reality. There were a rapidly increasing number of schools of the National Society and the British and Foreign Schools Society, there were the Sunday Schools, the Mechanics Institutes, the Literary and Philosophical Societies, home tuition and independent schools. There were rapidly spreading libraries with a growing selection of books, newspapers and periodicals. The first subvention of the national government to education came in 1833 when an annual grant of £20,000 was paid to the National Society and the British and Foreign School Society.

Was even this first subvention necessary? Probably not, since the number of school places provided by these two Societies doubled between 1818 and 1828 before a penny of state money came their way. It is also now estimated that even before 1833 60 per cent of the population could read and write and another 20 per cent could read.

There was a mass reading public long before 1870. William Cobbett's *Address to the Journeymen and Labourers* sold 200,000 copies in the early nineteenth century and Bibles, booklets and tracts had huge circulations. Charity and ragged schools were free or low priced and the fees of other schools were usually well within the pockets of working families.

It is possible, even probable, that the move towards compulsory state education from 1870, enforced from 1880, was a mistake and totally unnecessary. By the 1860s some 90 per cent of the public, according to recent studies, could read and write and the number of schools were still expanding to meet the rising demand. As late as 1869 two-thirds of school expenditure came from voluntary sources and this is especially remarkable when it is realised that taxation was then very regressive, falling heavily on food and tobacco. The meticulously researched and written Newcastle Commission on Popular Education, 1858-61, concluded that few children did not go to school.

The mistake of compulsory school education of 1870/80, however, wasn't just that school attendance was made compulsory but that the state, via the Board Schools, would provide the schools out of public funds. This meant that the bottomless purse of the state would pour money into its own schools and drive out of business thousands of independent schools dependent upon private funds and the fees of the parents of the pupils. Bread was rationed in World War II but people did not have to buy their bread from state bakeries. People could take their bread coupons to any shop to purchase the product they required. Similarly in 1870/80 the state could have decided to provide vouchers or grants to help those who could not afford education for their children and the parents could have used these to choose between different independent schools.

If, alternatively, the state was only concerned about educational standards then it could have laid down a standard to be attained at each age whether children went to school or not. People pass a driving test according to an assessment of their ability to drive not according to the number of driving lessons they have attended. Unfortunately the Forster 1870 Act heralded an age of state intervention and paternalism which following the Benthamites would lead to the Fabians and present-day collectivist socialism.

Before 1870 children attended school from the age of five or six until the ages of 11 and 12. They were often in classes of up to 120 taught by a qualified teacher with some three assistants. Yet 90% of people could read and write by the 1860s and the percentage was still increasing. This figure compares with the 85% who are literate now, the 10 per cent who are semi-literate and the 5% who are totally illiterate. We could thus wonder what a hundred years of state education has achieved particularly when one realises that pupils are now at school for 11 years from 5 to 16 compared with the six years of the late 1860s.

While I was researching in nineteenth-century history I came across the work of R. K. Webb and E. G. West on educational standards in the nineteenth century: their research, however, only bears out thousands of pieces of local research and the experience of anyone who has studied the wide range and vocabulary of nineteenth-century local newspapers. When I was doing research for my *Ashworth Cotton Enterprise* I was astonished to find that in 1833 Henry Ashworth claimed that of his 561 mill operatives in his two Bolton Mills 98 per cent could read and 45 per cent could write. Yet these figures were never challenged by Lord Ashley and the factory commissioners who visited these mills and had no love for the Ashworths. Many neutral observers who also called at these mills supported Ashworth's claim.

The comparison of standards in basic literacy and numeracy today with the 1860s must allow for two changes: the length of the years of schooling for all pupils has doubled; there has been a great reduction in the pupil-teacher ratio which should surely be productive of higher standards. The pupil-teacher ratio in Britain is now 17 pupils per trained teacher in secondary schools and 24 to one trained teacher in primary schools. This figure is very much smaller than the very high pupil-teacher ratios of the 1860s. It has been reduced by some 25 per cent over a generation and it is now one of the smallest in the world. If this great reduction has not led to improved standards then it would seem either that there is no particular advantage in reduced size of classes or that state-run schools are generally inefficient. It is very probable that both these factors are valid.

Evidence is now accumulating that there has been little improvement from the two state raisings of the school leaving age since 1945, first to 15 years and then to 16 years. The Somerset Education and Training Group reported in February 1978 that adolescents who had obtained a reasonable grade in CSE English could not write a satisfactory letter and that the weaknesses were in construction, punctuation and spelling.

In mathematics standards are appallingly low. The Institute of Mathematics Report of March 1978, covering 8,500 15-16 year olds showed very low standards. Only one 15 year old in every form in Inner London could give correct answers to 12 simple questions such as '7 times 8' and divide '24 by 6' and only 18 boys and 2 girls out of the 1,400 examined in Inner London obtained full marks in straightforward everyday problems such as, 'If milk is 12p a pint and I use 2 pints a day, what is my weekly milk bill?'

The Director-General of the City and Guilds in giving evidence to the Expenditure Committee of the House of Commons commented that 30 per cent of the first year courses for craft apprentices might be taken up by remedial work which should have been covered in school. No doubt this is the cause of apprenticeship vacancies even in areas of high juvenile unemployment which I have observed. In 1978 I spoke to an Industrialists Dinner in Glasgow where 17 employers employed 55,000 workers and only one had no unfilled apprenticeship vacancies because of lack of suitable applicants. Hugh Scanlon in July 1978 deplored as 'woefully inadequate' the literacy and numeracy standards of school leavers.

Thus it appears that after a hundred years of state education my third proviso of education is also not being fulfilled: that pupils are prepared in habits and knowledge for the world of work. This was made very clear by Mr. Merrick Spanlon, the National Coal Board Director for North Nottinghamshire, in a speech in May 1978. He said that the lack of basic literacy and numeracy had prevented a hundred young men from becoming miners in that area the previous year. He added 'It is a great shame that at the end of their schooldays there are juveniles unable to pass very simple tests.' A CBI report in 1976 concluded 'employers are becoming increasingly concerned that many school leavers have not acquired a minimum acceptable standard in the fundamental skills involved in reading, writing, arithmetic and communications.

School leavers today, after a hundred years of state education, are often without proper habits of work as well as being deficient in knowledge.

State education has failed to create attitudes of work reliability. In January 1978, the *Gazette* of the Department of Employment reported that many employers preferred taking on married women returners rather than school leavers because of the latter's 'attitude and personality, their experience and manners, and their lack of basic education'.

The before-mentioned Institute of Mathematics Report clearly shows the size of the problem of truancy in our schools. Some 18 per cent of 15-16 year olds were missing on the day the test was given and in Inner London 28 per cent! This was a genuine spot check because pupils did not know on what day the test was going to be made. This means that in Inner London each 15-16 year old is absent one day in three, or one-third of these pupils are absent all the time. No wonder so many school leavers are now unemployable and that the 16-29 year olds are the fastest growing unemployment group and their numbers have risen 120 per cent between 1974 and 1978. The 20-24 year olds now make up almost 18 per cent of all the unemployed. They have all left school in the last eight years.

The 12-year-old school leaver of 1869 was generally literate and numerate, he was well disciplined and he was usually keen to work. In 1978 it would appear that a considerable section of the 16 year olds have inadequate literacy and numeracy standards, many are not keen to work and they are trained not for apprenticeships but for a career of truant idleness. Maybe the employers of 1978 demand higher standards in literacy and numeracy, but it is the task of any system to respond to the demands upon it. I would certainly like to see further research into the standards of school leavers at 12 in 1869 compared with those of 16 in 1978. Certainly one would have to be a short-sighted collectivist to believe that the state takeover of education was justified by results.

It is often alleged when comparisons are made of present-day standards with those of a century ago that the curriculum then was very limited with undue, if not total, concentration on the three Rs. Before 1862 all schools taught scripture, the three Rs and often needlework, but other subjects were often introduced. Grammar and geography were quite common subjects, singing, drawing and mathematics proper were sometimes taught and some schools even found time for etymology, history and physical exercise.

It is perhaps ironic that it was state intervention by Lowe's revised Code of 1862 which restricted the curriculum. This provided that all children should be examined in reading, writing and arithmetic, according to a clearly defined syllabus issued by the central authority and that girls should also be examined in plain needlework. Grants for schools for all children over the age of six were then made dependent partly on the child passing an examination in these subjects conducted by Her Majesty's Inspector when he visited the school. A child who attended no less than 200 school sessions, and passed the examinations, could earn for the school a grant of 12s: 4s for attendance, 2s 8d for each of the three basic subjects. Perhaps it would be a good idea if the grant for attendance came back and the income for a school out of which the teachers' salaries were paid was made dependent upon the children actually attending school. The registers of course would have to be checked again by outside inspectors if they were to be meaningful.

Despite the 1862 state limitation on a general curriculum the subjects were soon increased. From 1867 onwards subjects like geography, grammar and history were admitted for grant purposes. In 1871 not only was the standard raised but the list of grant-earning subjects was further extended to include algebra and geometry, natural philosophy and the natural sciences, political economy and physical geography, English Literature, French, Latin, German and other subjects approved by H.M.I. Singing was also encouraged by the 1871 Code and 'military drill' introduced which became physical exercises in 1890. In 1875 botany and domestic science (for girls) were approved for grant. Cookery was also encouraged. The curriculum could by then be much wider than is now provided by many Inner City comprehensive schools.

I think, however, that the nineteenth-century emphasis on reading, writing and arithmetic was fully defensible. On these foundations all other subjects are built and without them there can be no genuine broadening of the curriculum. I must add, however, that my earlier acquaintance with people who went to school in the 1870s and 1880s indicated that their depth of knowledge of history and geography certainly far exceeded that of almost all young people of the present time. The modern project method whereby a pupil does not cover a full syllabus but only odd events accounts for these deficiencies.

It is difficult to compare standards in my fourth test of education: general cultural participation. There was little secondary and higher education a 100 years ago, yet a study of any local newspaper in 1869 would provide a surprising depth of serious and informed discussion in the news, leader and correspondence columns. There was generally as much coverage of parliamentary news in a weekly or a bi-weekly local town newspaper as is now given daily in *The Times*. Certainly the interest was in major debates and major issues.

There were huge public meetings on every possible subject covering political, religious and social issues in every English town. People did not talk, as now, about participation because their participation was real. Churches, debating, dramatic and improvement classes were crowded.

In the 1860s there was mass participation in the trade union, cooperative and political movements. In the North cooperative mills were common. Music was very popular and every small town could boast its chamber, orchestral and choral societies and in the North and Midlands and Wales each community also had brass bands by the dozen.

A study of local newspapers even shows a far greater number of town specialist societies in the 1860s than in the 1970s. The Mechanics Institutes also had their evening classes, sponsored concerts and poetry readings open to the public. A return to earth of one of the self-help believers of the 1860s would be horrified to see the smaller participation of the present time.

It is a sad commentary on a hundred years of state education that politicians now demand, in my view erroneously, political education in schools because people are not interested in politics. There was considerable interest in politics a hundred years ago and it was not taught in schools. On the other side of the coin I do not believe that there has been any heightening of general cultural standards despite compulsory music, art and literature in school curriculae. It is probable that culture is now more a minority pursuit than it was a hundred years ago. Is it possible that compulsory art and music in schools for all pupils has been counterproductive? Pupils gladly drop these subjects when they leave school just as they throw off their school uniform.

Let us, however, return to our major question. Why has a hundred years of state education not raised standards? The first answer is that anything done by the state stifles and does not stimulate. It is only successful if linked with intolerably repressive measures. In the 1860s children and adults wanted to learn and they strove for success by their own efforts. Now that almost everything is provided free, people do not care. The public generally say if something is free, 'If it's useful I'll have two, if I can't see its use I want none of it' and in education the second attitude is very common. People treasure what they fight and pay for, not what is thrust upon them.

The second failing of the state in education as elsewhere is that it is not responsive to what the public wants. The bureaucrats who organise it, and the professionals who work within it, believe they know what the public should have and this is what they provide. There is no response to a changing market and few education officers and teachers know what the world of outside work is really like. Every trendy fashion is followed in education to ease the boredom of teachers not for the benefit of children.

The third failing of the state is that it does not provide for individual or area differences. Section 76 of the 1944 Act stipulating that children should be educated according to the wishes of their parents is largely unenforced. The educational administrator considers parental choice and individual pupil differences to be nuisances and finds his solution in zoning and no choice. Each child is an individual. Standards would be much higher if parents could find schools which fitted their children.

It is very probable that the movement of the state into education was a mistake in 1870/80. The state should at the most have topped up the income of the very few parents who could not pay their children's school fees and could not find them a free place. The state is a dead monopoly which by its power and finances largely drives out all competitors.

There are only two ways schooling standards can be improved: more rigid central control with standards firmly enforced which is dangerous to the free society or the stimulus of a variety of schools operating in a market financed through parental choice, or a voucher system. We cannot just return overnight to the 1860s system. The educational voucher—a voucher worth the average cost of present-day education with which people 'buy' a place in the school of their choice—is the key as the only way to bring real participation, self-help and response back to the consumer in education.

Let no one cheer in 1980 for a hundred years of state education. It is undoubtedly a factor in the British decline in self-help, personal confidence and standards. We can't relive history, but it might help if we started learning lessons from it!

Lewis Elton

Lewis Elton was born in Germany and came to England just before the war. He was educated and has taught in both state and public schools, and he studied at the universities of Cambridge and London and at the Polytechnic, Regent Street. He has taught at King's College, London, Battersea College of Technology and the University of Surrey, where he was Head of the Physics Department and is now Head of the Institute for Educational Technology. He has held Visiting Professorships at the University of Washington in Seattle, Sao Paulo University, University College, London, University of Sydney and Universiti Sains Malaysia.

Education can change society?

One day in 1957 the American public woke up to find a Russian satellite circling the earth. The shock of this discovery led to a searching debate about the effectiveness of American education. Scientists at the prestigious Massachusetts Institute of Technology began to take an interest in school science teaching. By 1967, the Americans had won the moon race and landed the first man on the moon.

It's a neat story to illustrate how education can change society. Or is it? Every sentence, on its own, is correct, but actually Friedman and Weisskopf at MIT started discussions about changes in school physics teaching six months before the launching of the first Sputnik. The resulting curriculum which, while more interesting than the old one, was even less concerned with practical applications, was introduced into American high schools in the early 1960s. However, getting a man on to the moon had in any case little to do with physics, though much with engineering and management, and neither of these subjects underwent major curricular changes at that time. Finally, the men and women who put Neil Armstrong on to the moon in 1967 had all had their school education and most their university education before 1957. Thus traditional education had vindicated itself against the charges levied against it ten years earlier. By then changes which may or may not have been desirable for other reasons, but which had certainly been pushed through on the basis of a wrong diagnosis, had altered both school and university science teaching. Greatly enlarged physics departments were pouring out graduates who, to their dismay, found that by now the space programme was being curtailed and jobs were scarce.

The story, as analysed, exemplifies aspects of the three main purposes of education[1]: to fit people to society, to develop them as persons and to change society. It also illustrates that these functions may well be in

72

conflict with each other. The new curricula largely aimed at developing the individual, while the strong backing for them arose from a desire to make society more oriented towards modern technology. In the event, the old education was actually found to have met the expressed societal aims. The story also illustrates the important fact that the needs of society change far too rapidly for education to be able to respond to them. As Bowden puts it[2]:

After a schoolboy decides to read engineering, he spends a couple of years in the sixth form preparing himself, then he has to go to university for three years, then he has to undergo that extraordinary experience which converts a college graduate into an engineer.... Meanwhile we have had a couple of general elections and half-a-dozen changes of national policy. There are either too many graduates or too few, and people will blame the universities for lack of foresight.

This brings me to what at present is an issue for much debate and discussion of which we shall find useful in trying to answer the question in the title of this article: how should education change so that we get better at maintaining our position in a technological world? The pressure is on for teachers to become better acquainted with the industrial world, to make their teaching more relevant to it and to persuade more of their best pupils to enter it. The implication is that such changes are needed and that they will succeed in the desired aim. Unfortunately, the evidence on both counts is to the contrary. No such programme appears to be required to persuade pupils to choose careers in medicine, law or accountancy, or indeed—in many continental countries—in engineering. On the other hand, it is notorious that science teachers have failed to persuade their pupils to enter the one profession of which their own knowledge is unparalleled—that of science teaching. A prosaic but reasonable explanation of these observations is that students are more likely to go for professions where they can see good salary prospects.

There is a naive cause-and-effect model behind the above prescription for change which is contrary to all our knowledge and understanding of change in society. It is now over thirty years since Kurt Lewin first developed his field theory of social change[3], which postulates that social equilibria result from a balance of opposing forces and that the degree of conflict inherent in a particular social situation depends on the strength of the opposing forces. If therefore we desire to change an existing social situation, we must first plot the field of opposing forces. We shall then find that change is more likely to happen if we reduce the forces against change—since this reduces the degree of conflict, than if we increase the forces for change, which increases the degree of conflict. Further, social equilibria have an inherent resistance to change, so that any attempt at change will lead, at least at first, to an increase in the forces against change. This effect will be greater if the attempt at change has been made through an increase in the forces in support of the change—since this increases the degree of conflict—than if the attempt has been made through a decrease in the forces against change. Finally, since the forces which keep a given situation in equilibrium are strongly coupled to each other, a change in any one will affect all. Any attempt therefore to change a situation in a particular way by changing just one of the forces affecting it—and this is what the naive cause-and-effect model amounts to—is therefore likely to result in a change, but not the one desired.

Having plotted the force field, we shall have to analyse it and estimate what changes in it are most likely to produce the desired change in the social system. We already know that it will usually be more profitable to reduce some of the forces against change than to increase those which favour change. We might further conjecture that it will in general be sensible to look first at large forces, since it is unlikely that a change in a small one will significantly alter the force field as long as the large forces are unchanged. Beyond this there are few if any general maxims. Indeed, the fact that we can at best only partially predict the changes in the system that result from any changes in the force field and that there are always changes which have not been predicted is the reason why a simple cause and effect model is so inapplicable to social systems.

Let us look then at some of the forces which oppose a change towards a more technologically oriented society. Does industry really want thinking people when it recruits graduates? No doubt it often does, but the complaints of young graduates that they are not being properly used in their first employment are too persistent to be ignored[4]. They are likely to be endorsed by the Finniston Committee which at present is looking into the future of British manufacturing industry. There is indeed much evidence that what is wrong with British industry is not so much the quality of its engineers as the values and attitudes of the managers who employ them, who as a rule are not engineers.

The next force to which I therefore wish to refer relates to the values that our society places on technology and industry. Dahrendorf puts his view bluntly[5]:

No-one should believe that universities and other educational institutions can decide to instil industrial values in their students whereupon British industry will flourish. Unless the country itself gives industry a higher place in its system of values, educational institutions cannot do so.

Elsewhere in the same article he stresses that—with some minor qualifications—

education does not create the values of a society, but it reflects them.

I shall return to this dictum, which in the present context is most depressing, later in this article.

The values of our society are perhaps indicated by certain features of the 'great debate' on education which the then Prime Minister started in 1977. This confined itself to state education and, although it was concerned with all aspects of this sector, concentrated primarily on the apparent deterioration in the kinds of skills associated with clerkly virtues, such as correctness in spelling, grammar and elementary arithmetic. By now we have an Assessment of Performance Unit in the Department of Education and Science, and some well-heeled research projects in universities, all in the main concerned with the standards of achievement of the less able. Am I alone in finding this preoccupation with the hewers of wood rather extraordinary, quite apart from the fact that it seems to be mainly concerned with deteriorations that may have occurred in recent years in accepted standards of traditional skills?

The ills of this country are not of recent origin. Our industrial decline was first noted as a result of the Brussels exhibition of 1862—eight years before the introduction of universal elementary education—which showed stark contrasts compared to the Great Exhibition of 1851, few to our advantage. At that time and since, we have been managed and governed—irrespective of the party in power—almost entirely by men educated in the so quaintly misnamed Public Schools and in the two universities most closely associated with them, Oxford and Cambridge. Might it not have been appropriate for the Prime Minister at least to consider whether the independent sector of education also needed scrutiny and whether there were not aspects of our education to be questioned which were not concerned with purely academic achievements and skills? The Public Schools, as we know them today, were created by and helped to create Victorian Society. Their greatest success is likely to have been the creation and maintenance of the British Empire. How well did they and how well do they serve the home country which their products still very largely govern?

The Headmaster of Westminster in an analysis[6] of what Westminster boys learned in the 1870s, quotes Corelli Barnett's thesis that 'the whole bias of British upper-class education in the Victorian age was against the realities of the industrial world' and confirms this dictum by noting a complete absence of science in the curriculum of that time. Also, he finds that none of the boys of the 1870 class entered commerce or industry, while the great majority made their career in the public service and the professions. This bias is likely to have contributed to Britain's subsequent industrial decline, and although the Public Schools can by now not be accused of neglecting the teaching of science, the values created by their teaching in the past are still with us, as is shown for instance by the statistics for entry to the top ranks of the Civil Service. It would appear— although it would be difficult to produce conclusive evidence—that our ruling classes and those who educate them may have borne and may continue to bear a heavy responsibility for our present ills.

However, it is possible that a still weightier and quite separate fault may have to be ascribed to the Public Schools. This is epitomised in Disraeli's famous phrase of the two nations, 'the privileged and the people'. Again it would be difficult to provide conclusive evidence, but in no other developed country has the division in education been so complete, a division that was not seriously affected by the spread of grammar school education in the first half of this century. Also, it is generally accepted that Britain is unique in this age in its preoccupation with the differences of class. Is it too far-fetched to see a link between these two peculiar features of our society? This is not to say that there may not be other factors that have contributed to our present divisions, such as our early industrialization, our lack of revolutions and defeat in war which have allowed us to continue an unbroken past into the present, our island isolation—but we cannot change our history or geography.

The mutual ignorance created by this almost total separation of the rulers and the ruled from a very early age has created a wall between them which was only slightly cracked by the Second World War, as is for instance indicated by this reminiscence of one of the Bevin Boys[7]:

It was an eye-opener to my family that I didn't find it more disagreeable mixing with totally different people and doing manual work. I got on well with the miners and used to come home on holiday and tell my family in Barnes about my experiences. They came to understand a lot more about the miners' way of life, especially after my lifelong friend was killed in a shaft only six months after joining.

Looking back over the past thirty years it is difficult to avoid the conclusion that the cracks have not spread, and that the wall is as strong as ever. Its existence is visible in many places; and it has led to a massive defensiveness and an 'us and them' attitude which again is unique to this country. The Government Think Tank in its report on the car industry spoke of[8]:

trench warfare attitudes of management and labour (which) will not serve in the assembly industries of 20th-century Western Europe

and a German businessman expressed the opinion of many when he said[9]:

More important than paying them properly is treating them properly.

Most curiously, the *Daily Express*[10] tried to contradict this generally held criticism of British management by producing a Swiss-born head of an organisation which employs 8,000 people in Britain. 'He treats all of them as his fellow-workers.' Exactly.

Of course, the shooting in this trench war is from both sides and many young graduates are disillusioned with industry through the attitudes of trade unions which can lead to[11]:

organisations being hamstrung by restrictive practices, which are methods of reducing the freedom of managers to make desirable changes.

However, the old dictum that there are no bad soldiers, only bad generals, is still applicable.

I have been concentrating on the forces which oppose change and in fairness I must add that there are many progressive employers and that there is no doubt where the government's heart is. Also, there *are* of course still forces in education which oppose change. With these additions we can now plot the force field relevant to technological change:

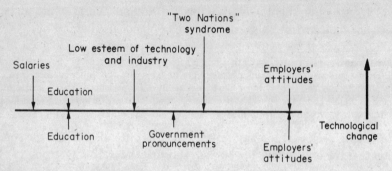

The length of each arrow is meant to give some qualitative estimate of the strength of the corresponding force.

Our analysis of the force field has taken us far from education and has indicated what powerful forces are arraigned against the puny force of the teacher in the classroom. Following Lewin, I postulate that even a small reduction of these powerful forces is likely to be more effective than anything that teachers can achieve directly. Of these forces, the strongest are those against technology and industry, and those that divide our nation. Both are very firmly entrenched—what a suitable metaphor—in the value system of our society and to reduce them will therefore require a change in that value system. This means that if we want to change the technological aspect of our society, we have to change that society as a whole. We should not be surprised by this conclusion in the light of Lewin's requirement that forces should not be treated in isolation.

This brings us back to the central question of this article. No longer can we ask whether education can change our society towards a more techno-logically oriented one, but quite simply whether education can change society *tout court*, and in particular, whether it can change its values. If Dahrendorf is right, then education cannot do this; it merely reflects the values of society. Is there a way out?

We have to distinguish here between the actual values of a society and the way its rulers desire its members to behave. It is perfectly possible for autocratic rulers, whether they are benevolent or malevolent, to change the actions of those in the society over which they rule, and it is not impossible for even a democratic government to do this, as our recent legislation on the death penalty and, to some extent, on homosexuality, may indicate[12]. The task of education is then to consolidate this change by moving the values which individuals hold nearer to their newly created behaviour, i.e. to bring the values of society closer to its laws. Sometimes, on the other hand, the task of education may be to influence people to change their values so that they will accept certain legislative changes. How difficult this is may be illustrated by the recent sorry attempts at legislation on seat belts or on smoking.

Clearly, legislation in advance of public opinion will be easier if it does not affect people too much. It will be hardest when it seriously affects the legislators themselves. It is probable that if a referendum had been held at any time during the past twenty years on the subject of grammar schools as against comprehensive schools, the majority of supporters of all parties would have voted for grammar schools. As late as 1963, Harold Wilson stated that grammar schools would be abolished 'only over his dead body' and it is likely that when he nevertheless eventually changed, he was well ahead of the opinions of his supporters. That legislation on comprehensive education has been possible at all may well have owed something to the fact that it has never been impossible for Cabinet Ministers to circumvent it by sending their own children to private schools.

If our analysis of the values of British society which hinder our technological progress is sound, then our situation is indeed parlous. I have suggested that the two strongest forces opposing change are due to the influence of the Public Schools, and I have suggested that the stronger of the two is rooted in our consciousness of and preoccupation with class, which in turn is related to the divisions in our nation. To ask that this force be reduced amounts to asking that two armies engaged in trench warfare —or whatever is the equivalent metaphor when the corresponding warfare takes place on the floor of the House of Commons—should agree to stop their fratricidal and suicidal battles and agree on a lasting peace. Recent failed attempts at a 'peace treaty' have included legislation on prices and incomes, and the Bullock report on industrial partnership. At the moment we seem to be back to square one[13], but this is never quite true. However, any circumspect dominie had better wait until the government is at least firmly ensconced on square two before he starts on his consolidation task.

The reason why these attempts at peace-making could not succeed is apparent at once from a force-field analysis of this particular situation. For while the forces of employers and employees are so powerfully balanced against each other in the industrial arena, any attempt at change will bring into play a stabilizing reaction of great strength. This manifests itself in both sides turning on the peacemaker. Mrs. Castle was the first person who got herself a bloody nose in this way; she is unlikely to have been the last.

What is needed and what was so eloquently expressed by the Bevin Boy is a means for bringing the two nations together so that they get to know each other better and reduce their mutual suspicions. This would seem to be one of those tasks where people might be influenced by education ahead of legislation. Indeed I believe that here education has its greatest chance, but only if it involves *all* children. As the last grammar schools disappear, there are signs of a euphoria that soon all schools will be equal. But this is not true, for the gulf between the comprehensive schools and the Public Schools may well remain greater than that between the grammar schools and Public Schools had ever been.

The logic of my argument seems to drive me to an apparently paradoxical conclusion—that in order to save this country from its present predicaments it may be necessary to abolish the Public Schools. The reason why this conclusion may seem paradoxical is that the Public Schools maintain recognisedly high academic standards and that the Great Debate has concentrated on the possible inadequacy of academic standards in state schools. I do not deny these standards, although I shall question below the way that the products of this education apply their academic excellence to the problems of today. However, my main argument against the Public Schools has not been educational; it has been sociological, in that I hypothesize that any temporary loss in trained personnel will be more than outweighed by greater social cohesion and the opportunity for the two nations to merge. To put it another way, and to link it to the general purpose of this article: the continuing argument about the Public Schools has been conducted almost wholly in educational terms; I want to stress the need for conducting this argument—and, by implication, the argument in any educational matter—on more general sociological lines and see where this takes us. Only in this way can we explore the relationship between education and society, and how change in one may lead to change in the other.

Let me now turn briefly to the next strongest opposing force, that due to the comparatively low esteem in which technology and industry are held.

I conjecture that the same radical prescription—the abolition of the Public Schools—may assist here too. For not only are our rulers being educated separately, but their education is still rooted in that amalgam of Greek and Judaic traditions which devalues those who do compared with those who think, whether in the form of Plato's philosopher-king or that of the learned man in Ecclesiasticus (ch. 38, v. 24), whose 'wisdom cometh of leisure: and he that hath little business shall become wise'. Perhaps the most pernicious result of this tradition has been our cult of the amateur and our suspicion of the truly professional.

The abolition of the Public Schools may thus help to reduce both the major forces opposing change towards a more technologically oriented society, but the main reason for this drastic measure must still lie in the need to bring together the two nations. And while it may indeed be sensible to think of the forces of education as in advance of those of legislation when it comes to the problem of reconciling the two nations, the opposite is the case when it comes to bringing pupils together in the first place. In other words, if we go back to the problem which we set out to tackle, it is my opinion that education can only make a significant contribution to the problems of our position in a technological world, if legislation ensures in the first place that all children are taught in the same schools. How to persuade our legislators to do that is another matter[14].

The argument in the last paragraph has drawn attention to three general matters. The first is that the relationship between education and society is more complex than is indicated by Dahrendorf's dictum that education reflects society. We must distinguish between the education of the individual which indeed tends to reflect the values of society and the educational system which society can modify so that it in turn modifies society. Thus the education of the individual is in general governed by Dahrendorf's dictum, but the educational system interacts with society in a more complex way, in that the interaction between the two is mutual. In technological language, we are dealing with a feedback loop, in which a change in either one affects the other and hence in turn the first.

Secondly, I want to draw attention to the very long time spans that may be required for changes in education to result in changes in society. While the 'Great Debate' appeared to be based on the premise that changes in the curriculum could significantly affect our technological effectiveness, possibly within the lifetime of one Parliament, the way that the two nations could be brought closer together through education clearly requires periods that are measured in decades, if not centuries. Which does not mean that we should not start now.

Thirdly, we should perhaps look not only a century into the future, but also a century into the past. We then may think that we can see in the society of today the results of the education which our great grandfathers received as well as the results of the education which they did not receive. This latter consideration may in fact be the more important of the two and, since omissions are in general less deliberate than commissions, we may conclude that if education is at times effective in changing society, it may be so in ways often not intended by the educators.

The argument of the last two paragraphs indicates just how long a time span we have to consider if we wish to investigate the effects of education on society and just how tenuous the connection may become in the course of that time. Educationists—like the landscape gardeners of the eighteenth century—can only hope that the fruits of their labours may be appreciated by generations yet unborn, and the apparent lack of success within five or ten years of for instance such special programmes to help the disadvantaged as the Head Start programme in the United States becomes irrelevant to our argument. If we do want to consider the effect of education and educational expenditure on the lot of the poor then we should ask whether the efforts of the introduction of compulsory education in this country more than a hundred years ago have been by now on the whole beneficial or not.

So we finally return to the question which forms the title of this article. What answer can one give to it in general, in the light of the specific case which I have discussed? Can education change society? Can education not change society? Why should an article which started with one question not end with four?[15]

This article was written in November 1978.

Notes

1. Maurice Kogan, *The Politics of Educational Change*, Fontana, 1978.
2. Lord Bowden of Chesterfield, 'Is manpower planning necessary? Is it possible? What next?', *Bacie Journal*, September 1978, p. 132.
3. Kurt Lewin, *Field Theory in Social Science*, Harper, New York, 1947.
4. See, for instance: Tim Albert, 'The class of '75: where are they now?' *Times Higher Education Supplement*, 17.2.1978.
5. Ralph Dahrendorf, 'The case for strengthening what is strong', *Times Higher Education Supplement*, 26.8.1977.

6. John Rae, 'Smudges on the upper crust', *Times Educational Supplement*, 2.12.1977.
7. William Harrington and Peter Young, *The 1945 Revolution*, Davis-Poynter, 1978.
8. Reported by Stephen Fay, 'Britain's poverty: the role of union power', *The Sunday Times*, 5.3.1978.
9. Reported in 'Germans blame the British manager', *Guardian*, 1.8.1977.
10. Michael Evans, 'The real secret of success', *Daily Express*, 8.8.1977.
11. Letter by W. W. Sweet, Senior careers adviser, Lancaster University, in response to Tim Albert's article (ref. 4), *Times Higher Education Supplement*, 24.2.1978.
12. Bridget Pym, *Pressure Groups and the Permissive Society*, David and Charles, 1974.
13. Peter Stothard, 'Resounding "no" to plan for worker directors', *Sunday Times*, 5.11.1978.
14. As I write this, H. C. Dent in the *Times Educational Supplement* of 17.11.78, writes: 'Would public opinion (or Parliament) ever *compel* independent schools to conform to l.e.a. pupil-teacher ratios and not exceed Burnham salaries?'
15. My thanks are due to Bridget Pym for most helpful comment and criticism.

H. D. Purcell

Professor H. D. Purcell went up to Jesus College, Oxford, on a scholarship in 1950, and holds degrees from Oxford, London, and Cambridge universities.

After National Service with the Green Howards in Germany, he spent a year in North America. His first teaching post was at the British Institute of Rome, and since that time he has taught at a number of universities, in Turkey, Persia, Northern Ireland, Libya, Nepal and Qatar. He now teaches at the Economics University in Vienna.

Apart from articles in learned journals, he reviewed over forty books for *International Affairs* in the 1960s, mostly about political and economic problems in the Middle East. His history of *Cyprus* appeared in 1970. During the 1970s, he has contributed reviews to *Books and Bookmen*, besides articles in other journals. Over the past twelve years, he has concentrated on banking and finance.

He is married and has four sons.

His hobbies are judo, climbing, scuba diving, and collecting language records and tapes.

The fallacy of environmentalism

Si monumentum requiris, circumspice.

Environmentalism is the dominant fallacy of our times. Its devotees include all those who believe, or profess to believe, in the relative unimportance of genetic inheritance and a correspondingly enormous scope for improvement on nature. Whether they be Marxists, anarchists, liberals, or neo-Christians, they all share this basic tenet.

It might be suggested that I have no right to express an opinion on a subject relating to genetics because my qualifications are in the humanities, and my practical experience otherwise has been in the field of economics. But the same objection would apply, *a fortiori*, to those influential journalists and well-funded sociologists who have set themselves up as scientific commentators and taken it upon themselves to attack hereditarianism—not indeed with arguments, but with the weapons of personal vilification and emotive insinuation. I can at least claim to have read widely in the subject and to understand the workings of scientific method. Also, I have had the privilege of discussing their findings with several of the scholars I shall mention (though of course they cannot be held collectively responsible for every detail of my argument).

When I went up to Trinity, Cambridge, in 1963, I found that the college authorities had arranged talks for us doctoral students to be given by various distinguished persons on topics of general interest. One of these was Sir Fred Hoyle, who told us: 'When your mathematicians emigrate, you mustn't think you can replace them by means of training schemes; they take their genes with them'. Another was Sir Francis Crick, who had recently won the Nobel Prize together with Professor J. B. Watson. He explained to us the actual mechanism whereby life is transmitted, and discussed a few of the implications of his discovery. Soon after, at a meeting of the Cambridge Humanist Society which he addressed, I asked him whether he agreed that what he had to say about the overriding importance of inherited characteristics was destructive of the assumptions which underlay most of what passed for religion, politics and sociology. He replied that indeed it was. In 1966, he published a book, *Of Molecules and Men*, which stressed the factual basis of hereditarian theory.

At Cambridge, as at other universities, I found that most of those engaged in legitimate scientific work (I do not count most 'social scientists') were of the opinion that heredity is much more important than environment. On the other hand, those studying Arts subjects either refused to consider the matter because it was outside their scope, or else conformed to the prevailing environmentalist view, with all its social implications.

The scientists might be expected to know rather more about the matter than the Arts men, and I was disappointed that so few of them dared voice in public opinions which they had expressed to me privately. They were not committed to their utterances, and I attributed this to moral cowardice. Leftist 'liberals' were gaining ground in nearly all Western universities at that time, and were only too ready to denounce a man as a rightist, or even as a fascist, if he advanced such views. (As always, they preferred labels to arguments.)

Cowardice was certainly part of the problem. It never ceases to amaze me how the educated Englishman can combine so much moral trepidation with physical bravery and pleasant human qualities. Confront him with a little righteous abuse, and he curls up like a snail when salt is sprinkled on it.

But I no longer think that cowardice is the sole reason for such behaviour. Condemning the environmentalist viewpoint involves questioning assumptions which have tended to dominate Western thinking since the eighteenth century: egalitarianism, cosmopolitanism, and belief in the power of education fundamentally to change people for the better. A single individual seldom has the time, the resources, or the inclination, to challenge rooted assumptions—especially when to do so makes him an automatic target for every hysteric that comes along. But concealing what one knows to be true gives one a quite unjustified feeling of guilt, and this feeling is increased by being associated with the misdeeds, real or alleged, of anyone who ever held similar views. Here indeed is guilt by association, and it is absurd. Do you hold every religious person responsible for misdeeds committed by his co-religionists? More to the point, do you hold every Marxist responsible for crimes committed by other Marxists?

At this juncture, a certain amount of background is indicated, in order to give an idea of the overwhelming strength of the hereditarian case. A fairly full and very readable history of genetics is to be found in Professor C. D. Darlington's *Genetics and Man*, and the human implications of the science are further discussed in his recent study, *The Little Universe of Man*.

The mathematical foundations of genetics were laid by Gregor Mendel, later Abbot of Brünn, whose *Experiments with Plant Hybrids* was published in 1866. It filled a great gap in Darwin's thinking because it explained the way in which characteristics are transmitted. Yet Mendel's findings were ignored for thirty-four years, perhaps because he was a priest, and so was presumed at that time to be out of touch with the modern world. Incidentally, he was not technically qualified either, having failed his examination in biology. What is more, he appears to have tidied up his results somewhat, since they are more clear-cut than could be expected from the limited experimental means at his disposal. Nevertheless, his conclusions are unchallengeable and their implications are profound.

What Mendel had discovered was that genetic traits are inherited in statistically predictable patterns, and his findings apply to *all forms of life*—not just to his sweet-peas. This fact throws an interesting light on the ignorance of people who say that Darlington ought not to write about human genetics because he is only a botanist! As a matter of fact, Mendel had originally intended to experiment with mice, but his ecclesiastical superiors felt that that went too near the bone! No species, and that includes man, is exempt from Mendelian laws.

From 1900 onwards, Mendel's discoveries were confirmed and acknowledged, and the science of genetics was placed on a firm foundation. On this base was erected the whole structure of modern genetics, with Crick and Watson's achievement in molecular biology as the keystone of the arch.

The practical effects of genetic research have been almost as impressive as its theoretical implications—and much more widely recognised. New breeds of animals and plants have enormously improved production and yields. Yet few of the people who enthuse over the new wheat, maize, and rice hybrids, yielding crops several times bigger than before, realise that without the discovery of Mendel's laws, such results would have been impossible. Similarly, when a genetic cocktail of a horse wins a race, its hybrid nature is stressed, and not the fact that it was produced by means of Mendelian recombination—and will tend to degenerate in the next filial generation according to the same laws. The whole point about hybrids is that they are unstable genetically. That is why pure stocks have to be preserved.

Let us pause a little here, and consider the remarks made at the end of the previous paragraph. Would I be encouraged to make them in a modern British comprehensive school? I doubt it. Yet they will remain true whether or not they are taught in schools, and those who proceed in ignorance of them will undoubtedly suffer for it.

Of course, the main objection to the application of Mendelian thinking to man is that it implies pretty clearly that evolution proceeds through subspecific differentiation. (Were not Darwin's Galapagos finches differentiated in precisely this way?) And the name for human subspecies is races. If races do not exist (as Ashley Montagu argues in the UN declaration on race, and as a recent NUT pamphlet continues to argue), then man is the only species without any subspecific differentiation! A little thought should convince the reader that this is ridiculous. Overlapping does not invalidate subspecific differences in man, any more than it does in the rest of the animal kingdom. Also subspecies are by definition able to interbreed, though they will not do so by preference. Sir Arthur Keith recognised this when he emphasized the importance of instinctive prejudice in preserving contiguous breeding-groups (see *A New Theory of Human Evolution, passim*). Anyone still in doubt as to the existence of races should read John R. Baker's excellent study of the subject in his *Race*, O.U.P., 1974.

There are perfectly respectable arguments against race-mixing which are not allowed to be taught in universities, let alone in schools. Every breeding-group has a reservoir of unfavourable recessive alleles, and these tend to be transmitted heterozygously (i.e. from one side only). The favourable ones tend to be transmitted homozygously, if the breeding-group is in equilibrium. (That is to say, they tend to be identical in composition on both sides.) The breeding-group may take in alleles from another breeding-group, provided these are only introduced in small numbers. This is in fact the process whereby races lower in evolutionary grade appear to have been hominised. See Carleton S. Coon's *The Origin of the Races*. However, if cross-breeding occurs on too large a scale, then the genetic equilibrium of both groups is upset. Not only is the common pool of unfavourable alleles increased in size and complexity (since different races have some different ones), but the favourable alleles in both breeding-groups tend to be transmitted heterozygously as well (because they also differ in certain cases). Thus the fact that human races may share over ninety per cent of their genetic inheritance is offset by the differences in the remaining few per cent (as indeed is the case where all species are concerned). Race-mixing destroys the balance in favour of the beneficial genes which has been established through a long process of selection, and all the alleles tend to compete on a free and equal basis—with unfortunate results. For a time, the phenomenon of hybrid vigour may mask the effects of intermixing, but the later stages must show the effects of enlarging the reservoir of unfavourable alleles and the detrimental effects even of combining different favourable ones.

There are indeed indications that widespread intermixing, accompanied by the emigration of outstanding individuals (the brain drain), does irreparable harm to a people; and it is no surprise to find that cross-bred peoples (as opposed to mosaics of ethnic groups) are lacking in civic sense and social cohesion. Certainly, if we compare the crime rates in more and less mixed societies, we find an astonishing difference in favour of the latter. To quote Franz Boas, in the 1911 edition of *The Mind of Primitive Man*: 'Differences of structure must be accompanied by differences of function, physiological as well as psychological; and as we found clear evidence of differences in structure between the races, so we must anticipate that differences in mental characteristics will be found'. In 1912, Boas went on to claim that his research showed how American immigrants of East European origin showed definite changes in head shape over the generations, but this Lamarckian claim was discredited when checked. The 1938 edition of *The Mind of Primitive Man* lacks the above-quoted passage but, as has been remarked, research in between the two dates had tended strongly to confirm it. The point is of more than academic interest, since Boas gathered round him a number of environmentalist sociologists who in turn influenced others and eventually imposed their spurious orthodoxy on the whole of American (and British) sociology until very recently.

Mere denial of the existence of races is now wearing thin as a form of argument, and various compromises have been suggested that would permit things to go on as they are. For example, many Christians and liberals have felt drawn towards the compromise proposed by Pierre Teilhard de Chardin. He did not deny the importance of physical evolution—he knew too much for that—but he postulated the existence of a 'noösphere' in which human evolution would henceforth continue. By 'noösphere' he meant the cloud of mind. That cloud has yet to discharge any collective lightning, but the theory has given comfort to those who wish to overlook the clear acceptance of human variety found in the Bible, and who prefer to see mankind in undifferentiated terms.

The sincere liberal is confronted with a problem—what to do about the mounting evidence for the decisive part played by heredity in human affairs. He cannot just ignore it, dearly as he would like to. The reason is a propaganda phenomenon known as the credibility gap, which is never discussed in editorials, but enters into the calculations of editors all the same. Once a point of view is sufficiently well known, it becomes positively damaging to ignore it any more. It has to be tamed in some way. (So when important problems, ignored for years, are finally ventilated in the Press, there is no reason for us to feel any exaggerated gratitude.)

At the same time, if the offending viewpoint is to any extent accepted, it leaves its opponents with another problem; namely, that counter-arguments, in so far as they can be created, have to be lifted on to the same plane. The best parallel that I can find is with Christian arguments after publication of Darwin and Wallace's findings (backed by the formidable eloquence of T. H. Huxley). So long as the Christians stuck to Archbishop Ussher's chronology, they were fairly safe—though they ran the risk of being left as an absurd anachronism by the receding tide. But the moment they tried to achieve a compromise, the question arose as to how far they could go without damaging their case irremediably. New wine has a well-known effect on old bottles.

Similarly, opponents of hereditarianism today are being forced to admit for the sake of argument, that heredity does play some part in life, though much subordinate as a factor to the environment. They could of course argue that the environment is decisive in evolution, because it amounts to the circumstances under which life-forms are selected out. But this ultimate importance of the environment is rather too long term for the liberals' liking. Naturally, they can argue that man now controls his environment to some extent, but this line is less popular than formerly,

(a) because he makes awful mistakes while doing so, and (b) because his control over the environment is equally an argument for heredity controlling environment. I mean that if man is himself mainly genetically programmed, then his control of the environment is hereditarian at one remove. It is not all such plain sailing as it once seemed!

But argument with liberals is an unrewarding exercise—even if one wins, which is not too difficult. They are not really concerned with objective truth, but rather with moral imperatives. In fact, one of the main planks in their platform is a denial of the possibility of objectivity—which leaves us all exactly where we were to begin with. Their driving force is a deep sense of outrage with nature as it is, coupled with resentment against those favoured by nature. No lasting compromise can be made with such an attitude of mind, and any attempt to achieve one is a waste of time.

I do indeed believe that most of those who support environmentalist causes are genuinely deluded—that is to say, wrong but well-meaning. However, I cannot bring myself to believe that the 'opinion-formers' are often equally sincere. What about those three founder members of the Institute of Race Relations (which is apparently dedicated to race-mixing for the British majority) who are at the same time members of the Race Relations sub-committee of an organisation which is against such inter-marriage for a particular minority? One of them became the Home Secretary's adviser on race relations, I believe. To call this sinister would not be to overstate the case.

For those environmentalists who have accepted the logic of their position and become Marxists, no difficulties remain. All the answers are implicit in Marxist writings. It is merely a matter of interpreting the world in the light of these. The concept of objective truth is dismissed as a bourgeois illusion, and argument becomes a dialectical exercise, the only purpose of which is to gain converts and destroy adversaries. If the evidence is against the environmentalist case, so much worse for the evidence. In the West, Marxists harness the moral disapproval of liberals and turn it into a weapon of moral blackmail and intellectual terrorism. In the East, they use naked power.

For the Marxist, people are perfectly adaptable and susceptible to conditioning. The true collectivist reveres the name of Pavlov and Skinner. As for Mendel's laws, they were replaced before the war by Lysenko—with a lot of theoretical help from Lamarck. This involved the liquidation of dissident scientists and public acceptance in the Soviet Union of all Lysenko's faked experiments.

Stalin supported Lysenko because he saw that a behaviourist society was far easier for him to manage than one in which all sorts of intractable differences had to be taken into account. All tyrants prefer to coerce people with punishments, as Pavlov did with his unfortunate laboratory animals, or bribe them with rewards, as Skinner did with his. And when they find themselves up against a body of doctrine which conflicts with such theories, they lie—just as Lysenko did with Stalin's support. Even now, when the credibility gap has forced a reappraisal of the subject, the heirs of Lysenko come up with unverifiable experiments which purport to have rehabilitated him as a scientist.

In the West, the methods used are scarcely more subtle. Just as Pavlov's dogs were given electric shocks whenever they behaved instinctively, so scientists who promote hereditarian views are subjected to defamation, economic and social pressure, and physical violence. Such are the electric cattle prods applied to the rogue bulls of the majority herd.

Shockley and Jensen, for example, based their initial conclusions regarding American Negro intelligence on a mass of data, much of it collected over years by the US Army. Yet they have received the full treatment from intellectual terrorists posing as guardians of political morality. Their motives have been impugned, their lectures broken up, and their lives made miserable. One *canard*, obviously based on the presupposition that people will not take the trouble to check it, is that Jensen has done no original research on this matter. I recommend those interested to read his *Environment, Heredity and Intelligence* (1963) and his *Educability and Group Differences* (1973). In private, liberals will sometimes admit that there is probably something in his findings—Marxists never. But all are equally determined to deny them a platform. Intellectual dishonesty has been elevated to the status of a moral virtue.

Similarly, Carleton S. Coon, the respected doyen of American anthropologists, a great scholar and good writer, has been insulted in public by vastly inferior but influential colleagues. There is a definite pattern in the operations of such gentlemen. They emerge from the woodwork the moment there is any danger of hereditarian theory reaching a wider audience.

Konrad Lorenz, whose name is synonymous with the study of inherited behaviour patterns, was prevented from rehabilitating himself for years, and even now there is a whispering campaign against him. Professor Hans Eysenck was assaulted when he tried to speak at the London School of Economics, and all such speakers were 'blacked' by the National Union of Students.

Even more despicable have been the attempts to blacken the posthumous reputations of hereditarian scientists. Thus, Sir Arthur Keith was accused after his death of being responsible for the Piltdown hoax, but now that more evidence is available it points in quite a different direction. Recently, the reputation of Sir Cyril Burt has been besmirched as if by smoke from a belching chimney. A selective study of the allegations made against him does indeed indicate that in old age Burt succumbed to a temptation to bring his data more exactly into line with his thesis, but the tendency of the evidence is still in favour of that thesis, which is concerned with the relationship between intelligence and social mobility. What is more, one of his colleagues whose existence has been denied, Margaret Howard, turns out not only to have existed but to have been mathematically competent. Given the notorious animus of his detractors, it is likely that in retrospect his offence will seem no more heinous than Mendel's.

The attack on Burt's reputation was particularly significant because it also involved a rejection of the whole principle of identical twin studies, and so struck at the very basis of hereditarian theory. But the validity of such studies is by no means dependent on evidence offered by Burt. The fact is that identical twins come from the same fertilised ovum; they are literally one flesh and blood, and there is a positively vast body of evidence to show that they do in fact resemble each other more than other people. Their psychology, behaviour, and even gestures, continue to have extraordinary resemblances even if they are separated at birth. Rejection of such studies must lead one to question the *bona fides* of the critics, not that of Cyril Burt.

Nor is it only a question of defaming or terrorising outstanding individuals. All researchers into human genetics are liable to be demonstrated against by agitators posing as humanitarians, and to have their funds quietly withdrawn unless they concentrate on helping the unfit to procreate rather than on the study of eugenics. Since the groups of demonstrators can claim the support of extensive race relations legislation and have contacts which enable them to bring pressure to bear upon those who control funds for research, their influence is virtually irresistible.

Of course, they claim that they are motivated by considerations of kindness, but those who insist on the perpetuation of misery are morally responsible for it. Differential breeding in favour of the less fit, coupled with the widespread practice of abortion among the healthy majority, has a compound interest effect in genetic terms. If it is allowed to continue unchecked, our civilisation is doomed.

To be sure, there are signs that the techniques of intimidation have been overdone. Articles have appeared denouncing Eysenck's persecutors, and the two egregious gentlemen who orchestrated the hymn of hate against Professor Edward O. Wilson of Harvard and his new science of Sociobiology have been forced to admit that they made a tactical mistake. Hysteria becomes counter-productive as more people become aware that it is not a sincere expression of 'concern', but a coercive act put on for effect.

Amazingly enough, one of the charges made against Wilson is that he is 'only' an expert on insects, and so has no right to speak about mankind. Once again, we find a rooted unwillingness to come to terms with the basic unity of all life, together with a refusal to accept its variety.

Ye shall know a tree by its fruit, and the environmentalist tree bears the bitter fruit of collectivism. The pace of 'change' over the past forty years (change only in one direction) has accelerated to the point where collectivism has become a rampant menace. Its destructive effects are there for all to see: in our educational, immigration, and social engineering policies. All levelling must result in levelling down, simply because people's innate abilities differ. The Chinese, at least, have learnt this lesson.

There is a democratic Australian poem which forsees the millennium in the following stirring terms:

> Then the curse of class distinctions into ruins shall be hurled
> And a sense of human kinship revolutionise the world,
> There'll be higher education for the toilin', starvin' clown,
> And the rich and educated shall be educated down.

All around us we see projections of this state of mind. Has it reduced racial or class animosity? Is it really meant to? Has it promoted prosperity? Is it really meant to? Has it improved educational opportunities? Is it really meant to? Or is it meant to bring about the collapse of our society and the replacement of our demoralised meritocrats with a New Class of former conspirators who will be vastly more callous and authoritarian? In preparation for the brave new world of the future, increasing numbers of our people emerge from school as functional illiterates, injected with the poison of egalitarianism, and ready to take their place as serfs in a manipulated society.

The environmentalist dream is fast becoming a nightmare. But you ain't seen nothing yet. As the pace of 'change' accelerates—like a roller-coaster leaving the rails—good people will be saying to themselves, 'What have I done to deserve this?' The answer will be, 'Nothing. That is why you deserve it.'

You may rest assured, however, that the liberal answer to the problems created by environmentalism will merely be more environmentalism. If people don't fit into the predetermined pattern, then obviously that is the people's fault. As for the facts, environmentalist spokesmen will continue to have an infallible answer to them all: compulsive, systematic lying.

Sir Peter Medawar

Sir Peter Medawar, CH 1972, Kt 1965, CBE 1958, FRS 1949, was born in 1915. His appointments include Director, National Institute for Medical Research, London, 1962-71, and Professor of Experimental Medicine at the Royal Institution. His publications include *The Uniqueness of the Individual*, 1956, *The Future of Man*, 1960, *The Art of the Soluble*, 1967, *Induction and Intuition in Scientific Thought*, 1969, *The Hope of Progress*, 1972, *The Life Science* (with J. S. Medawar), 1977, and *Advice to a Young Scientist*, 1979.

A bouquet of fallacies from medicine and medical science with a sideways glance at mathematics and logic

My favourite fallacy—favourite because it is so rich and devious in concealed assumptions and unspoken implications—runs 'Medicine cannot even cure the common cold'. Taken at its face value and disregarding the pejorative adverb the statement is not false. There is indeed no cure for the common cold though many of its symptoms can be ameliorated; the concealed fallacy lies in the implication that it is folly to spend huge sums of public money upon, for example, cancer research when 'medicine cannot even . . .'

What is wrong here is the assumption almost everybody makes until they come to learn how grievously mistaken it is—the assumption that grave diseases have complex causes while comparatively mild diseases have simple causes and are proportionately easy to cure.

Nothing could be further from the truth: the common cold is a dismayingly complex disease, caused by one or more of upwards of fifty so-called 'rhinoviruses' and bedevilled by a complex overlay of allergic reactivities. No known antibiotic acts upon viruses as penicillin and the sulphonamide drugs act upon bacteria: we recover from our cold because of the mobilisation of our own body's natural immunological defences. We shan't get *that* cold again for several weeks—though we could get a cold caused by other viruses. We need not worry then about 'reinfecting ourselves from our own handkerchiefs' or by exposure to someone who got his or her cold from us, as if the same cold could go round and round in circles or shuttle to and fro between two victims.

What about cancer, then?—and the hundreds of millions of pounds spent on cancer research.

This costly research has made it clear that some of the causes of cancer are quite simple: it has been said that 80% of all tumours are of environmental origin—are caused by hydrocarbon tars, tarry smokes, asbestos dusts, industrial chemicals and the like. This circumstance does not make established tumours any easier to cure, but it does point the way to preventive measures such as abstention from smoking—a procedure that has already saved thousands of lives.

Fallacies about cancer abound: *cancer is a disease of civilisation,* for example. This is half true inasmuch as most of the identifiable cancer-causing agents referred to in the preceding paragraph developed as a concomitant of industrial civilisation.

But that is not really what people have in mind when they speak of cancer as a disease of civilisation. No: nearly all WASPS believe in the punishment theory of illness and what they really mean is that contracting cancer is a punishment for our having adopted an effete and unnatural way of life: central heating and CHW have weakened the natural defences in proportion as they have attenuated the moral fibre.

It is perfectly true that a far higher proportion of people die of cancer in the industrial Western world than die of cancer in the third world in the developing countries; but before we compare the mortality statistics of different populations we must make quite sure that the populations are genuinely comparable—and of course they are not. The mean expectation of life at all ages is much higher in the effete industrialised Western countries than it is in the third world and insofar as cancer tends to be a disease of middle and later life we in the Western world are more gravely at risk: elsewhere people are less likely to die of cancer because they are so much more likely to die earlier of something else.

Cancer is so grave a disease and held so greatly in dread that we need not wonder at the growing up of many folkloristic fallacies about it. One such fallacy is that cancer of the breast may be the consequence of a blow upon the breast. I can suggest two reasons why this belief arose: the first is that which I have described as one of the fallacies due to 'selective memory'. Women unlucky enough to contract a breast cancer are likely to remember and make mention of the fact that they once received a blow upon the breast, but there is no comparable body of evidence relating to women who have had a blow upon the breast and who have *not* contracted a breast cancer, so the evidence is inherently biased. The second possible reason is that a blow upon the breast, because of the anxious palpitation that follows it or the disproportionate pain it causes may show up a hitherto unsuspected cyst or abnormal growth. This again is a source of biased evidence because women who have not received such a blow have not the incentive for the scrutiny which might reveal a tumour.

The incentive—even willingness—to believe that cancer is a disease of civilisation represents a cast of thought that reveals itself in many different ways: for example, very many people take it entirely for granted that brown (i.e. unrefined) sugar is better for one than refined white sugar. The parallel upon which this reasoning is based is of course the well-known and genuine superiority of brown (wholemeal) flour and bread, which is superior to refined white flour and the bread that is made from it for at least three reasons: (a) flours and breads made from whole grain will retain the highly important vitamins of the B complex and other vitamins to be found in wheat germ, including vitamin E; (b) the chemical agents used in the bleaching or refining process may themselves be harmful; and (c) it is now known that consumption of cereal fibre is specially important for the correct working of the bowel and a preventive against ailments peculiar to the bowel such as diverticulitis.

The case of 'brown *v.* white sugar' is by no means comparable. Crystalline sugar (originally an extremely murky substance) was a rare and expensive treat until about the middle of the eighteenth century: it has not been a natural article of diet long enough to have brought about any selective change in human populations. It is far otherwise with cereal flours which have been in use for hundreds of years. The use of polished (as opposed to whole) rice is in some ways comparable to the use of white versus wholemeal flours; populations subsisting upon polished as opposed to whole rice may be the victims of the deficiency disease beri-beri, one of the clues that led to the recognition of vitamins as essential ingredients of diet. Here then strong selective forces may be at work.

Demography is full of pitfalls for people not used to the ways of thought that become second nature to demographers. Everybody realises the desirability of stabilising the population numbers of the more prolific peoples of the world: an idea which gained widespread currency, particularly in the United States, was that if all couples were to limit the number of their children to two the population would be stabilised and would neither enlarge nor diminish. 'This proposal,' the Medawars[1] said

'. . . has that air of commonsensical rightness about it which is almost invariably a symptom of some aberration of reasoning. The trouble is that the two-child proposal gives no weight either to mortality or to infertility— factors of the utmost importance for the reproductive vitality of a population.' Two children per couple would not even provide for replacement.

Another demographic aberration of thought which is usually raised in any discussion of the rights and wrongs of the exercise of the power to terminate pregnancy is that which the Medawars describe as the *Beethoven fallacy*. It owes its name to the particular form in which the argument was put by Mr. Maurice Baring and it was recounted by Mr. Norman St John Stevas, MP, in the following terms:

One doctor to another: 'About the terminating of pregnancy, I want your opinion. The father was syphilitic. The mother tuberculous. Of the four children born, the first was blind, the second died, the third was deaf and dumb, the fourth was also tuberculous. What would you have done?' 'I would have ended the pregnancy'. 'Then you would have murdered Beethoven.'[2]

The reasoning involved in this argument is breathtakingly fallacious, for unless it is being suggested that there is some causal connection between having a tubercular mother and a syphilitic father and giving birth to a musical genius, the world is no more likely to be deprived of a Beethoven by abortion than by chaste abstention from intercourse or even by a woman's having a menstrual period; for by either means the world may be deprived of whatever genetic make-up conduces to the development of a musical genius.

The rejection of the Beethoven fallacy makes it inevitable that I should devote some attention to the analysis of a fallacy which I have made the basis of an intelligence test to quite large audiences at lectures during which I have discussed the notion of 'intelligence'. Following the precedent set above I shall call this the *Greco fallacy*.

The Cretan painter Domenikos Theotokopoulos spent most of his life in Spain where he was known, understandably enough, as the Greek, El Greco.

To many eyes the figures in El Greco's paintings, particularly the holy ones, seem unnaturally tall and thin.

This was clearly what El Greco intended, but an incautious ophthalmologist expressed the opinion that El Greco painted this way because he had a defect of vision which made him see people this way—and as he saw them so he would naturally draw them.

Having given this background information in the lecture I have then told the audience that anyone who could see instantly that this argument is totally fallacious—for philosophical, not for aesthetic reasons—was undoubtedly very bright. On the other hand, anyone who couldn't see that the argument was fallacious when the error of reasoning involved in it was made clear must surely be rather dull. I went on to explain that if the ophthalmologist's argument were true then any painter who suffered from diplopia—from seeing things double—would necessarily paint everything double: twenty-four at the Last Supper, two Laughing Cavaliers, two Stags at Bay, etc.

But if the painter did anything of the kind then when he came to inspect his own handiwork he would at once suspect that something was amiss: four Stags now at Bay, four Laughing Cavaliers, etc.; the point need not be laboured: the point is epistemological, i.e. has to do with the theory of knowledge: if the painter depicts his subjects in such a way that they look normal to him if they will also look normal to us. By 'normal' I mean of course normally representational.

Criticisms and critical analyses of the kind I have just been engaged in often cause a good deal of resentment, particularly among those who have cherished the beliefs shown to be without foundation. I write as a scientist, though, and scientists soon learn not to feel aggrieved at criticisms of their ideas and experiments—they soon come to learn, indeed, that science cannot prosper without continuous criticism of the imaginative exploits by which they try to make sense of the natural world, for without criticism, science would consist of no more than fanciful invention, whereas science is the outcome of a synergistic collaboration between the imaginative and critical faculties.[3]

The point I am making is that the exposure and rectification of error is part of the ordinary hurly-burly of scientific life. In science, however, aberrations of reasoning do not declare themselves by any one sign: in science correspondence with reality is always the ultimate court of appeal: in mathematics, logic and philosophy generally, aberrations of reasoning declare themselves by the characteristic that they lead to self-contradictions, i.e. to the derivation of mutually contradictory theorems, or to paradoxes, examples of which I shall give below. A paradox has the same significance for a logician or a mathematician as the smell of burning rubber for an electronics engineer.

The most famous logico-mathematical paradoxes are the paradoxes of continuity discovered by Zeno who was able to demonstrate to his own satisfaction (and to the discomfiture of almost everyone who has thought about them since) that Achilles can never overtake the tortoise, nor an arrow reach its target. Zeno's reasoning is as follows: while Achilles runs to reach the place the tortoise started from, the tortoise will have moved on a little more and will have done so again while Achilles is making up the extra distance and so on *ad infinitum*—so Achilles never quite catches up. Galileo's paradoxes of infinity show that, unlikely though it may seem, one infinite number may be larger than or smaller than another. Consider the following reasoning, for example: by putting one on top of the other it becomes obvious by inspection that every number has a square:

Integers	1	2	3	4	5	6 . . . . .
Squares	1	4	9	16	25	36 . . . . .

We may thus confidently say that the number of numbers is equal to the number of squares, because they pair off exactly 1-1. On the other hand, it will certainly be agreed that some numbers are not squares—for example, 7, 17, 27. It therefore follows that the number of numbers must be greater than the number of squares.

Another famous paradox which is soon picked up by bright school-children who are taking mathematics seriously is that which shows that the square root of 2 (i.e. the length of the diagonal square of unit length of side) cannot be represented as a ratio of simple integers. It is accordingly described as 'irrational'.

Logical paradoxes make a more immediate appeal to those who have no taste for numbers. A famous logical paradox is that of Sextus Empiricus. It is that which called attention to the element of question-begging (*petitio principii* as they used to say in ancient Rome) in one of the forms of the syllogism. Given as premises that Socrates is a man and that all men are mortals, most people would confidently infer that Socrates was mortal, but, Sextus Empiricus asked, in effect, how can you know that all men are mortal unless you *already* know that Socrates is mortal? It's a good point, but not such as to undermine one's faith in the validity of deduction.

Another famous paradox belongs to a class that has been described as the class of '*All*' paradoxes. The most famous is that of the Cretan spokesman who said 'All Cretans are liars'. Was he telling the truth or not? Whichever answer one gives leads to a contradiction. Another paradox of this kind which I learned from Max Black runs thus: In a village there's one barber. The barber shaves everyone who does not shave himself. Does the barber shave himself or not? Whichever answer we give leads to self-contradiction.

Another famous logical paradox is one which seems to strike at the heart of the notion that general truth can be established by mere iterative induction. If asked to give an example of such an inductive generalisation philosophers are very apt to say 'all swans are white'. Indeed, their habit of saying this and also of teasing themselves with the idea of looking at tomatoes through blue spectacles is one of the methods by which one can tell they are philosophers. Sensible people are offended by the notion that such a grave generalisation as 'all swans are white' can be corroborated by the discovery of an old black boot, but the reasoning is perfectly in order: if all swans are white it follows logically that all non-white objects are non-swans and the discovery of an old black boot gives us a God-sent opportunity to test this logical implication. If it *is* black, and if anxious scrutiny convinces us it is not a swan then we gain extra confidence in the generalisation that all swans are white.

An interesting logical—or rather sematological—paradox can be shown to grow out of the assumption that all words—even 'nothing' must *stand for* something. Consider, for example, the following exhilarating train of thought:

> A Ford is better than nothing
> Nothing is better than a Rolls Royce
> *Therefore a Ford is better than a Rolls Royce*

In formal reasoning paradoxes invariably call for some degree of reconsideration: they are evidence that somewhere or other we are thinking on the wrong lines.

In real life, however, we are obliged to come to terms with paradoxes, however much they may dismay us. The paradox of free speech is a case in point: if speech is to be unconditionally free, are we to give ear to those who denounce it? Again, Oliver Wendell Holmes asked if freedom of speech extended to the right to cry out 'Fire!' in a crowded cinema. In real life we are obliged to live with and reconcile ourselves to paradoxes such as these: indeed someone should prepare an anthology of them. Examples come readily to mind: advertising, being costly, raises the prices of goods but by promoting sales it reduces the prices. It is wicked to make weapons of destruction in secret but wicked also to divulge the secret. If it is true that the misdemeanours of children are the fault of their parents, why were their parents so gravely at fault as to rear them badly? it must have been that *their* parents' fault and so on—an infinite regress.

I don't think it wildly exaggerated to say that our success as a working society depends upon our good judgement in coming to terms with our reconciling ourselves in a pragmatic spirit to the paradoxes and self-contradictions that surround us on all sides.

References

1. P. B. & J. S. Medawar, *The Life Science*, Wildwood House, London, 1977.
2. Norman St John Stevas, *Life or Death: Ethics and Options*, ed. D. H. Labby, University of Washington Press, Washington, 1970.
3. See P. B. Medawar, 'Science and Literature' in *The Hope of Progress*, Wildwood House, London, 1974.

We should like to thank the Wildwood House Press for permission to reproduce passages from the above.

Stuart Sutherland

Stuart Sutherland was born in 1927. He took first-class honours in Ancient Greats at Magdalen College, Oxford 1949, and subsequently studied Experimental Psychology. He held a prize fellowship at Magdalen College (1954-1958) and became Oxford University lecturer in Experimental Psychology and Fellow of Merton College. He spent two years as visiting professor at the Massachusetts Institute of Technology.

In 1965 he took the Chair of Experimental Psychology at the University of Sussex and built up a new department there. He is currently Professor of Experimental Psychology, Director of the Centre for Research on Perception and Cognition at the University of Sussex, and President of the Experimental Psychology Society. He has written and edited six books including *Breakdown: A Personal Crisis and a Medical Dilemma* and has published numerous scientific and philosophical papers. Most of his research has been on problems of perception and learning and he is currently working on computer modelling of mental activities.

The myth of mind control

Nowadays, many laymen and some scientists believe that it is possible to modify and control beliefs, feelings, and behaviour by using techniques based on recent discoveries in psychology and the brain sciences. B. F. Skinner has written, 'The behaviour of the individual is easily changed by designing new contingencies of reinforcement'.[1] Some of his disciples have been more extreme: James V. McConnell announced, 'We should reshape our society so that we would all be trained from birth to do what society wants us to do. We have the techniques now to do it . . . I believe that the day has come when we can combine sensory deprivation with drugs, hypnosis, and astute manipulation of reward and punishment to gain almost absolute control over any individual's behaviour'.[2]

Unthinking faith in such techniques has led to their being widely applied in many disparate fields including psychiatry, education, the reform of criminals, and the treatment of political prisoners, suspected spies and prisoners of war. In America prisoners have been subjected to vicious routines of behavioural reform, including the use of 'succinylcholine', a drug that paralyses the muscles used for breathing so that the fully conscious victim feels as though he is suffocating. In Britain a magistrate recently ordered a brain operation to 'cure' compulsive gambling. The CIA and the American Army have invested millions of dollars in programmes to discover more effective techniques for controlling the mind. In the course of their investigations, two American citizens died after being administered LSD without their knowledge.[3] Despite the furore provoked by the use of techniques of behavioural control, it is seldom realised that, obnoxious as they are, for the most part the methods do not work.

As studies of the effects of psychiatric treatment demonstrate, it is extremely difficult to change anyone's feelings and behaviour even when he or she earnestly desires to make the change in question. I shall argue that it is impossible at present—and is likely to remain so—to alter anyone's beliefs against his will; moreover, the vaunted 'new' psychological techniques are not in fact new and the psychological and pharmacological methods, some of which are of value in treating the mentally ill, are ineffective in changing the beliefs of the sane.

Skinner's belief in the possibility of controlling behaviour is based on the unsurprising observation that rats and pigeons when hungry or thirsty can be induced to perform responses that are rewarded by access to food or water. It is popularly assumed that Skinner and his disciples have evolved a number of specific techniques for controlling behaviour. In fact, apart from the systematic application of reward and punishment ('reinforcement'), only two such techniques can be readily identified. The first is known as 'shaping'. Before an action can be reinforced, it must be performed by the animal: if we are trying to teach an animal a response that it is unlikely to make spontaneously, we might have to wait for ever before the response first occurred. Shaping overcomes this problem. Initially the experimenter rewards the animal for a response that only approximates to the desired behaviour but which the animal is likely to make spontaneously: as the frequency of this response increases, the criterion for reinforcement is gradually narrowed until eventually only the final behaviour the experimenter desires to produce is reinforced. Thus a rat being taught to press a bar might initially be rewarded merely for approaching it; then, as it learns to approach frequently, for touching it; and finally only for depressing it.

The second technique is used to teach animals to make a series of successive responses and is known as 'chaining'. The final response in the chain is taught first, and only after the animal has thoroughly mastered that response is the preceding response taught: once an animal has learned to make one response for a reward, it will learn to make another response that provides it with the opportunity to make the original one.

Using these methods Skinner was able to teach a rat to pull a chain which released a marble from a rack, and then to pick up the marble, carry it across the cage and drop it into a slot in order to obtain a food reward. He also taught pigeons to play a crude version of ping-pong. Although it is to Skinner's credit to have analysed these techniques, neither is new: both have been used for centuries in the training of animals in the circus, the

home and the farmyard. As it happens, the techniques are seldom useful
in training people since we can usually tell them what it is that we want
them to do and then reward them for doing it: we do not normally have to
wait for a response to be emitted, and people can grasp how to make a
chain of responses without going through the labour of learning each part
of the chain separately.

If Skinnerians have not actually discovered new techniques, one can ask
what is the basis for their claim that behaviour can be controlled. It lies in
their belief that any act that is repeatedly reinforced in the presence of a
stimulus will come to be automatically emitted whenever that stimulus is
present. To control behaviour, therefore, one needs only to analyse the stimuli
that give rise to it and to manipulate the rewards and punishments that follow it.

One of the curiosities of Skinner's theory is his assumption that it is
unnecessary to take into account mental processes in order to predict and
control what someone will do: indeed, he advocates abandoning the use of
all such terms as 'thoughts', 'expectancies', 'motives', 'intentions',
'drives', and so on. It is an article of faith for him that behaviour can be
predicted and controlled with no knowledge of the mental state of the
organism. He argues that since all we can observe of another person is his
behaviour, there is no need to postulate mental terms to understand it. It is
as though a physicist were to argue that since we can never observe atoms
or forces directly, it is unnecessary to postulate their existence. Just as it
may be doubted how far physicists would have succeeded in understanding
and controlling the physical world without inferring such entities, so it is
questionable how far techniques based on a theory as impoverished as that
of Skinner can succeed in controlling behaviour. I shall cite three reasons
why Skinnerian techniques of behaviour control are bound to fail: the first
two set theoretical limits to control, the third imposes a practical limit.

First, unless we take into account what is going on in someone's mind, it
is impossible to be sure just what behaviour it is that is being reinforced.
Noam Chomsky has given a nice example of this dilemma. Suppose someone derives pleasure (reinforcement) from reading Skinner's book, *Beyond
Freedom and Dignity*: Skinner should predict that he will read it again
because reinforced behaviour becomes more probable. Skinner might
perhaps retort that the behaviour reinforced was *reading the book for the
first time* and since people are not in general reinforced for reading the
same book twice, most readers will not immediately start upon it again.

But this reply begs the question of how to choose in advance a description of an action that will correctly predict what the effects of reinforcement will be. We certainly cannot do so merely by observing overt behaviour: we must infer the knowledge, beliefs, and intentions that underlie the behaviour, in other words we must know the structure of someone else's mind. But this structure is notoriously difficult to infer, and although cognitive psychologists work on such problems, their theories are still so inadequate that they are of little practical help.

In summary, it is because only action, not beliefs, can be rewarded and punished that reinforcement cannot be used to indoctrinate others against their will. False confessions were obtained through torture and the threat of further torture by the Catholic Inquisition, and the Russians have repeatedly used similar methods with political prisoners. But although true and false confessions may be extracted under duress, there is no evidence that long-term changes in the victim's beliefs occur. The Hungarians obtained false confessions from Cardinal Mindszentsy, but as his autobiography demonstrates they failed to convert him.

A second obstacle to changing human behaviour by the manipulation of reinforcers is that it is both practically and theoretically impossible to gain control over all sources of reinforcement. Men are not merely motivated by external rewards and punishments such as money, praise, pain and blame, they are also influenced by inner satisfactions and dissatisfactions. Skinner is himself aware of this fact, although he never faces up to it: he writes, for example: 'Perceptual responses (*sic*) which clarify stimuli and resolve puzzlement may be automatically reinforcing'.[4] There is no way in which the would-be manipulator of others' behaviour can gain control over such internal reinforcements. No matter what external rewards or threats are offered, a man may stick to his beliefs and even persist in a given course of action out of sheer pride: the reward he obtains through increased self-esteem may outweigh all external blandishments and threats.

Moreover, there is evidence[5] that extrinsic rewards given in order to induce someone to perform a task may be counter-productive. In a typical study, students were asked to solve a series of puzzles that had nothing to do with their ordinary curriculum. Half of them were rewarded with money for performing the task, the remainder received no external reward. The latter students found the task more interesting than did those who were paid, and when given the opportunity spent more of their own free time solving puzzles of a similar type. In common-sense terms, their behaviour is readily explicable: the promise of rewards for performing a task suggests that the task is not a very interesting one.

The third problem for the application of Skinnerian methods is that they often require complete control over a person's environment. Such control can only be exercised within an institution such as a mental hospital or a prison. By manipulating the rewards and punishments within such an institutional framework, it is sometimes possible to effect some modification of the inmates' behaviour. As soon as the inmate is returned to the community, however, the habits that he has learned to practise in the institution are no longer subject to the same schedule of reinforcements and he often gives them up. There are two theoretical reasons why behaviour taught within an institution should cease on discharge. First, the behaviour has been conditioned to the environment of the institution and should become less frequent when the external stimuli are changed ('generalisation decrement'). Second, it is well established that behaviour based on external rewards rapidly 'extinguishes' when the rewards are withdrawn.

'Token economy' programmes often fail for these reasons. Such programmes have been introduced, often without the patients' consent, in many mental hospitals. Long-stay patients live in conditions of extreme monotony, become accustomed to being taken care of by others, and often sink into a state of apathy in which they lose all sense of personal responsibility. In token economy programmes, the patients can earn tokens by behaving in more responsible ways; for example, by washing themselves, cleaning their teeth, making their beds, washing dishes, sorting laundry, or gardening. The tokens can be exchanged for goods or privileges, such as sweets, cigarettes, access to television or a chance to talk with the hospital staff. Some but not all patients do alter their habits under the influence of such programmes: the problem is that when the patient is discharged into the community, and the habits are no longer maintained by tokens, he tends to abandon them.

In summary, then, the technology of behaviour modification as practised by Skinner's disciples fails because it is based on a crude model of behaviour that does not take into account the structure of the mind. One of the first applications of Skinner's ideas was to the treatment of mental disorder, using the techniques of behaviour therapy. By a curious irony, many behaviour therapists have come to realise the inadequacy of Skinner's theory as a basis for treatment and a new school has come into being known by the name of 'Cognitive Behaviour Therapy', a splendid and unintentional oxymoron. In essence, the practitioners of this new therapy have realised that to effect any permanent change in behaviour it is necessary to change the patient's beliefs and that the best way of accomplishing this aim is to use rational forms of persuasion supported by direct demonstrations of the folly of the patient's current ways of behaving.

As an example of such methods, consider the treatment of phobias. There is growing evidence[6] that the best way to cure a simple phobia is by a combination of the techniques known as 'modelling' and 'flooding'. In modelling, the therapist himself approaches the object of the patient's phobia and demonstrates to the patient that no harm ensues. In flooding, the patient is persuaded to approach the object of which he or she is afraid and to stay in its vicinity until the fear it arouses begins to decrease. Flooding is thought to work because it gives the patient a chance to learn that no harm will come from the object of which he is afraid. A disorder such as agoraphobia is self-sustaining in so far as whenever the patient approaches a public place, intense fear is aroused: the fear causes him to withdraw and the ensuing reduction in fear reinforces the act of withdrawal and thus perpetuates this kind of behaviour. Only if the patient can be induced to stay in the situation, can he learn that no harm will come to him. Flooding and modelling differ radically from the use of arbitrary rewards and punishments, and owe nothing to Skinnerian theory. These techniques were developed within the framework of learning theories proposed by others, and they have been refined through careful tests of their efficacy.

Cognitive behaviour therapy, then, attempts to change the way patients view themselves and others, by reasoning them out of their irrational beliefs, and where necessary giving systematic training in skills in which they are lacking. For example, the excessively shy person may receive instruction and practice on how to assert himself. The methods used owe more to common sense than to any advances in scientific psychology. It is too early to say how successful this approach to mental disorder will be, but it is far removed from 'mind-control', being based on nothing more sinister than rational argument and persuasion. It is no more likely to succeed in changing the firmly held convictions of a sane man than would any other attempt to argue him out of them.

The most notorious technique for controlling the mind by psychological methods is known as 'brainwashing'. The term was first coined in 1950 by an employee of the CIA. At the time of the Korean War the American security services deliberately set out to convince the public that there existed a set of new and mysterious scientific techniques for the efficacious control of the mind, and that these techniques were being practised by the North Koreans. The security services had three motives for publicising and sensationalising the efficacy of brainwashing. First, they wished to inspire hatred of the North Koreans and of Communists in general; second, brainwashing provided a comforting explanation of why many American prisoners of war made statements favouring the enemy; and third, they wished to aggrandise their own role by arguing that they themselves must investigate brainwashing techniques in order to keep up with the enemy.[7] Brainwashing is in fact not mysterious, it is of limited efficacy, and it owes little or nothing to new scientific discoveries: it was practised by the Catholic Inquisition.

Brainwashing is the collective name for a set of techniques aimed at breaking the will and at inducing collaboration. Starvation, torture, and drugs are often used to weaken the prisoner's physical condition. He may be kept in isolation in the dark in order to produce a sense of disorientation and loss of personal identity. Systematic efforts to reduce the victim's self-esteem by ridicule and obloquy may also be made. Teams of vicious interrogators may alternate with teams who simulate kindness. The sudden contrast between the brutality of one team of interrogators and the kindness of the other encourages the prisoner to feel grateful to the latter and to develop trust in them: his judgement is weakened and he may begin to collaborate out of gratitude. These techniques are again based more on common sense and practical experience than on scientific discoveries. Determination to resist is likely to be lowered by physical weakness, confusion of mind, and loss of pride in oneself. There is no question that such techniques can often break a prisoner's resistance and force the confessions, whether true or false, that the captors are seeking to extract. Brainwashing does not, however, result in long-term control over the victim's mind: it changes his behaviour not his beliefs and when no longer under duress his beliefs are once again evinced in his actions. The 4500 American prisoners taken by the North Koreans were subjected to one of the most prolonged and systematic regimes of brainwashing ever used, but only 22 elected to stay in North Korea at the end of the war.[8]

Hypnotism is a further psychological method that has been used in efforts to control the mind: it is a topic in which it is difficult to separate fact from fiction. With willing subjects, hypnotic suggestion can increase the tolerance for pain, and is sometimes used in minor dental treatment. It is not employed on its own for major surgery, although there are claims that patients who have been told under hypnosis that they will not feel the pain of an operation need smaller doses of anaesthetic. The reports of the use of hypnotism to assist athletes are largely anecdotal, and the few well--controlled studies of its use to break addiction to cigarettes are discouraging. There is little doubt that hypnotic suggestion can sometimes help people to perform tasks that they wish to undertake but find difficult: but its effects are limited and uncertain, and its mode of operation is poorly understood. There is much debate about whether it can ever force people to do anything against their will. On this question, it is impossible to obtain reliable evidence since it would be grossly unethical to instruct someone under hypnosis to do anything to which he strongly objected.[9] We are therefore dependent on purely anecdotal evidence, none of which is satisfactory. The most famous case is that of an American model, Candy Jones, who claims to have been hypnotised against her will by the CIA, provided with an alternative personality and sent on dangerous missions under the guise of that personality. On her final mission, she was instructed to commit suicide, but the hypnotic control was apparently imperfect since fortunately for her she failed to complete her mission, and lived to broadcast the story to an avid public.[10]

The efforts that have been made to develop physiological and pharmacological techniques for controlling the mind may be dealt with more briefly, since they have been less frequently used than psychological methods and their limitations are more obvious. They have moreover been carefully evaluated in a recent book.[11]

Perhaps the most notorious of these techniques is psychosurgery—the mutilation of the healthy brain. Psychosurgery was introduced as a treatment for mental illness in 1936. Originally a massive cut was made in order to sever the fibres connecting the front half of the cerebral cortex to the remainder, a procedure known as prefrontal leucotomy in England and prefrontal lobotomy in the USA. This operation tends to render patients more tractable for a time, but the effect is often short-lived and many patients revert to their original disturbed behaviour. Moreover, the majority are left with permanent deficits: their emotions become shallow and inconsistent, with a tendency to euphoria, tactlessness and sudden changes of mood. Many leucotomised patients are incapable of forming and executing long-term plans, and are unable to concentrate: if interrupted in the performance of some task, they fail to resume it, having apparently forgotten what they were doing. A few hospitals both in Britain and in the United States still practise a less drastic form of this operation.

More recently, attempts have been made to control aggression by bilateral destruction of the amygdala, a brain nucleus that is implicated in anger and other forms of emotion. The effects of this operation are similar to those of prefrontal leucotomy, but to the best of my knowledge no careful study of it has been undertaken by an independent research worker: its long-term effects are therefore unpredictable, though likely to be severely damaging to the patient. Moreover, the operation often fails to reduce violent behaviour even in the short-term. Of three violent criminals from Vacaville prison who volunteered to have partial removal of their amygdalas, the only one who showed substantial improvement was paroled. He was subsequently jailed again after committing a robbery, and he complained that he was again losing control of his emotions.[12]

In summary, the most that psychosurgery can do is to blunt emotions, often at terrible cost to the individual. The selective destruction of other areas of the brain could of course be used to produce a range of specific defects such as loss of the ability to learn anything new, the incapacity to use language, blindness, and so on but such operations merely impair mental functioning, they do not result in control over the victim's mind. Our ignorance of the detailed workings of the brain makes it impossible to produce selective changes in beliefs by direct interference with it. It should of course be remembered that whilst there can be little or no justification for the destruction of healthy brain tissue, brain operations involving the removal or isolation of damaged tissue are often necessary to save life and restore normal mental function.

A second physiological technique that has been investigated with a view to using it for mind control is stimulation of parts of the brain with implanted electrodes. It is possible to make an animal repeat a particular response for hours on end by electrically stimulating certain sites in the brain every time the response occurs. Stimulation at corresponding brain sites has been administered to mental patients who report sensations of pleasure and sometimes euphoria, often accompanied by sexual arousal. Stimulation may also be used to produce sleep, to arrest ongoing activity, and to block various forms of behaviour such as eating and aggression. Despite its dramatic effects, there are several reasons why this technique cannot be used to control the mind. First, an implanted electrode usually has multiple effects—it stimulates more than one system in the brain. Second, its effects vary with the temperament of the subject and often vary within the same subject depending on his current mood or preoccupations. Third, it is not possible to produce specific well-integrated sequences of behaviour through electrical stimulation of the brain. Finally, the actions carried out as a result of brain stimulation have an automaton-like quality and stimulation cannot be used to induce changes in beliefs or goals.[13]

The effects of psychotropic drugs on behaviour and on the mind are more predictable, and judiciously used they have brought relief to many mental patients.[14] The neuroleptic drugs, of which chlorpromazine is one of the most common, can be helpful in the treatment of schizophrenia. Chlorpromazine has been called 'a chemical strait-jacket': it makes patients less violent and more tractable, though at the cost of inducing apathy and with the risk of producing the symptoms of Parkinson's disease. Chlorpromazine has been administered, sometimes surreptitiously, to criminals in both British and American jails. In Russia, political dissidents are frequently diagnosed as schizophrenic and are committed to mental hospitals where they are heavily dosed with chlorpromazine.[15] Although the drug may make them apathetic and may eventually result in permanent damage to the brain, it does not of course make it any easier to manipulate their beliefs, as is attested by those dissidents who have undergone such treatment and subsequently emigrated to the West.

One further use of drugs merits brief discussion. The CIA has investigated over 150 substances ranging from alcohol to strychnine in search of a truth-drug. It is not known whether the search was successful, but it is known that it was conducted with remarkable ineptitude. One investigator after testing one particular truth-serum commented: 'We know practically nothing about these drugs: but the little we know was confirmed yesterday', and his remark sums up nicely the current state of knowledge. Since truth-drugs have been administered only in secret and by intelligence agencies, there is no available evidence of their efficacy. Perhaps the most commonly used is pentothal, a barbiturate, which produces euphoria and light-headedness. Although it may sometimes be a useful adjunct to other techniques, it is unlikely to have proven very effective or it would have replaced the systematic torture still practised in most nations.[16]

Other drugs, such as LSD or amphetamines, may produce altered states of consciousness and lead to excitement, ecstasy or despair, but prolonged use produces psychosis. In short, drugs can be used to influence mood but no known drug can assist in systematically altering a sane person's beliefs or values.

I conclude that mind control remains in the realm of science fiction not scientific fact. Under sufficient duress, a person may be forced to do things against his wishes, but the techniques used have a long history and owe little to recent scientific findings.

It is possible that more effective methods of manipulating the mind will be developed, but it is unlikely to happen in the foreseeable future. Our present knowledge of how the brain works is rudimentary, and we know almost nothing about how it governs emotions, values or beliefs. New psychotropic drugs have for the most part been discovered by accident and we have little or no understanding of their mode of action. Although psychologists have advanced our understanding of some topics such as visual perception and the use of language, little is known about the roots of personality or the origins of human values. There is a nineteenth-century canard falsely attributing to Ignatius Loyola the saying: 'Give me a child under the age of seven, and he is mine for ever'. As any parent knows, this boast is empty and despite a century of scientific work on mental development, we are no nearer to knowing today how to bring up a child in order to produce an adult with specified characteristics. The fact that the human mind cannot be controlled should of course not make us any less vigilant in resisting the use of the vile but ineffective techniques that are directed to this end.

Modern methods of mind control may be a myth, but old-fashioned persuasion and propaganda are known to work: the technology of mass communication and mass surveillance poses a more serious and more immediate threat to freedom of opinion than do the sinister sounding techniques of mind control. The deliberate manipulation and control of information, as practised in Nazi Germany and Soviet Russia, can subvert the beliefs of whole nations. If the citizen is to be free to make up his own mind, it is imperative that he should have access to all the information and to information from all sources. With commendable prescience, the founding fathers of the United States built this freedom into the constitution. Recent attempts by British governments to suppress information suggest that even in the oldest existing democracy the importance of free access to information is not understood—or perhaps it is understood only too well.

Acknowledgement

I am much indebted to Phil Johnson-Laird for reading the draft manuscript and making many helpful suggestions. His ability to sniff out a cliché, a solecism, a clumsy sentence or an exaggerated claim has helped me greatly in the writing of this chapter and of many other pieces.

References

1. Skinner, B. F. *About behaviourism* (London: Cape, 1974), p. 206.
2. McConnell, J. V. *Psychology Today* (April 1970), p. 14.
3. For a thorough account of such attempts at mind control, see Scheflin, A. W. & Opton, E. M. Jr., *The mind manipulators* (New York: Paddington Press, 1978).
4. Skinner, B. F. (*op. cit.*), p. 141.
5. See, for example, Notz, W. W. *American Psychologist*, 1975, **30**, 884-891.
6. On phobias, see Marks, I. M. *Living with fear* (Washington: McGraw-Hill, 1978) for a readable and detailed account; or for a briefer treatment, Teasdale, J. D. in Sutherland, N. S. (Ed.), *Tutorial essays in psychology*, Vol. 1 (Hillsdale, N. J.: Lawrence Erlbaum Associates, 1977), pp. 137-163.
7. On brainwashing and the role of the CIA, see Scheflin, A. W. & Opton, E. M. Jr. (*op. cit.*).
8. Russell, A. W. *Journal of Clinical Psychology*, 1974, **30**, Special Monograph Supplement, pp. 111-136.
9. For a discussion of this problem, see Orne, M. T. *International Journal of Clinical and Experimental Hypnosis*, 1972, **20**, 101-117.
10. Bain, D. *The control of Candy Jones* (New York: Playboy, 1977).

11. Valenstein, E. S. *Brain Control: A critical examination of brain simulation and psychosurgery* (New York: Wiley, 1973).

12. Pines, M. *The brain changers* (New York: Harcourt Brace Jovanovitch, 1973), pp. 205-206.

13. For a review of research on self-stimulation, see Valenstein, E. S. (*op. cit.*), pp. 162-196, and Scheflin, A. W. & Opton, E. M. Jr. (*op. cit.*), pp. 325-353.

14. For a simple account of the use of drugs and other forms of physical treatment in mental illness, see Sutherland, N. S. *Breakdown, A personal crisis and a medical dilemma* (London: Weidenfeld & Nicolson, 1976), pp. 184-209.

15. For a scholarly but highly readable account of the treatment of Russian dissidents as mental patients, see Bloch, S. & Reddaway, P. *Russia's Political Hospitals: the abuse of psychiatry in the Soviet Union* (London: Gollanz, 1977).

16. On truth drugs and their investigation by the CIA, see Scheflin, A. W. & Opton, E. M. Jr. (*op. cit.*), pp. 106-169.

Thomas Szasz

Thomas Szasz, MD, was born in Budapest, Hungary, in 1920, and emigrated to the United States in 1938. Trained in psychiatry and psycho-analysis in Chicago, he has held a professorship in psychiatry at the State University of New York in Syracuse since 1956. He is the author of many well-known works on psychiatry and human affairs, among them *The Myth of Mental Illness, The Manufacture of Madness, Ceremonial Chemistry, Karl Kraus and the Soul-Doctors, Heresies,* and *The Myth of Psychotherapy.* Dr. Szasz is a co-founder of the American Association for the Abolition of Involuntary Mental Hospitalization and a contributing editor to *Inquiry* magazine. Among the honours he has received are the Humanist of the Year Award of the American Humanist Association and the Jefferson Award of the American Institute for Public Service.

The lying truths of psychiatry

We have been forced to stop all intercourse between Adler's splinter group and our own association, and our medical guests are also requested to choose which of the two they will visit. . . . It is not my purpose, my dear lady, to enforce such limitations in your case. I only request of you that with due regard for the situation you make use of an artificial psychic split, so to speak, and make no mention there of your role here and vice versa.

Sigmund Freud (1912)[1]

During my whole life I have endeavoured to uncover truths. I had no other intention and everything else was completely a matter of indifference to me. My single motive was the love of truth.

Sigmund Freud (1930)[2]

Of all the lying truths popular today, one of the most important is surely the mendacity inherent in the term 'mental illness'. In addition to asserting a falsehood concealed as a truth, this term also generates and justifies a host of related mendacious propositions and deceitful practices. As I noted in *Heresies*, 'The subject matter of psychiatry is neither minds nor mental diseases, but lies—the "patient's" and the "psychiatrist's"'. These lies begin with the names of the participants in the transaction—the designation of one party as 'patient' even though he is not ill, and of the other as 'therapist' even though he is not treating illness. They continue with the lies that form the very substance of the discipline—psychiatric 'diagnoses', 'prognoses', and 'treatments'. And they end with the lies that follow ex-mental patients like shadows through the rest of their lives—the records of imprecations and imprisonments called 'depression', 'schizophrenia', and 'hospitalization'.[3]

The nature and scope of psychiatric lies

The concept of mental illness is the pivotal mendacity of psychiatry. How this literalized metaphor is affirmed and used as if it were a scientific truth is best conveyed by means of illustrative quotations (a few of which follow without internal comment).

Mental Illness is Top U.S. Health Problem
Mental illness is 'America's primary health problem', afflicting at least 10 per cent of the population, the National Institute of Mental Health said today.[4]

Mental Health in America: 1978
For the past few years the most commonly used estimate has been that, at any one time, 10 per cent of the population needs some form of mental health services. . . . There is new evidence that this figure might be nearer 15 per cent of the population. . . . As many as 25 per cent of the population are estimated to suffer from mild to moderate depression, anxiety, and other indicators of emotional disorder at any given time.[5]

The Unmotivated Patient Syndrome
The unmotivated patient syndrome, characterized by a reluctance to accept treatment and an unwillingness to cooperate in therapy, pervades the spectrum of services for the emotionally disturbed. . . . Yesterday's 'brat' is today's hyperkinetic youngster, and the 'drunk' has become the alcoholic with deeply rooted psychosocial problems. These new target populations represent diverse aspects of psychopathology.[6]

Birth of a New Speciality—'Torture-ology'
'Torture is a disease that can be treated and cured just like many other diseases,' said Dr. Inge Kemp Genefke of the Danish Medical Group. . . . 'The medical profession is responsible for dealing with the problem of those doctors who are torturers themselves,' said Dr. Erik Karup Pedersen. 'We are all responsible for recognizing that torture is a disease . . .'[7]

The status of these statements as lying truths is obvious from the fact that they are Sunday truths: on weekdays, men and women display their belief in truths that belie these psychiatric prevarications. For example, opinion polls about which diseases Americans fear the most consistently fail to mention mental illness as a disease they fear at all. According to a 1976 Gallup poll, Americans fear cancer the most, 58 per cent of the population ranking it first.[8] Deafness is trailing the list, 1 per cent rating it as the most feared. Not on the list at all: mental illness. Likewise, survey after survey reveals that although the American media ceaselessly evangelize mental illness as 'just like any other illness', American behaviour testifies that mental illness carries a stigma and that the mental hospital is a prison. From a report entitled 'Mental care at bottom of list', we learn: 'Most Americans have been trained to call a doctor when they feel sick . . . but when it comes to mental health, the majority would rather suffer in silence. . . . Two of the biggest obstacles are the fear of being thought "nuts" and the fear of being "locked up" once psychiatric care is sought. Until these misconceptions are cleared up, mental health care is going to come last on the list.'[9] Ironically, the correct perception of the truth is here labelled a 'misconception'. Let us consider the specifics of this 'misconception'.

Just how severe is the stigma attached to mental illness was revealed by another recent survey: 'Employes seeking psychiatric care are less likely to be promoted in their jobs than others, according to a survey of 126 supervisors in Philadelphia. . . . Bosses surveyed reported a more negative attitude towards employees under treatment for mental illness than toward those who smoked marijuana on weekends, are obese, had a heart ailment, were age 60, being treated for skin cancer, atheists, or part of a racially mixed marriage.'[10]

This popular perception of psychiatry is, of course, consistent with psychiatry's intimate involvement with murder and mayhem—and, more specifically, with the psychiatrists' insistence that murder and mayhem are the manifestations of mental illness curable by means of compulsory psychiatric interventions. Furthermore, because this popular perception rests on the fact that psychiatrists, unlike other physicians, use legally formalized and enforced compulsion both in 'hospitalizing' and in 'treating' persons who refuse to consent to psychiatric interventions, psychiatric apologists and propagandists—unwilling to acknowledge, much less alter, the realities of psychiatry—systematically lie about its supposedly false image. For example, responding to an article in *Newsweek* magazine in which hospitalized mental patients were called 'inmates', Rosalynn Carter, Honorary Chairperson of the President's Commission on Mental Health, writes:

I was dismayed . . . by your use of the term 'inmate' in describing these individuals. Many of the difficulties they face stem from negative public attitudes towards the mentally ill. Inaccurate labeling feeds the public's fear of those with mental problems. Mental patients are not inmates and are rarely dangerous.[11]

But individuals incarcerated in institutions are correctly labelled 'inmates', notwithstanding Mrs. Carter's efforts to deny that fact. The reality we face here is, of course, painful: hundreds of thousands of individuals innocent of lawbreaking are deprived of their liberty by psychiatrists and incarcerated in so-called hospitals. Confronted with this fact, we have only two real options: we can acknowledge the evil inherent in compulsory psychiatry and oppose it; or we can deny that evil by believing the lying language of madness and mad-doctoring.

Psychiatric coercion sticks in the throats of the psychiatric apologists. In trying to rid themselves of this threat, which they correctly perceive as a danger to the very survival of psychiatry, they only incriminate themselves more deeply. Thus, in an article in the *Washington Post* devoted to an analysis of the 'rights of the mentally ill', Alan Stone, a professor of law and psychiatry at Harvard University, offers the following comment on 'dangerousness' as a requisite for civil commitment:

No one, including psychiatrists or judges, can predict with 100 per cent certainty who will become dangerous. But waiting for a person to commit an overt act simply won't work. If we just wait until someone has already committed a crime, we'll just collapse the civil commitment procedure into the criminal justice system. Mentally ill persons will have to be treated as criminals.[12]

Without civil commitment laws then, according to Stone, 'mentally ill' persons would 'have to be treated as criminals'. In fact, 'mentally ill' persons would then have to be treated like everyone else—which is the avowed goal of those who most loudly bewail the stigma of mental illness! Like so-called normal people, some so-called mentally ill persons break the law; they should be regarded as criminals , not because they are mentally ill, but because they broke the law. And like most 'normal' people, most 'mentally ill' persons do not break the law; they should be regarded as innocent persons no more subject to involuntary confinement and treatment than anyone else.

The lies of psychiatric history

Psychiatric history, insofar as it pretends to be the history of the diagnosis and treatment of mental illnesses, is largely a tissue of lies. Actually, the history of psychiatry is the history of the stigmatization, persecution, and incarceration of individuals exhibiting various types of socially deviant behaviour. Evidence supporting this interpretation abounds. For example, Philippe Pinel, hailed as the 'liberator' of the madman, offered the following recommendation for apprehending individuals deemed insane:

As he [the manager of the madhouse] advances he speaks to him [the madman] in a firm and menacing tone, and gives his calm advice or issues his threatening summons, in such a manner as to fix the attention of the hero exclusively upon himself. This ceremony is continued with more or less variation until the assistants have had time, by imperceptible advances, to surround the maniac, when, upon a certain signal being given, he finds himself in instant and unexpected confinement.[13]

For dealing with the madman who seeks his freedom, Pinel recommended the following policy: 'Improper application for liberty, or any other favour, must be received with acquiescence, taken graciously into consideration, and withheld under some plausible pretext.'[14] Pinel also embraced deception as a form of treatment, illustrating its effectiveness by the report of a case in which the cure failed because the mad-doctor's mendacity was exposed.[15]

Benjamin Rush, the undisputed father of American psychiatry, regarded deception as a veritable panacea. The following account is an example of his practice:

If our patient imagines he has a living animal in his body, and he cannot be reasoned out of a belief of it, medicines must be given to destroy it; and if an animal, such as he supposes to be in his body, should be secretly conveyed into his close stool, the deception would be a justifiable one, if it served to cure him of his disease.[16]

I cite another similar account to illustrate how deeply deception was ingrained in the mind of the man who wrote the first American textbook of *Diseases of the Mind*:

Cures of patients, who suppose themselves to be glass, may be easily performed by pulling a chair, upon which they are about to sit, from under them, and afterward showing them a large collection of pieces of glass as the fragments of their bodies.[17]

Psychiatric patients often propound lies, and psychiatric physicians counter-lies. Much of modern psychiatry rests on the compounding of such prevarications—an intepretation dramatically illustrated by Freud's early psychiatric experiences.

The prevarications of Freud's hysterical patients—who claimed they were seduced as children by their fathers or other male authority figures—have achieved a psychoanalytic status bordering on the legendary.[18] However, although the story of Freud's life and work is well known, the fact that psychoanalysis rests squarely on two crucial deceptions has somehow eluded both the adherents and critics of this mendacious cult. The first deception was perpetrated by the patients on Freud; the second was perpetrated by Freud on his followers, the public, and perhaps himself. The patients lied about sexual activity, claiming they had been subjected to traumatic sexual acts as children; Freud lied about the etiological significance of childhood sexual traumas in hysteria, claiming that these traumas caused that 'disease', regardless of whether the sexual seductions actually occurred. A brief recounting of these lies and the psychoanalytic legends based on them deserves our attention here.

It is important to keep in mind that, at the beginning of his career, Freud thought of himself as a psychopathologist. Accepting the literal reality of mental diseases, he sought to discover their causes or 'etiologies', just as other medical investigators had discovered the causes of the major infectious diseases that then plagued mankind. In 'The Aetiology of Hysteria' (1896), Freud asserts that he possesses a special method for investigating the 'etiology' of this 'disease' and that its etiology is invariably a sexual trauma in childhood:

But the most important finding that is arrived at if an analysis is thus consistently pursued is this. Whatever case and whatever symptom we take as our point of departure, *in the end we infallibly come to the field of sexual experience*. So here for the first time we seem to have discovered an aetiological precondition for hysterical symptoms.[19]

Freud's view that hysteria is a disease (which has an 'etiology') must, in fairness, be regarded as evidence of his acceptance of the conventional perspective on it rather than of his making any special claims about it. It is Freud's proposition that he has discovered the etiology of hysteria that deserves our special attention. That claim was solely his and it is fair to hold him fully responsible for it.

Only the most laborious and detailed investigations [writes Freud] have converted me, and that slowly enough, to the view I hold today. If you submit my assertion that the aetiology of hysteria lies in sexual life to the strictest examination, you will find that it is supported by the fact that in some eighteen cases of hysteria I have been able to discover this connection in every single symptom, and, where circumstances allowed, to confirm it by therapeutic success.[20]

Freud here elevates his own *interpretations* of various symptoms to the status of scientific discoveries. Moreover, he claims that his therapeutic successes support his etiological speculations. That sort of reasoning— inferring etiology from intervention—has long been popular among mad-doctors. The same reasoning prevails today in psychiatry—when, for example, a chemical etiology of the psychoses is inferred from their allegedly successful chemical treatment.

Freud's claims could hardly have been more grandiose: he had discovered, he insisted, both the cause and the cure of one of the most common and disabling mental illnesses of his age:

Now we are really at the end of our wearisome and laborious analytic work, and here we find the fulfilment of all the claims and expectations upon which we have so far insisted. . . . I therefore put forward the thesis that at the bottom of every case of hysteria there are *one or more occurrences of premature sexual experience*, occurrences which belong to the earliest years of childhood but which can be reproduced through the work of psycho-analysis in spite of the intervening decades. I believe that this is an important finding, the discovery of the *caput Nili* [source of the Nile] in neuropathology.[21]

Freud here claims to have made a medical or scientific 'discovery'— namely, of the etiology of hysteria. The questions I now want to raise are: Was his assertion about the cause of hysteria true? If not, what did he do about his erroneous or false claim? Here are Ernest Jones's answers to these questions:

Up to the spring of 1897 he [Freud] still held firmly to his conviction of the reality of these childhood traumas. . . . At that time doubts began to creep in, although he made no mention of them in his records of his progress he was regularly sending to his friend Fliess. Then, quite suddenly, he decided to confide to him 'the great secret of something that in the past few months has gradually dawned on me'. It was the awful truth that most—not all—of the seductions in childhood which his patients had revealed, and about which he had built his whole theory of hysteria, had never occurred.[22]

Why Freud should have believed the stories of 'mental patients'—whose reputation for veracity was no better then than it is now—need not concern us here. The fact is that Freud believed these stories or acted as if he did. What we need to consider is what Freud did when it became impossible for him to deny that he had been wrong. He did two things: he stopped believing his patients; and he concluded that, although his patients had deceived him, he was still right. Jones says that this crisis 'was a turning point in his [Freud's] scientific career, and it tested his integrity, courage, and psychological insight to the full. . . . It was at this moment that Freud rose to his full stature'.[23] I submit, and shall document, that this, too, is a mendacity. Actually, Freud resolved this crisis by a daringly deceptive strategy: abandoning all efforts to demonstrate empirically the validity of his claims, Freud shifted the ground on which his 'depth psychology' rested from the 'actual reality' of science to the 'psychical reality' of his patients' minds—as that 'reality' was revealed to him (and his loyal lackeys) by means of the 'psychoanalytic method'. It is this shift and the resulting arbitrary—and usually demeaning—judgements of persons, on and off the analytic couch, that I have elsewhere identified as the 'base rhetoric' characteristic of psychoanalysis.[24] The evidence for the foregoing interpretation lies, first of all, in a letter to Wilhelm Fliess dated September 21, 1897. Freud writes:

Let me tell you straight away the great secret that has been slowly dawning on me in recent months. I no longer believe in my *neurotica*.[25]

Freud then gives Fliess four convoluted reasons for having decided to no longer believe his patients' supposed recollections of their childhood experiences—reasons that seem to impress Jones very deeply indeed. What Freud fails to mention is that these stories were so patently contrived that when he presented this theory of the etiology of hysteria to a group of physicians in April, 1896, Richard von Krafft-Ebing, then professor of psychiatry at the University of Vienna, called it a 'scientific fairy-tale'.[26] Perhaps Freud did not mention that to Fliess because he had already decided to transform his fairy-tale into the epistemological bedrock of his new science of psychoanalysis. In the same letter to Fliess, Freud writes:

Were I depressed, jaded, unclear in my mind, such doubts [about the 'explanation of neuroses'] might be taken for signs of weakness. But as I am in just the opposite state, I must acknowledge them to be the result of honest and effective intellectual labor. . . . It is curious that I feel not in the least disgraced, though the occasion might seem to require it. Certainly I shall not tell it in Gath, or publish it in the streets of Askalon, in the land of the Philistines—but between ourselves I have a feeling more of triumph than of defeat (which cannot be right).[27]

Why was Freud so exuberant? Because he hit upon the formula that enabled him to be free, once and for all, of the burden of tailoring his theories to fit the facts of external reality. Henceforth, he could fit the facts to his conjectures. His formula, in effect, was this: when he was right, he was right; and when he seemed to be wrong, he was still right, because his seeming error actually embodied the '*psychical* reality' of his patients (as 'discovered' by the 'psychoanalytic method'). This boundlessly arrogant, and amazingly successful, re-interpretation of the etiology of hysteria became the linchpin of psychoanalytic theory. This is Freud's own account of it in 'The History of the Psycho-Analytic Movement' (1914):

Influenced by Charcot's view of the traumatic origin of hysteria, one was readily inclined to accept as true and aetiologically significant the statements made by patients in which they ascribed their symptoms to passive sexual experiences in the first years of childhood—to put it bluntly, to seduction. When this aetiology broke down under the weight of its own improbability and contradiction in definitely ascertainable circumstances, the result at first was helpless bewilderment. . . . The firm ground of reality was gone. . . . At last came the reflection that, after all, one had no right to despair because one has been deceived in one's expectations; one must revise those expectations. If hysterical subjects trace back their symptoms to traumas that are fictitious, then the new fact which emerges is precisely that they create such scenes in phantasy, and this psychical reality requires to be taken into account alongside practical reality.[28]

Here Freud displays his skills as a master con-man. He writes as if he had been deceived, when he was, in fact, the deceiver. Hysterical patients were always ready to attribute their illness to whatever they believed would flatter their doctors' vanity. Freud grew up in an atmosphere saturated with the admonition not to believe the claims of mental patients. Thus, if Freud believed some of his hysterical patients' claims, it was not because he was deceived, but because he wanted to believe them (or pretended to believe them) in order the better to deceive his listeners about his 'etiology of hysteria'. Then, when he realized that it was hopeless to maintain that the sexual seduction stories of his patients were true, instead of scuttling his theory, Freud merely transformed actual unreality into 'psychical reality', historical falsehood into mental truth. Such is the mendacity on which psychoanalysis—pretending to be a scientific procedure—rests.

The lies of psychiatric diagnosis

The fact that healthy persons assume the sick role or impersonate patients, has, of course, always been known. Called 'malingering', the phenomenon was, for centuries, correctly categorized as a species of counterfeiting. In the nineteenth century, such counterfeiting became redefined as itself a form of sickness—a 'mental illness'. This then led to defining feigned mental illness as itself a severe mental illness, demonstrating the limitless possibilities of deceptions masquerading as diagnoses.[29]

In *The Myth of Mental Illness*, I showed that the concept of psychopathology rests on the misleading metaphorization of personal displeasure or social deviance as bona fide illness or pathology. In view of the ideological, economic, and political interests of psychiatry—as well as its relation to the modern nation states which support it, and which psychiatry, in turn, supports—mental illness is bound to be an omnivorous category, swallowing up any behaviour displeasing to a person himself or to certain others.[30] That such is the case is supported by the perusal of any contemporary newspaper or magazine.

For example, in 1977, the Vatican newspaper, *L'Osservatore Romano*, declared that feminists demonstrating for sexual freedom and abortion on demand 'represented a pathological phenomenon'.[31] In a similar defence of traditional sexual values, a psychiatrist writing in the *American Journal of Psychiatry* claimed to have identified a new 'pathological symptom' called 'pathological tolerance'. This term, he explained, 'refers to the acceptance of the triangular relationship by the member of the primary dyad who is the same sex as the triadic addition'.[32] In other words, 'pathological tolerance' is not being jealous of your sexual partner when the psychiatrist believes you ought to be jealous of him or her. The deception of defining such a personal judgement as a 'pathological symptom'—requiring 'treatment'—is concealed by the additional deception of couching it in an opaque and pretentious pseudomedical jargon.

The prevarications implicit in psychiatric diagnoses are perhaps most obvious when such diagnoses are affixed to prominent political figures. For example, in 1968, Dr. Robert Cancro, an authority on schizophrenia, declared that if he had been asked 'to screen the candidacy of Charles de Gaulle for the presidency of France a few years ago, he might have said de Gaulle was a paranoid with delusions of grandeur'.[33]

President Carter's wife, Rosalynn, seems to be another devout psychopathologist. In the 1978 presidential commission *Report* on 'Mental Health in America', she enthusiastically endorsed the proposition that 25 per cent of her countrymen are mentally ill. Especially distressed by the madness of black Americans, she categorized that group, en masse, as psychiatrically 'underserved'.[34] Mrs. Carter's psychiatric judgement about Americans, and especially black Americans, is, to say the least, astonishing, if it is compared to one of her earlier remarks, offered in response to a question about Idi Amin's mental health. 'I do not think,' she said 'that Amin Dada is crazy. He is a very intelligent man.'[35] It is worth recalling, in this connection, that in 1972, President Amin sent a telegram to Secretary General Kurt Waldheim of the United Nations in which he not only urged the removal of all Israelis from the Middle East to Britain, but also endorsed Hitler's policies. 'When Hitler was the Prime Minister and Supreme Commander,' declared President Amin, 'he burnt over six million Jews. This is because Hitler and the German people knew that the Israelis are not people who are working in the interests of the people of the world.'[36] Displeased with Amin's words and deeds (such as his expulsion of 55,000 Asians from Uganda), Harold Wilson, then the leader of the British Labour Party, had not the slightest difficulty in diagnosing the Ugandan President as an 'unbalanced paranoiac'.[37]

I submit that Mrs. Carter and Mr. Wilson are both wrong. Idi Amin may be called a good or bad president of his country, a good or bad person. However, calling him mentally healthy or mentally sick is a dangerous mendacity.

The contention that psychiatric diagnoses are themselves deceptions may be further illustrated by certain metamorphoses in modern American psychodiagnostics. For example, in 1974, with much fanfare, the American Psychiatric Association dropped homosexuality from its official list of mental diseases. In the years since then, psychiatrists have laboured mightily to make up for that loss. They have thus invented several new psychopathological conditions, listed in the proposed draft of the third edition of the Association's official roster of mental illnesses. For children, the mad-doctors manufactured the 'Academic Underachievement Disorder', which they identify as follows:

> The essential feature is a clinical picture in which the predominant disturbance is failure to achieve in most school tasks despite adequate intellectual capacity, supportive and encouraging social environment, and apparent effort. . . . The disorder is relatively common and found equally in males and females.[38]

If this fails to compensate psychiatrists for the loss they suffered relinquishing homosexuality 'per se' as a disease, another newly discovered illness should more than make up for it. The new mental disease is 'Tobacco Use Disorder', a diagnostic entity that converts a good part of mankind into psychiatric cannonfodder. Here is what the Task Force on Nomenclature and Statistics of the American Psychiatric Association says about this disease:

This is the first time that certain forms of tobacco use are included in this classification of mental disorders. . . . Chronic use of tobacco has been shown conclusively to predispose to a variety of medical diseases. . . . Health authorities have estimated that 15% of the annual mortality in the United States is directly due to diseases caused or aggravated by the consumption of tobacco. Tobacco use is therefore clearly a major health problem. . . . In this manual, the use of tobacco is considered a disorder either when the use of the substance is directly associated with distress at the need to use the substance repeatedly; or there is evidence of a serious tobacco-related physical disorder in an individual who is judged to be currently physiologically dependent upon tobacco.[39]

Concerning the 'prevalance and sex ratio' of Tobacco Use Disorder, its discoverers have this to say:

A large proportion of the adult population of the United States uses tobacco, with the prevalence among men greater than among women. . . . The prevalance of Tobacco Use Disorder as defined here is not known. . . . However, since surveys have shown that approximately 50% of smokers express a desire to be able to stop, and since tobacco-related physical problems that are aggravated by smoking are common, Tobacco Use Disorder is obviously common. Assuming that the prevalence of smoking does not decline rapidly, that there are no breakthroughs in the development of a 'safe' cigarette, that social acceptability for tobacco use will decrease, and that restrictions in public use will become more widespread, then it follows that the proportion of smokers who are distressed by their inability to stop will increase, and therefore the prevalence of Tobacco Use Disorder will increase.[40]

Evidently, psychiatrists have come to believe their own lies—a mental condition which, although not a disease, is exceedingly dangerous to the body politic. It has often been observed that no one is as zealously intolerant as a person intoxicated with abstinence. Traditionally the heaviest of smokers, psychiatrists, once they embrace anti-smoking, can be counted on to be as hard on smokers as they have been on other psychiatric scapegoats. Indicative of the nascent psychiatric passion against smoking is the invention of still another mental disease related to smoking: Tobacco Withdrawal. Concerning this disease, we learn:

Withdrawal is not seen in all smokers, but in many heavy cigarette smokers, changes in mood and performance which are probably related to withdrawal can be detected within two hours after the last cigarette. The sense of craving appears to reach a peak within the first 24 hours after the last cigarette. . . . The most common symptoms of withdrawal are irritability, restlessness, dullness, sleep disturbances, gastrointestinal disturbances, headache, impairment of concentration and memory, anxiety, and increased appetite. . . . The diagnosis is usually self-evident and the disappearance of symptoms upon resumption of smoking is confirmatory.[41]

In view of the obviousness and severity of these symptoms, one wonders why the disease of Tobacco Withdrawal was not discovered until now. But then perhaps it was discovered: Mark Twain, in his inimitable style, once remarked that it was exceedingly easy to stop smoking; he had done it himself a thousand times. If the American Psychiatric Association had a sense of humour, it would have called Tobacco Withdrawal the Mark Twain Syndrome.

The lies of psychiatric treatment

As in *The Myth of Mental Illness* I showed that any behaviour disapproved of by oneself or others may be categorized as psychopathology, so in *The Myth of Psychotherapy* I showed that any behaviour approved of by oneself or others may be categorized as mental treatment.[42] The lying truth inherent in the term 'mental illness' is likewise evident in the term 'mental treatment' (and its synonyms).

Clairvoyance was not necessary, in the past, to recognize many prevailing methods of psychiatric treatment as dangerous and harmful, just as clairvoyance is not necessary now to recognize many presently fashionable methods of psychiatric treatment as dangerous and harmful. Venesection, sadistic restraints, and incarceration in the madhouse were among leading psychiatric treatments in the nineteenth century; insulin shock, electric shock, psychosurgery, powerful 'antipsychotic' drugs, and incarceration in a mental hospital have been and are some of the leading psychiatric treatments in the twentieth century. Insulin shock and lobotomy have few defenders any more. Their passing, however, has not affected either psychiatric mendacity or public gullibility about the supposed therapeutic benefits of electroshock and the so-called antipsychotic drugs.

Of course, not all psychiatric treatments are dangerous in the same ways as the procedures mentioned above; that is, they do not all cause brain damage or loss of liberty. Indeed, some psychiatric treatments are harmless, even helpful—because they do not go beyond conversation and because they increase rather than diminish the client's autonomy. Nevertheless, even these benign methods are, in my opinion, deceptive if they pretend to be bona fide treatments of bona fide diseases. My point here is that just as everything bad in the world is not a disease, so everything good in it is not a treatment. Yet there is hardly any pleasant or 'health'-promoting activity that has not been mendaciously proffered as a psychiatric treatment. Thus everything from reading books ('bibliotherapy') to engaging in sexual activity ('sex therapy') is now psychiatrically promoted, and often popularly accepted, as a mental treatment. A typical example of this psychotherapeutic con-game came in the mail as I was writing this essay. It was an article entitled 'Antidepressant running: Running as a treatment for non-psychotic depression', published in the June, 1978 issue of *Behavioral Medicine*.[43] The senior author, John Greist, was identified as an associate professor of psychiatry at the University of Wisconsin, and one of the junior authors, Mr. Roger R. Eischens, as a 'running therapist'. This could be, and indeed is, funny—but psychiatrists, politicians, and the Internal Revenue Service take it all quite seriously. This particular six-page article contains two very scientific-looking tables and a special set of instructions on 'Treatment techniques', duly medicalizing the subject, transforming just plain running into 'running therapy'.

The lies of psychiatric research

With the growth of psychiatric research in the modern era, deception—long the stock-in-trade of the mental patient and the mental healer—became a favourite methodological device of the psychiatric investigator as well. Although accounts of modern psychiatric research are singularly lacking in information that is both significant and reliable, they display a remarkable array of lies.

For example, in 1972, Dr. David Rosenhan and his associates set out to deliberately deceive a number of hospital psychiatrists by assuming the role of what they called 'pseudopatients': pretending to be hearing voices, they called mental hospitals and gained admission to them on the basis of that complaint.[44] Once inside the 'insane' asylum, regardless of how 'sane' the pseudopatients acted, they continued to be regarded as crazy. 'With the exception of myself (I was the first pseudopatient and my presence was known to the hospital administrator and chief psychologist, and, so far as I can tell, to them alone),' wrote Rosenhan, 'the presence of the pseudopatients and the nature of the research program was not known to the

hospital staff.' This deception was supposedly necessitated by the problem
to be investigated. 'However distasteful such concealment is, it was a
necessary first step to examining these questions,' explained Rosenhan.
The questions to which he was referring were: 'If sanity and insanity exist,
how shall we know them?' and '. . . whether the sane can be distinguished
from the insane (and whether the insane can be distinguished from each
other).' But this 'experiment' was not premised on concealment (as are
double-blind studies), but rather on deception: the 'researchers' imper-
sonated psychotics and deliberately lied to the psychiatrists whose help
they ostensibly solicited. Nevertheless, not only was this study accepted
for publication in *Science*, but it was also hailed as an important piece of
research—supposedly proving the 'labeling theory' of mental illness and
the 'unreliability' of the psychiatric-diagnostic process. To me it proved
only that it is easy to deceive people, especially when they don't expect to
be deceived.

Two recent events illustrate the prevalance of deception in contemporary psychiatric research. One is reported in a letter to the editor of
Psychiatric News, by Natalie Shainess, recounting a personal encounter
with such 'research' at the annual meeting of the American Psychiatric
Association in Atlanta, in May, 1978.[45] 'Arriving late in the evening at the
Omni Hotel,' she writes, 'I was unpacking when my phone rang at about
11.30 p.m. Wondering who might be calling at that hour, I picked up the
phone receiver to hear a man's voice say, "Would you like us to send up a
gentleman to pleasure you?".' Offended by this offer, Dr. Shainess
interrogated the hotel manager about the incident, only to learn that 'a
member of the American Psychiatric Association was conducting a piece of
sex research and had arranged for 25 women arriving alone to receive this
call'. By representing himself as a scientific investigator, this unidentified
psychiatrist deceived not only his victims, but also the hotel manager. It
remains to be seen what steps, if any, the American Psychiatric Association
will take to expose and punish this 'researcher'.

The other event involves some of the most prominent 'scientific' investigators of mental illness in the United States. On January 12, 1978, four
researchers published a paper in the *New England Journal of Medicine*,
entitled 'Are paranoid schizophrenics biologically different from other
schizophrenics?'[46] Their answer was yes. They claimed to have demonstrated that the blood platelets of chronic non-paranoid schizophrenics

exhibited a significantly lower level of monoamine oxidase activity than did the platelets of chronic paranoid schizophrenics or normal controls. In the same month, five researchers published a paper in the *American Journal of Psychiatry* entitled 'Platelet monoamine oxidase in chronic schizophrenic patients'.[47] Their conclusion was that 'There were no significant differences between the mean platelet MAO activities of 21 chronic paranoid schizophrenic patients compared with 18 chronic undifferentiated schizophrenic patients'. What makes these two articles uniquely relevant is that both were co-authored by Dennis L. Murphy, Chief, Clinical Neuropharmacology Branch, National Institute of Mental Health, Bethesda, Maryland, and Richard J. Wyatt, Chief, Laboratory of Clinical Psychopharmacology, St. Elizabeths Hospital, Washington, D.C.

The discrepancy between these two reports has created a furor in the pages of the *New England Journal of Medicine*—but not, so far, in the pages of the *American Journal of Psychiatry*. On May 18, 1978, the *New England Journal* published a series of letters, as well as a scathing editorial note, concerning this affair. In the lead letter, Dr. Karen Pajari notes the contradiction between the two articles cited, and concludes with this observation: 'It seems worthwhile to clarify how the same authors can come to such diametrically opposed conclusions—a clarification that I have been unable to extract from either article.'[48]

In their reply, the authors 'explain' their action by asserting that 'We could not previously address ourselves to the then unpublished study by Berger *et al.* because it has been our policy not to discuss unpublished data in a published paper'.[49]

The editors were not satisfied. 'We are as puzzled as Dr. Pajari', they wrote, 'by the virtually simultaneous publication of two apparently contradictory papers, one in the *Journal* and the other in the *American Journal of Psychiatry*. Despite the fact that these papers share two co-authors in common, neither manuscript, as submitted, referred to the existence of the other. . . . We cannot be satisfied with the explanation given of this bizarre event. . . . To dismiss one's own discrepant results as being "unpublished data" and therefore not open to comment defies common sense and is, to say the least, disingenuous.'[50]

Such discrepancy may defy common sense, but it does not defy—has never defied—psychiatric sense. Psychiatrists never had difficulty reconciling other troublesome discrepancies—such as the discrepancy between asserting that schizophrenia is a disease of the brain like pellagra or Parkinsonism, and yet claiming a special legal status for it to justify its involuntary treatment; between asserting that 'mental illness is like any other illness', and yet insisting that mere talking is treatment ('psycho--therapy'); or between denouncing psychiatric coercion in Russia, and yet practising such coercion, on an even larger scale, in America.

Viewed in a psychiatric rather than a scientific context there is, therefore, nothing 'bizarre' about Murphy and Wyatt reporting in one paper, published in January, 1978, that there is a significant difference in the platelet monoamine oxidase activities of chronic paranoid schizophrenics and chronic non-paranoid schizophrenics, and reporting in another paper, published in the same month, that there is no such difference between them. By psychiatric context, I refer, for example, to a moral arena in which Leonardo da Vinci is defamed as a homosexual and Barry Goldwater as a schizophrenic—and where such defamation is officially accredited as diagnosis.[51] Such conduct, practised consistently over many generations, inexorably affects every aspect of psychiatry— from the deceptive manipulation of the mental patient in the name of treatment to the deceptive manipulation of research methods and results in the name of science.

The lies of psychiatric education

The lies of psychiatric education are inherent in, and follow from, the lies inherent in the concepts of psychiatric illness, diagnosis, hospitalization, and treatment. Ostensibly, psychiatric education consists of training the young physician in the diagnosis and treatment of mental diseases; actually it consists of indoctrinating him into the theory and practice of psychiatric mendacity and violence.

In 1972, a psychiatrist actually performed an experiment which, albeit unwittingly, illustrates the deliberate use of deception in psychiatric education as well as the pervasively mendacious content of that education. Independently of David Rosenhan's scheme to deceive psychiatrists by means of pseudopatients, Donald Naftulin, a University of Southern California psychiatrist, devised a scheme to deceive mental health educators by means of a pseudopsychiatrist.[52] The result was predictable: just as psychiatrists were unable to distinguish pseudopatients from real patients, so mental health educators were unable to distinguish the pseudo-psychiatrist from real psychiatrists. In fact, the pseudopsychiatrist was rated an outstanding psychiatrist.

The purpose of this experiment, according to the investigators, 'was to determine if there is a correlation between a student's satisfaction with a lecturer and the degree of cognitive knowledge required. . . . We hypothesized that given a sufficiently impressive lecture paradigm, even experienced educators participating in a new learning experience can be seduced into feeling satisfied that they have learned, despite irrelevant, conflicting and meaningless content conveyed by the lecturer.'

To this end, the team hired a professional actor 'who looked distinguished and sounded authoritative', named him Dr. Myron L. Fox, bestowed upon him the persona of 'an authority on the application of mathematics to human behaviour', created a bogus curriculum vitae, and coached him in a speech entitled 'Mathematical Game Theory as Applied to Physician Education'. The experimenters coached 'Dr. Fox' to teach 'charismatically and non-substantively on a topic about which he knew nothing', instructing him to use double-talk and other trickery in the question-and-answer period and to intersperse the nonsense 'with parenthetical humour and meaningless references to unrelated topics'. The lecture was first presented to a group of 11 psychiatrists, psychologists, and social work educators and was videotaped. The tape was then shown to a group of 11 psychiatrists, psychologists, and psychiatric social workers, and finally to a group of 33 educators and administrators taking a graduate course in educational philosophy. All 55 subjects were asked to answer a questionnaire evaluating their response to the lecture. The audience loved 'Dr. Fox': 'All respondents had significantly more favorable than unfavorable responses. . . . One even believed he [had] read Dr. Fox's publications.' Among the subjective responses quoted by the investigators were the following: 'Excellent presentation, enjoyed listening. . . Good analysis of the subject . . . Knowledgeable.'

What does this experiment about the 'pseudopsychiatrist as educator' prove? To Naftulin and his colleagues, it proves that 'If a lecturer talks at a group, with no participation permitted to the group [a question-and-answer period was, however, permitted], then a mellifluous, trained actor might do just as well, possibly better than, an uncharismatic physician.'* That is not what it proves to me. Like the Rosenhan pseudopatient study, the Naftulin pseudopsychiatrist study proves only that when it comes to the institutionalized deception and gobbledygook of psychiatry, observers trained in mental health are unable to distinguish fake fakes from real fakes—not exactly a surprising conclusion. As if to support this contention, Naftulin and his co-workers offer this conclusion, couched in the appropriate gobbledygook: '[The] study supports the possibility of training actors to give legitimate lectures as an innovative educational approach toward student-perceived satisfaction with the learning process.' The authors do not explain why medical students (or their parents) would want to pay $5,000 or more to listen to actors talk about nonexistent subjects they know nothing about. No doubt they envision a system of psychiatric education patterned in the tradition of psychiatric 'diagnosis' and 'treatment'—true facts being mendaciously misdescribed each step of the way.

Conclusion

Psychiatry, paraphrasing Ambrose Bierce, is the pretentious art of lying for one's profession. The psychiatrist, paraphrasing Sir Henry Wotton, is a dishonest man sent to lie wherever he can for the good of his guild. The psychopathologist lies about the prevalence and severity of psychiatric illness, the psychotherapist lies about the efficacy and safety of psychiatric treatment, and the forensic psychiatrist lies about the 'mental health' and 'mental illness' of the defendant.

Behind the massive structure of psychiatric lies there are, of course, grains of genuine truths. These are the truths of real human suffering honestly expressed, and of real human succoring conveyed by honest healing words.[53] Unfortunately, but perhaps inevitably, organized psychiatry has been largely a struggle against, rather than for, such truths and 'therapies'.

---

* This observation, by a group of respected academics, is astonishingly similar to Hitler's famous remark that, in politics, a big lie works better than a small one. Hitler did not mention truth at all; he knew it was useless for capturing crowds and was therefore not interested in it. In the main, psychiatrists and psychiatric patients exhibit the same thirst for big 'mental health' lies, as do crowds of disaffected people thirsting for the redemptive messages of messiahs, whether religious or political.

References

1. Freud, S.: Sigmund Freud to Lou Andreas Salomé, November 4, 1912; in Levy, S. A., ed., *The Freud Journal of Lou Andreas Salomé* (New York: Basic Books, 1964), p. 41.
2. Freud, S.: Quoted in Sterba, R. F., Discussions of Sigmund Freud, *The Psychoanalytic Quarterly*, **47**: 173-191, 1978.
3. Szasz, T. S.: *Heresies* (Garden City, N.Y.: Doubleday Anchor, 1976), p. 113.
4. Palmer, C. A.: Mental illness is top U.S. health problem, *Syracuse Herald-Journal*, July 13, 1975, p. 1.
5. The President's Commission on Mental Health: *Mental Health in America—1978* (Washington, D.C.: U.S. Government Printing Office, 1978), p. 8.
6. Nir, Y. and Cutler, R.: The unmotivated patient syndrome: Survey of therapeutic interventions, *American Journal of Psychiatry*, **135**: 442-447 (April), 1978.
7. Elliott, J.: Birth of a new specialty—'Torture-ology', *Medical Tribune*, April 5, 1978, p. 5.
8. Most feared diseases, *Parade*, February 6, 1977, p. 12.
9. Mental care at bottom of list, *Psychiatric Newsletter*, **36**: 15 (June), 1975, p. 15.
10. National news, *American Medical News*, June 9, 1975, p. 2.
11. Carter, R.: Mental illness myths (Letters), *Newsweek*, June 19, 1978, p. 8.
12. Wilson, M.: Rights of the mentally ill, *The Washington Post*, June 11, 1978, p. F-4.
13. Pinel, P.: *A Treatise on Insanity* (1806) (New York: Hafner, 1962), p. 94.
14. Ibid., p. 87.
15. Ibid., p. 228.
16. Rush, B.: *Medical Inquiries and Observations upon the Diseases of the Mind* (1812) (New York: Hafner, 1962), p. 109.
17. Ibid., p. 110.
18. Jones, E.: *The Life and Work of Sigmund Freud*, 3 vols. (New York: Basic Books, 1953-1957), vol. 1, Chapter XI.
19. Freud, S.: The aetiology of hysteria (1896), in *The Standard Edition of the Complete Psychological Works of Sigmund Freud*, 24 vols. (London: Hogarth Press, 1953-1974), Vol. III, pp. 187-221; p. 199.
20. Ibid.
21. Ibid., pp. 202-203.
22. Jones, op. cit., Vol. I, p. 265.
23. Ibid.
24. Szasz, T. S.: *Karl Kraus and the Soul-Doctors* (Baton Rouge, La.: Louisiana State University Press, 1976).
25. Freud, S.: *The Origins of Psycho-Analysis* (New York: Basic Books, 1954), p. 215.
26. Freud, S.: The aetiology of hysteria, op. cit., p. 189.
27. Freud, *Origins*, op. cit., pp. 216-217.
28. Freud, S.: On the history of the psycho-analytic movement (1914), in *The Standard Edition*, op. cit., Vol. XIV, pp. 1-66; pp. 17-18.
29. Szasz, T. S.: *The Myth of Mental Illness* (1961), rev. ed. (New York: Harper & Row, 1974), Chapter 2.
30. Ibid., especially Chapter 4.
31. 'Pathological' feminism deplored by Vatican, *The New York Times*, January 21, 1977, p. 4.
32. Pinata, E. R.: Pathological tolerance, *American Journal of Psychiatry* **135**: 698-701 (June), 1978.
33. Politicians safe, *Syracuse Herald-Journal*, May 13, 1968, p. 1.

34. The President's Commission, op. cit., pp. 4-6.
35. Carter, R.: Interview with the Associate Press (retranslated), *Jeune Afrique*, March 25, 1977, p. 55.
36. Uganda: Hitler's friend, *The New York Times*, September 17, 1972, p. E-3.
37. Wilson calls Amin 'unbalanced paranoiac', *The International Herald-Tribune*, September 7, 1972, p. 1.
38. American Psychiatric Association: *DSM-III, Draft—Diagnostic and Statistical Manual of Mental Disorders*, third edition (Washington, D.C.: American Psychiatric Association, 1978), p. M: 59.
39. Ibid., p. B: 21.
40. Ibid., pp. B: 22-23.
41. Ibid., pp. A: 75-76.
42. Szasz, T. S.: *The Myth of Psychotherapy* (Garden City, N.Y.: Doubleday Anchor, 1978).
43. Greist, J. H. *et al.*: Antidepressant running, *Behavioral Medicine*, June 1978, pp. 19-24.
44. Rosenhan, D. L.: Being sane in insane places, *Science*, **179**: 250-258, 1973.
45. Shainess, N.: Ethics and sex research (Letters), *Psychiatric News*, **13**: 2 (June 2), 1978.
46. Potkin, S. G., *et al.*: Are paranoid schizophrenics biologically different from other schizophrenics? *New England Journal of Medicine*, **298**: 61-66 (January 12), 1978.
47. Berger, P. A. *et al.*: Platelet monoamine oxidase in chronic schizophrenic patients, *American Journal of Psychiatry*, **135**: 95-99 (January), 1978.
48. Pajari, K.: Monoamine oxidase in schizophrenia (Letters), *New England Journal of Medicine*, **298**: 1150 (May 18), 1978.
49. Potkin, S. G. *et al.*: ibid., pp. 1151-1152.
50. The editors: Schizophrenia and publication, ibid., p. 1152.
51. Szasz, T. S.; *Ideology and Insanity* (Garden City, N.Y.: Doubleday Anchor, 1970), especially Chapters 3, 4, and 12.
52. Naftulin, D. *et al.*: The Doctor Fox lecture: A paradigm of educational seduction, *Journal of Medical Education*, **48**: 630-635 (July), 1973.
53. Szasz, T. S.: *The Myth of Psychotherapy* (Garden City, N.Y.: Doubleday Anchor, 1978).

P. C. W. Davies

Dr. P. C. W. Davies is 33, married, with three children. He gained a BSc (first), PhD from Department of Physics, University College, London (1967, 1970). He was Visiting Fellow, Institute of Theoretical Astronomy, University of Cambridge (1970-72) and is currently lecturer in Applied Mathematics, King's College, London. He is the author of over forty specialized research papers, many popular and review articles and four books: *The Physics of Time Asymmetry*, 1974; *Space and Time in the Modern Universe*, 1977; *The Runaway Universe*, 1978; *The Forces of Nature*, 1979. His main research interests are cosmology, gravity, quantum field theory, structure of space and time.

Reality exists outside us?

Is there really a world 'out there'? It may seem startling, that a physical scientist should pose such a blunt question. Philosophers, psychologists and artists are frequently disposed to struggle with their own constructions of the meaning of reality, but of all disciplines, physical science is supposed to be rooted in the concrete reality of the objective universe. In the coming pages I shall explain how, since the momentous discoveries during the first quarter of the twentieth century, physicists have generally (though by no means universally) come to suppose the answer to be negative.

It is obvious to all that the world of our daily experience cannot be totally objective, because we experience the world by interacting with it. The act of experience requires two components: the observer and the observed. It is the mutual interaction between them that supplies our sensations of a surrounding 'reality'. It is equally obvious that our version of this 'reality' will be coloured by our model of the world as constructed by previous experience, emotional predisposition, expectation and so on. Clearly, then, in daily life we do not experience an objective reality at all but a sort of cocktail of internal and external perspectives.

Naturally, the purpose of physical science has been to disengage from this personalized and semi-subjective view of the world and to build a model of reality which is *independent* of the observer. The reader will be familiar with the traditional procedures to attain this goal—repeatable experiments, measurement by machine, mathematical formulation, etc. How successful is this objective model provided by science? Can it actually describe a world which exists independently of the people who perceive it?

The world as a machine

Several early cultures possessed enough information about the eclipses of the sun and moon for the next one to be predicted. Presumably none of

144

them could supply the reason *why* the particular numerical sequences work. In the seventeenth century Isaac Newton, the founder of real science, formulated the mathematical principles which govern the motions of material bodies, and was able to solve his equations describing the behaviour of planets in the solar system. Using Newton's mechanics, astronomers have been able to compute precisely when eclipses will occur. The 'magic' formulae of the ancients are now a trivial consequence of a proper mathematical understanding of gravity and the laws of motion.

I mention the example of eclipses because they are a good illustration of 'objective science' at work. Who would deny that the eclipses will come on schedule whether anyone is around to see them? There is a powerful image of a machine—the solar system—turning about like the cogs of a clock, oblivious of its audience. We can go further than this. An eclipse could be witnessed by automatic cameras only, and our faith in objective reality would compel us to fit the event recorded on the film into our model of a universe 'out there', operating quite independently of our perceptual whims.

Newton's laws have been applied to other bodies besides planets; indeed, everything from galaxies to atoms. In particular, the operation of the engineer's machine has been designed with these laws in mind. This picture has suggested a model of the entire universe as a machine, with each individual atom following its own predetermined career with the inexorable certainty of the sun and moon; a gigantic cosmic clockwork unwinding itself according to immutable principles.

Where does the observer fit into this tidy, though rather sterile, scheme of things? Let us examine the act of observation in greater detail. To take a typical example of a scientific observation: suppose we wish to measure the temperature of a cup of hot water, how is this to be accomplished? A good method is to immerse a thermometer in the water and read off the temperature. However, as likely as not the thermometer itself is cold, and in heating up to water-temperature to give an accurate reading, it cools the liquid somewhat. So the temperature we record is not the temperature we really wanted, but a slightly reduced one. This example illustrates the general principle that *any* sort of observation necessarily involves some kind of disturbance to the system that we are trying to observe, and this is true whether the observation takes place through the intermediary of an instrument (thermometer) or by direct observation (finger?).

It might be thought that the interfering effect of all observations deals a death blow to the idea of the universe as a machine, but this is not so. A measuring instrument is as much a machine as the system it measures, so by regarding the total system (apparatus + system to be measured) as one big machine re-establishes the predetermined inevitability of the outcome of measurement. Indeed, in practice one can simply allow for the effect of the measurement disturbance in calibrating the measuring device. Using Newton's mechanistic laws one can compute just how much a given thermometer will lower the water temperature and simply add the discrepancy to the measured result.

From this position it is possible to retreat a stage further and point out that the very act of the experimenter *looking at the thermometer* will cause a minute though significant disturbance, because of the passage of light from the thermometer to the eye, etc. (One is reminded of Francis Thompson's words: 'thou canst not stir a flower, without troubling a star'.) The mechanist would counter by including the observer's eye, brain and everything else into the greater system, and argue that the atoms of the experimenter's body are no less subject to the deterministic laws of physics than the atoms of the thermometer, or water, or whatever. The reader should not feel disenchanted with the fact that the disturbances due to measurement might be almost unthinkably minute in practice. Either the world is real or it is not; the magnitude of the unreality is of no consequence. We are dealing with deep issues of principle. The practical effects are irrelevant.

I do not want to get embroiled here in the old philosophical question of whether a part can ever know the whole of which it is a part, but merely point out that the total reality must clearly include the observer's body. This does not mean, of course, that the rest of the world is unreal, only that it is incomplete. The breakdown of reality which I shall discuss below is of a more direct nature than issues of this sort.

Nor do I want to address the thorny question of free will. It would appear that in a fully deterministic universe there is no room for free will of any sort, which has, over the centuries, provoked debate among philosophers about criminal responsibility and so forth. We shall see below that the universe cannot anyway be deterministic in the Newtonian sense after all, but whether or not that re-establishes the possibility of free will is another matter.

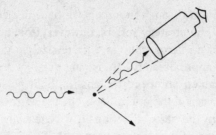

Figure 1. A photon of light (marked ⁓⁓⁓➤) bounces off an electron into a microscope. The recoil angle and velocity of the electron can only be computed by knowing exactly the direction of the rebounding photon. However, this can only be located within the cone of angles defined by the broken lines.

The indeterminate atom

The collapse of the mechanistic world model followed a sequence of stunning discoveries made between 1900 and 1930 by laboratory physicists. The idea of atoms as building blocks for all matter had been floated for more than two millenia. By the turn of the twentieth century, advances in technology enabled direct measurement and observation of atomic, and even subatomic, systems to be made. Whereas in macroscopic systems the disturbances due to measurement could be kept negligibly small in practice, it was by no means clear that atoms could be probed and manipulated by men without drastic disruption. Great attention was therefore devoted to analysing various idealized measuring devices.

One of the simplest atomic observations is to measure the position of an atom or, because we now know atoms are really composite bodies, one of the subatomic particles such as an electron. In principle we can do this by directing a beam of light towards the electron and looking for the illuminated particle through a powerful microscope. For the electron to show up, it is necessary for some light to scatter off it. When this happens the electron will recoil. The more energetic the light, the greater its impact on the particle. (This curious light pressure is the cause of the tails of comets—the tenuous cometary gases being blown off by the force of sunlight.) It thus seems that to know the position of an electron inevitably results in a disruption of its motion.

In spite of this, we could attempt to compute the effect of the light's kick to allow for it in our observation. This requires knowing the angle through which the light is deflected by the collision (see Fig. 1). We can fix this by varying the position of our microscope until it lies along the line of the deflected beam. This strategy suffers, however, from a fundamental limitation. The lens of a microscope has a finite size, so it can only locate the beam direction approximately. (It is not possible to tell when looking through a lens which point on the lens the light passed through.) Worse still, the more powerful the microscope, the bigger the lens and the greater the uncertainty in the beam direction. If we use a small lens then we cannot see the position of the electron very well. This is because light consists of *waves*; when light waves pass through a restricted aperture they smudge out the image. To improve it one can reduce the size of the waves (i.e. use shorter wavelength light) so the waves fit through the lens more comfortably. It is here that we run up against the first revolutionary discovery referred to above.

In the year 1900 it was suggested by the German physicist Max Planck that even though light consists of waves, it can only be emitted or absorbed in discrete lumps, or *quanta* as he called them. A quantum of light is now called a *photon*, and Planck proposed that each photon carry a fixed energy proportional to the frequency of the light. Thus, short wavelength photons are more energetic than long wavelength photons. The existence of photons was soon confirmed experimentally. One conspicuous effect is photoelectricity, where the quanta of light knock electrons out of metals after the fashion of the coconut shy.

The significance of photon quanta for our experiment on the location of electrons is the following. As remarked, to compute the recoil accurately requires using a small lens to observe, which in turn demands very short wavelength light to see with, so as to avoid compromising the position measurement. But according to the quantum hypothesis, this means using very energetic quanta, which implies a more violent recoil. Thus the two conditions—precise position location and accurate knowledge of recoil—are incompatible. We can either use a small lens and low energy photons to keep the recoil under control, in which case we won't get a very good image of where the electron is, or we can push up the photon energy (reduce the wavelength) and the power of the microscope (bigger lens), thereby improving our location measurement at the expense of knowledge about the recoil.

In spite of the rather specialised nature of this experiment, the outcome is completely general. The argument was originally given by the German physicist Werner Heisenberg and the conclusion is known as the Heisenberg uncertainty principle. It is a result of fundamental importance for science. Stated simply, it says that we cannot, by any means whatever, simultaneously measure *both* the location and the motion of a particle. The degree of uncertainty in each is determined, as expected, by Planck's constant—the fixed ratio of energy to frequency of the photon. This number is extremely small by everyday standards, so the Heisenberg uncertainty is only important on an atomic scale.

Probability waves

The discovery of the photon endowed light waves with some of the properties of particles—travelling in lumps with a definite energy and momentum. A second major discovery, in the 1920s, overturned centuries of belief about the nature of material particles.

Early ideas about atoms were based on the belief that the microworld is merely a scaled-down version of the everyday world of our experience. According to this view, atoms (and presumably subatomic particles too) move about, interact and generally behave like miniscule billiard balls. Even today, popular accounts of atomic structure paint a picture of little spheres rattling about. When it became possible to isolate and control beams of electrons, experiments were performed by the American physicist Clinton Davisson in which electrons were scattered off crystal surfaces.

The result was astonishing. Instead of bouncing off the crystal atoms in the way a stream of tiny particles should, the elctron beam behaved instead as though it were a *wave*, like light. Moreover, the wavelength turned out to depend on the *speed* of the electrons in inverse proportion, with a ratio determined by Planck's constant. Similar effects occur with all atomic and subatomic particles. Evidently, quantum effects 'particle-ize' light and 'wave-ize' particles.

The implication of this experiment (the result of which was actually predicted by Prince Louis de Broglie in 1924) is that the quantum theory applies as much to material particles, as to light. It means that we would be equally stymied if we attempted to use other particles rather than light as a method of locating our target electron. Thus, the uncertainty of Heisenberg is in fact an inherent *property of nature*, not just a limitation in the behaviour of light waves.

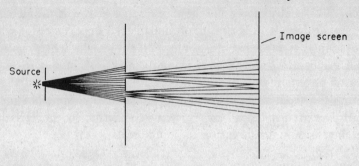

Figure 2. Young's experiment. A small source of light illuminates a screen with two apertures. The overlapping images are examined on another screen, revealing bright and dark interference fringes. Similar effects occur with electrons.

What is the meaning of these enigmatic matter waves? It must not be imagined that the Davisson experiment shows that electrons *are* waves, only that their motion is controlled by wavelike principles. There is no doubt whatever that electrons are particles in some respects. They can be counted and collected one at a time, and they have no measurable spatial extension, as does a conventional wave. This curious dichotomy, similar to that associated with photons, is sometimes referred to as wave-particle duality. Photons and material particles such as atoms and electrons display both wave- and particle-like behaviour, and it depends on what type of experiment or measurement we are trying to perform which of these two faces is manifested. There is no counterpart to such a 'wave-particle' in the everyday world. Clearly, then, atomic systems are *not* just scaled-down versions of the macroworld. Important new qualities reside in the microscopic recesses of matter.

To make sense of the meaning of matter waves it is helpful to imagine another simple experiment illustrated in Fig. 2. A small source of light illuminates a screen A containing two narrow slits close together. The image of the slits is examined on screen B. What do we see? The experiment was first performed by the English physicist and Egyptologist Thomas Young over a century and a half ago. It might be imagined that the image would consist of two strips of light directly behind the slits, rather fuzzy at the edges and overlapping somewhat. In fact one observes a sequence of light and dark *bands* called interference fringes. The reason for this rests with the wave nature of the light. The waves erupting from one slit partially overlap those from the other slit and where the two arrive at the screen B in step (i.e. peak to peak, trough to trough) they reinforce to give a bright image. However, where they arrive out of step (peak to trough) they cancel each other and give a dark band. If one of the slits is covered, the interference is removed, and the image of the remaining slit is 'normal'.

If the experiment is now repeated using *electrons* instead of light, the same pattern of interference bands is seen, as would be expected on the basis of the wave nature of matter described above. This time, though, we seem to have a paradox, because each individual electron can clearly only pass through *one* of the slits. To eliminate the possibility of some collective interference between two or more different electrons, one can turn down the source until *only one electron at a time* passes through the apparatus. The cumulative effect after a long period still produces the interference fringes. Indeed, the fringe pattern even appears if the arrival points of single electrons are recorded from a whole ensemble of different apparata! In some strange way each electron manages to interfere with itself. Even though a solitary electron passes through just one slit, the wave influence probes both slits and operates to direct the electron preferentially to certain regions of the image screen (i.e. those corresponding to the bright fringes).

This may seem like magic, and a mischievous experimenter might attempt to thwart nature by determining in advance which slit a given electron is headed for, then quickly cover up the other one. According to the wave picture the fringes should go away if only one slit is open, but the electron, moving in the vicinity of the other slit, could know nothing of the trickery. A careful analysis of these tactics reveals another victory for nature. To see in sufficient detail which slit the electron is headed for turns out to require a light source so energetic that the recoil imparted completely washes out the interference fringes anyway. Thus, although we know only *one* slit witnesses the passage of the electron, *which* one cannot be determined, even in principle, without disrupting the very phenomenon under investigation.

The fact that *solitary* electrons continue to display wave interference properties is a clue to the meaning of the matter waves. Evidently they represent some kind of *statistical* effect. We may say that any particular electron has a high *probability* of reaching the image screen at a point corresponding to a bright fringe, and a low probability of reaching a dark fringe region. When we accumulate vast numbers of electrons, then collectively they will form light and dark fringes. The matter waves are not, therefore, waves *of* matter, but *probability waves*. Where the wave is most intense, there the electron is most likely to be found. It is rather like a crime wave, which is also not a wave of any substance, but represents an enhanced probability of a felony in that place.

The significance of the probabilistic behaviour of subatomic matter for our world model is profound indeed. First, it is clear that the deterministic, mechanical picture cannot be correct. When an electron sets out to pass through the apparatus shown in Fig. 2 it does *not* move along some well-defined, in-principle completely knowable, trajectory. Instead, it can choose a whole range of possibilities, with greater or less likelihood. This implies that there are many *potential* worlds (involving the electron reaching a whole range of points on the image screen) only one of which becomes the actual world, with a certain probability.

The shifting worlds of the quantum

The probability interpretation of quantum theory may appear bizarre, but it has had widespread acceptance among physicists since the early 1930s. The idea that the world operates at random instead of along tightly controlled channels has seemed repugnant to some, though. Even Albert Einstein could not accept it and dismissed the interpretation with a famous phrase: 'God does not play dice'. In spite of this, alternative interpretations, for example those that involve a hidden substratum of deterministic physics, have not enjoyed much success. In what follows I shall adhere to the (conventional) probability interpretation, sometimes known as the Copenhagen interpretation since it was due largely to the work of the great Danish physicist Niels Bohr.

To fix ideas, consider a useful application of the quantum theory to a problem in nuclear physics, i.e. radioactivity. Some heavy atoms have nuclei that are unstable, and tend to disintegrate by ejecting a small charged body called an alpha particle. Using the wave mechanical theory outlined above, it is possible to compute the probability that, after a certain duration, a given nucleus will have decayed in this way. Suppose we choose a nucleus and a duration so that the probability at the end is one-half. There are then two potential worlds; one in which the nucleus is intact, one in which it has decayed. Both are equally likely. Which one is the 'real' world?

To answer this question, it is necessary to make an observation. We could, for example, station a Geiger counter nearby and examine it at the appointed time to see if it has registered the presence of an alpha particle. At first sight the situation seems no different from the usual indeterminacy associated with incomplete information about the world. If we toss a coin there are two potential worlds, a 'heads' world and a 'tails' world. Some sort of observation is necessary to decide which potential world is the *actual* world. However, the quantum version of indeterminacy is altogether more fundamental than this for two reasons. The first is that in the heads/tails dichotomy we suppose that, given sufficient information about the structure of the coin, the force of spin, height of flip, etc., it would (in principle) be possible to predict heads or tails, whereas, even in principle, and even with the most complete knowledge allowable about the atom, there is no way that the nuclear disintegration can be predicted. Only the betting odds can be calculated.

The second difference gets right to the root of the problem of a 'real world out there', and requires a careful explanation. The head/tails choice is between two alternative worlds, only one of which corresponds to the 'real' world. The situation is either/or. In the quantum case this is not so. We are only forced into an either/or choice *when a measurement or observation is actually made.* Until that time, the world consists of a curious overlapping combination of all its alternatives, a combination known to physicists as a *superposition.*

This idea is so revolutionary and so significant that I shall devote some considerable space to explaining it. To do so I shall consider an example frequently used by physicists which, moreover, can actually be used as the basis of laboratory measurements. We have seen how quantum effects control the motion of subatomic particles like electrons. It is found that electrons also have a kind of internal motion called *spin*, and this provides a clean example of the application of quantum principles. The spin of an electron can likewise be described after the fashion of a wave, especially in the way that interference effects occur.

It is helpful to think of the spinning electron as defining a direction in space. Imagine an axis of rotation with a little arrow directed along it. This arrow (i.e. the electron's spin) could be pointing in any direction. For convenience let us label them north, south, east, west, etc. Now, in the previous section it was described how, according to quantum principles, light energy only comes in lumps called photons. The same principles require that many other quantities also come in lumps, one of these being spin. Specifically, suppose we take a spinning electron and measure which direction its spin axis lies along. We find the bizarre result that it lies along whatever direction we care to choose. Choose N-S, measure the spin, and find it pointing either directly north or directly south. Choose E-W and find it pointing either E or W. It is as though the act of measurement *throws* the electron's spin into the direction we have chosen. Just as there are no 'in between' energies for photons, so there are no 'in between' directions for spin, only the two discrete choices—parallel or antiparallel ('up' or 'down') the particular direction of choice. We begin to see the tight interplay between the state of the world (i.e the electron in this case) and the act of measurement. Instead of regarding the world as made up of a collection of independently existing *objects* (electron, measuring apparatus, experimenter) we must think of it as a network of *interactions* or *observations* of one part on another. It is the *coupling together* of the system and the observer that apparently brings the reality into existence. It is meaningless to say that the electron spin was 'really' pointing NE, but the apparatus disturbed it, for there is no way whatever that we can tell which way the electron 'really' pointed *before* the observation was made. The very concept of the direction of electron spin only makes sense *within the context* of the experiment and its particular choice of direction.

But that is not all. Suppose we set up our apparatus to measure the spin E-W and find the result E. A further E-W measurement will certainly (i.e. with probability one) find the spin pointing E. But what about a subsequent N-S measurement? By symmetry it is clear that there is equal likelihood of finding the spin pointing N as pointing S. Now ask what happens if we make a NE-SW oblique measurement. If this is done directly after the E-W measurement then we find that in most cases the spin points NE; the probability is greater NE than SW. This is no great surprise, as we left the spin inclined eastwards at the outset. The catch is, if we intercede with the N-S measurement (i.e. follow the sequence E-W, N-S, NE-SW) then we end up with *equal* likelihood of finding SW as NE. That is, the effect of making the N-S measurement completely destroys the original E state, and *removes* the predeliction for NE.

These observations have a clear interpretation in terms of waves, and it is here that we reach the crucial stage in my entire argument. Viewed within the context of a N-S measurement, the original (E) state of the world is a superposition of *two* possible worlds: 'north' and 'south'. It is not possible to say which is the actual world without making a N-S measurement. I want now to demonstrate my contention that we are not simply faced with a N/S alternative, but an actual hybrid of the two. That conclusion follows by considering the subsequent NE-SW measurement. If this is undertaken directly, that is, on the N-S hybrid superposition set up by arranging the electron spin to be pointing E, then we get, as explained above, a preference for NE. If, on the other hand, we intercede with the N-S measurement, we find no such preference. (This effect is very real and has been measured in the laboratory.) In wave language it is easy to spot precisely where the NE bias originates. It is an *interference* effect caused by an *overlapping* between the 'north' world and the 'south' world. Crudely speaking the waves which describe these different potential worlds are in step towards the NE and out of step towards the SW. In fact, everything I have so far said goes through equally well if we set up the spin originally pointing W rather than E, only in this configuration, the 'north' and 'south' worlds are in step towards the SW and out of step towards the NE. Thus one finds a SW bias instead.

The effect outlined in the previous paragraph is so fundamental to quantum theory and its version of 'reality' that it should be thoroughly grasped. If the world merely consisted of the two *independent alternatives*, north and south, then no such interference effects would occur, and the NE bias would disappear. This is just what happens if we intercede with a N-S measurement. The act of measurement changes the hybrid world—the superposition—into a real alternative between the two, with the result that the overlap interference is destroyed and equal NE, SW likelihood results. The act of collapsing a superposition of overlapping worlds on to a set of mutually exclusive alternatives is the central role of the observation in quantum theory, and beautifully illustrates how such an observation inevitably disrupts the system under observation.

It may appear beyond belief that the world can be in a state where several alternative 'realities' may not only co-exist, but overlap with each other to cause real, physical interference effects. When we detect a NE bias, we are witnessing the collective and collaborative action of *two* overlapping worlds! Lest the reader should suppose that discussions of spinning electrons are inconsequential pedantry, I should point out that the interference effects of the type mentioned here lead directly to forces that help hold molecules together. They are central to our understanding of most of atomic and subatomic physics.

The role of the observer

The essential conclusion of the previous section is that, unless an observation is made, the world must be regarded as a superposition of alternative overlapping realities, *all* of which coherently operate to affect the outcome of subsequent measurements. The hybrid is *more* than just all the alternatives acting together. The alternatives actually interfere with each other. Moreover, *which* alternative worlds and *which* interference is entirely the choice of the experimenter, who may decide to perform one type of measurement on the other. (Let me repeat that this may not at all be the same thing as the usual notion of 'free will'.)

Such a fundamental role for the experimenter is alien to pre-quantum physics. According to the Newtonian mechanistic view, the experimenter is undeniably part of the world, but his whims cannot affect *which* world, for there is only one, and the observer is simply there for the ride. In contrast, the quantum observer seems almost to create his own world with him by choice. There are many potential worlds, existing with various probabilities. The experimenter has no actual control over the probabilities *themselves* (he cannot load the dice) but he can decide what are the alternatives (choose the game).

The purpose of this article is to refute the fallacy that reality exists outside us. So far I appear to have shown that the observer plays an essential role in determining what the reality might be, but once the observation is made, then the reality exists nonetheless. I shall now argue that even this position is untenable.

It is possible to study (in model systems) precisely how the act of measurement, say by some laboratory machine like a Geiger counter, actually brings about the destruction of the quantum interference, and changes the overlapping superposed worlds into mere separate alternatives, only one of which is the 'actual' world. This analysis was carried out by the mathematician John von Neumann in the 1930s. He showed that in order to measure an atomic system it is necessary to couple it temporarily to some large piece of apparatus which is 'triggered', thereby changing its state in a macroscopically observable way (e.g. click of a counter, deflection of a pointer). The alternative microworlds, such as decayed-nucleus or intact-nucleus, then become alternative macroworlds (clicked or unclicked-counter) where we can observe the difference.

Naturally this is true even on pre-quantum ideas. The crucial quantum difference is the role of the interference effects. The act of coupling and triggering the apparatus, von Neumann showed, destroys the overlapping of the different microworlds, changing it from a ghostly superposition to an ordinary set of separate alternatives, which alternative being displayed on the apparatus for the experimenter to see. However, the victory is a pyrrhic one, for these very interference effects which have disappeared from the atomic system under observation have, through the coupling, infested the measuring apparatus. The reason is actually rather obvious. There is no justification for separating the world into 'microscopic' and 'macroscopic' pieces. The laboratory apparatus is made of atoms also, and these too are subject to quantum laws. If we consider the quantum system of interest to be atom + apparatus, then there is *no way* in which, treated in isolation as a whole, it can collapse from a superposition of overlapping alternative realities, to one of a concrete set of distinct realities.

Von Neumann's analysis raises the disturbing spectre of an Alice-in-Wonderland laboratory in which schizophrenic apparata engage in the sort of antics already described for electron spin. In fact, that is not so. It turns out that in a chunk of machinery of everyday size, there are so many billions of atoms that the degree of overlap between macroscopically distinguishable states (e.g. positions of a pointer) is utterly negligible. It is as though, for all practical purposes, the overlapping worlds are very, very nearly separate. Thus, in practice, we do not notice insane wavelike interference effects.

Nevertheless, the fact that 'other realities' might overlap our own, however dilutely, raises such important points of principle that we cannot let matters drop here. Von Neumann argued that to rid the laboratory apparatus of interference effects, it is necessary for an observation of the apparatus to be made: for example, by the experimenter himself. This in turn shifts the superposition into the still larger system requiring a further observation and so on in an apparently endless sequence, popularly known as von Neumann's chain.

Where does von Neumann's chain end? This question has been the subject of intense debate among physicists for decades. Some proponents favour abandoning the Copenhagen interpretation of quantum theory altogether because of this apparent philosophical inconsistency. A number of paradoxes have been discussed to highlight it. One of these, due to Erwin Schrödinger, the Austrian co-founder of modern quantum theory, is known as the cat paradox. It envisages a mechanism, triggered by the radioactive decay of a nucleus, which releases a cyanide capsule and kills a cat. We know that the two worlds 'nucleus-intact' and 'nucleus-decayed' are an overlapping superposition. Are we to suppose that there can exist live-dead overlapping cats?

Problems also occur in cosmology. As von Neumann's chain grows and grows, what happens when it encompasses the entire universe? Who is to make the crucial observation from 'outside' the universe so that the whole cosmic panorama can collapse into reality? Faced with problems of this severity, some physicists have fallen back on bizarre speculations. Perhaps all the worlds are equally real, and co-exist in parallel? Perhaps the entry of the observation in the *consciousness* of the observer is the crucial step that breaks the chain of regression, implying as it does the supra-quantum status of mind over quantum-enslaved matter? There is no unanimous agreement.

To conclude this somewhat sketchy account of what is, after all, the most successful scientific theory ever known, it would appear that the concept of an independent reality 'out there' has been discredited. We see in its place a shifting world of uncertainty in which apparent realities can come and go in seemingly random fashion, and in which even the observer himself has dissolved into something evanescent and insubstantial. The central conclusion is that if reality has any meaning at all, it is only in the context of the observer and the observation itself. There is a kind of continuous creation— a new world every moment—brought into being by our own conscious awareness. Or so it seems. In a world full of uncertainty, who can be sure?

Sir Alan Cottrell

Sir Alan Cottrell is the Master of Jesus College, Cambridge. He was Deputy Chief Scientific Adviser to H.M. Government, 1968-71, and Chief Scientific Adviser to H.M. Government 1971-74. He has been awarded numerous honorary degrees and prizes, including the Harvey Prize, Technion, Israel, 1974, and the Rumford Medal of the Royal Society, London, 1974.

His main interest has been in the atomic theory of the properties of matter, especially those of metals, with emphasis on the theory of the strength, ductility and brittleness of steel, and also on problems of nuclear radiation in solids in connection with the development of nuclear power. More recently Sir Alan has become interested in the roles of science and technology in national affairs and also in industrial policy. Another recent interest of his is in the presentation of science to the general public.

Science is objective

Heads or Hearts?

Someone once remarked that, when a scientist says something, his colleagues need ask only whether it is true, whereas, when a politician says something, they must first ask 'why did he say it?'. Whatever this may imply about politics, it reflects a widely held view of science as the objective search for natural knowledge.

Yet, of course, scientists as human beings are the same as everyone else. Indeed, the published memoirs of those scientists who have ventured into the corridors of power are impressive as displays of that same old human nature—passionate, prejudiced, vain—in full flood. How does it happen then, that in scientific work ordinary human beings are able to turn themselves into impartial seekers of objective truth? How is it that, in this at least, they are able to rule their hearts so completely by their heads? It is a question that still perplexes the philosophers and sociologists of science, but several important factors are plain. The most obvious is that science gathers its knowledge—the facts of nature—by means of the experimental method, which distils the required information in a form largely separated from confusing extraneous factors; a method which replaces value-laden quality by irrefutable numbers as far as possible; which also replaces the observer's gullible eyes and fingers by photographic plates and graduated scales; and which insists that experimental results must be repeatable by independent observers, if they are to be believed.

In addition, *pure science* (as distinct from applied science) has achieved its success by its scientists themselves choosing the problems they work on, instead of taking up problems selected for them by external non-scientific authorities on grounds of extrinsic importance. In the words of Medawar (1967) science is 'the art of the soluble' and only those scientists working at the frontiers of knowledge know what they can reasonably expect to solve at any given time. There is also the point, stressed by Ziman (1968), that 'science is public knowledge'; new facts and theories have to survive an ordeal of independent testing and sceptical analysis in a public scientific arena, before they can expect to become generally accepted. In this way their objective quality is enhanced, since this no longer depends solely on the impartiality of the original discoverer but on the confirmation through a world-wide scientific community that is initially uncommitted and instinctively sceptical.

No one could deny that these methods have been enormously successful in uncovering the secrets of nature. The 300-year-old era of science is one of almost unbroken triumphal progress, which continues at full pace today. It is hardly surprising that many people outside science, dazzled by its brilliance, have reacted to it strongly in several ways. The reaction of the literary intellectuals has already been vividly told by Snow in *The Two Cultures* (1959). But there have been others. Some scholars have tried to imitate science, have tried to make similar advances in their own fields by applying the 'scientific method' of objective analysis to them. The impacts of this have been felt in philosophy, linguistics, history, literary studies, economics, politics, and other branches of scholarship. At its extreme, this reaction has led to *scientism*, to the view that only the methods of the natural sciences can yield true knowledge about anything, even man and society. In some respects this has been beneficial, serving rather like an Occam's razor to cut back the dense growths of wishful thinking that have smothered mankind's intellectual outlooks for centuries. In other respects it has been harmful, by 'atomising' scholarship—for example, replacing the grand sweeps of classical history by disjointed specks of analytical history; by 'dehumanizing' those subjects such as economics, where value-judgements have an essential part to play; and by enabling the purveyors of ideologies to claim intellectual respectability for their doctrines by labelling them 'scientific', in much the same way as they claim moral respectability for them by labelling them 'democratic'.

Of course, such excesses and abuses of scientism have produced their own highly-charged counter-reactions, particularly in the anti-scientific crusades of Marcuse, Ellul, Roszak, and others. This is the two-culture problem again, but now inflamed almost beyond recognition by an aversion to Western industrial society and everything to do with it, including science. Politics apart, the argument against science has been that the cold search for objective truth is alien to subjective human nature, alien to engagement, participation, involvement, to the 'existential absorption of experience'. In older times when language was simpler it would have been described as the conflict between heart and head. And if the heart is to win, then the head must be either discredited or captured.

Discrediting the head is the technique chosen for open societies, to be achieved through the doctrine of 'relativism' which claims that there is no absolute knowledge—only personal opinions—that objectivity is optional and that scholarship is therefore a waste of time. Of this doctrine perhaps no more need be said than that its authors ought not to mind too much if they find themselves among its first victims, by having their own thesis cast aside as a personal eccentricity.

Capturing the head is the technique for authoritarian societies. It is the reverse of relativism. The free market of individual thought is to be replaced by collective order of received doctrine, which the head is instructed to rationalize intellectually. If the facts do not agree, so much the worse for them; they must be rejected or 'massaged'. This is the control of science, so beloved by authoritarians, that led Bruno to the stake, Galileo to the Inquisition, and N. I. Vavilov to a concentration camp and death sentence. But it is a technique that can only fail in the long run, for truth will eventually out. In the words of Horace 'though you drive away Nature with a pitchfork she always returns' (Epistles).

Inside the Citadel

Not surprisingly, it is in the outposts of science, in the region of the social sciences, that the conflict of head and heart is most intense. How can we discuss problems of, say, population, natural resources, economics, or education, without bringing value-judgements into play? How can we remain coldly analytical about great social problems? But on the other hand, can they be solved by gusts of emotion? How can heart and head, subjectivity and objectivity, work together under such circumstances? Until this problem is solved the social sciences cannot but remain in turmoil, with little enduringly constructed. Deeper within the citadel of science the balance swings more decisively in favour of the head, as the topics become progressively 'harder'. But even here, the test of objectivity is sometimes severely strained. A cruel problem in genetics, for example, is that of the relation between race and intelligence. Are some 'races' more intelligent than others? This is a question to make the blood run hot, yet impossible to answer with scientific certainty except by means of huge statistical surveys under difficult conditions of environmental work. Why work on this question, when it is such a difficult one for the head and such a disturbing one for the heart?

Right in the centre of the citadel we meet the really 'hard' physical sciences, crystal-clear, coldly abstract, conceptually remote, mathematically exact, unsullied by human passions, the final strongholds of objectivity. The speed of light in space, the molecular weight of methane, the efficiency of an ideal engine, the crystal structure of diamond, the galactic structure of the universe, are exactly the same whatever one's race, creed, colour, sex, age, politics or purse. It is here above all that the true essence of the world seems to be discoverable.

Yet it is precisely in this central citadel of physical science that we shall raise questions about objectivity. We shall do this not in any effort to undermine the exact sciences. This is in no sense an essay in relativism. On the contrary, we do it because experience has shown that delving for previously unsuspected subjective features is one of the most effective methods of advancing the scientific understanding of nature. Thus, in the dawn of modern science, Copernicus realised that what everyone had previously taken for granted—i.e. that all things in the heavens rotate round an earth fixed at the centre of the universe—was merely a subjective point of view. Its exposure cleared the way for Galileo, Newton, and modern astronomy. Similarly, Einstein proved that subjective assumptions about the special position of observers confused our notions of space and time, especially the concept of simultaneity. The eradication of these subjective features immediately led to the great theory of relativity.

In the following we will raise questions of objectivity in three areas of present-day physics: (i) the emergence of new properties in bulk matter; (ii) the role of the observer in quantum mechanics; and (iii) the nature of time.

Emergent Properties

Classical physics was founded on the properties of large bodies, properties that were fairly directly abstracted from everyday experience, such as mass, inertia, volume, pressure, density, heat capacity, thermal expansion, conductivity, surface tension, magnetisation, electrical and optical properties, elasticity, viscosity, hardness and strength. Each such property was dealt with either *sui generis* or derived from a few others—as, for example, in the theory of sound waves derived from the elasticity and density of extended bodies—by an *ad hoc* theory which simply invested a hypothetical continuous and structureless medium with imagined functions necessary to enable it to perform like the real stuff. Only rarely—as in Laplace's deduction of a fundamental length in matter from a comparison of the energies of surfaces and volumes—was the internal consistency of the continuum hypothesis questioned.

It all changed with the atomic theory of the 19th century. Kinetic theory began brilliantly by deducing the properties of gases as the statistical effects of random molecular motions. The atomic theory of bulk matter has gone on triumphantly since then, so that today most scientists believe that all properties of large-scale bodies, even biological ones, are entirely the results of atomic behaviour. This is the *reductionist hypothesis*. In the words of Feynman (1963), 'everything that animals do, atoms do'.

Without challenging this, we can nevertheless consider the scope for subjective influences in the emergence of macroscopic single-body properties from microscopic multi-atomic behaviour. The atomic information which could in principle be gathered from a large body, e.g. a pebble of 10^{24} atoms, is gigantic. In practice we collect, with our senses or instruments, only a tiny fragment of this information, which means that many opportunities exist for making different selections of this small sample from the total. In making our choice we thus bring a subjective element into the emergence of a bulk property from atomic behaviour.

A simple example is provided by frictional properties. At the atomic level, where all processes are completely reversible, there is no friction. But in bulk matter, where there are just too many particles to analyse individually, it becomes convenient, even essential in practice, to neglect the microscopic details of their motions. As a consequence of this neglect, the properties of friction appear, accompanied by the extraordinary emergence of *irreversibility*. Although entirely 'real' to our ordinary senses and although they can be entirely studied in their own right as 'good' physical properties, the frictional properties are nevertheless subjective properties of matter. While it would be highly inconvenient to do so, we could if we wished dispense with them entirely and instead describe all the relevant effects in terms of what the atoms are doing.

The same argument applies more or less to all emergent properties of bulk matter. It is significant that the theoretical science of bulk matter— statistical thermodynamics—is incapable of describing such properties in terms purely of statistical particle mechanics; a 'non-mechanical' assumption has always to be brought in. Not surprisingly, subjective features appear throughout the theory. For example, if we stir up two paints, red and white, we do not at first produce a pink paint, but only an interlacing of red and white filaments. Eventually the mixture becomes so fine that, to our eyes, it emerges as an apparently new state, that of a single homogeneous pink paint. Something corresponding closely to this is done in statistical thermodynamics when, at a suffcently finely mixed stage, we redefine the mixed fluids as a *single* medium with a higher entropy. The second law of thermodynamics, which deals with such irreversible increases of entropy, thus has a subjective basis.

Another example is provided by the probability laws of statistics. The actual lifetime of an individual radioactive atom, for example, is unpredictable; the atom may disintegrate at any time. But a large number of such atoms behaves, collectively, in a statistically regular and predictable way, so that a bulk property of the collection—its *radioactive decay constant*— emerges as a well-defined and measurable physical quantity. We can then, if we wish, imagine each atom possessing the same constant, as a measure of its 'probability' of decaying within a given interval of time.

Such subjective interpretations as these, provided they are properly understood, are not wrong but highly convenient features of science. They are like stepping-stones which enable us to cross, to and fro, the immense gulf which separates the world of the atom from that of everyday experience. Their interest for the future is that not all features of everyday experience have yet been reduced to atomic behaviour. Psychology is still very tenuously connected to the natural sciences, for example. It may be that, by looking for subjective elements in such connections—elements which produce an almost transcendental change in the appearance of properties—we shall be able to understand those connections better.

The Engaged Observer

In classical physics the observer was a passive bystander, entirely innocent of the drama being played before his eyes. In the words of Eddington 'you won't hurt the moon by looking at it'.

But we now know that this is wrong. The bystander cannot help getting into the action, if he is to observe anything of it. Messages in the natural world come in chunks and require physical carriers. The smallest message consists of one *quantum*, as defined by Planck's constant, and this unit of action cannot be delivered from the object of observation to the subject (i.e. the observer) without leaving behind a disturbance in the object itself. For the moon it hardly matters, because Planck's constant is so extremely small by comparison. But for an electron or an atom it matters very much indeed and the atomic properties of matter are immensely influenced by it. We cannot avoid being physically involved with a system when we observe it. But we can choose the manner of our involvement and so exert a subjective influence over what we observe.

At root, we have only two notions—*particle* and *wave*—for visualising material things. Both come from classical physics, where they stand entirely separate in the sense that a given thing is always either a particle or a wave. But in quantum physics the same things—electrons, for example, or pulses of light—can be observed to be either particles or waves, according to our choice of the form of our compulsory interaction with them. By changing this choice, we can change their observed nature from wavelike to particlelike, and vice versa, as often as we wish. The choice of how they shall appear is ours. This dual allegiance of elementary things to two classically incompatible forms, which was given its clearest and most widely accepted expression in Bohr's *complementarity principle*, has the consequence that our most precise concept today for describing elementary things, which is the quantum-mechanical 'wave function', generally contains both objective and subjective features. Those features which are the same for all observers are objective; those which express what a particular observer may know about the object and which may change for other observers are subjective.

In the early days of quantum mechanics people wondered whether this latitude in nature left an opening in physical science for free will, which aroused much philosophical interest. This possibility was, perhaps prematurely, dismissed on the grounds that the quantum-mechanical complementarity is on much too fine a scale to have a significant direct effect on the behaviour of large bodies. Despite this early interest, however, philosophers generally seem not to have grasped the immensity of the change that has been brought about in physical science by the discovery of quantization. The prevalent impression, from outside science, of the exact sciences is still that of classical mechanics with its 'clockwork' world running, in a totally objective and deterministic way, in strict obedience to an exact set of Newtonian equations. It is an impression of a closed, complete, world, leaving no room for any physically undetermined influences. This is the world of physical science as imagined by many philosophers and non-scientists. But it is nothing like the world of today's physicist, a world in which natural processes are riddled with physically undetermined micro-events, a world in which the apparent determinism of large bodies emerges merely as a statistical result of their multi-particle constitutions.

Two Kinds of Time

Careful philosophers have introduced a third category between those of objective and subjective. It is 'intersubjective' and refers to common or *public* experiences, as distinct from the private and idiosyncratic experiences of the individual. Scientific knowledge thus comes from intersubjective experience. This raises an important question, put by Gold (1974):

> The basic concepts of physics—space, time, force, velocity—were singled out from other subjective notions because 'objective' measurements were possible . . . all observers had to agree about the result of the measurement. What if all observers bring the same subjective notion into the measurement? It is after all only the variations between humans that this criterion removes: what is common to all will survive the application of this criterion.

Gold himself gave the concept of the moving 'now' of flowing time as an example of such a notion. It is subjectively experienced, but it is the same for all of us and so is at least intersubjective (although this term was not used by Gold). Its objective status is, however, doubtful.

As human beings we live and act in the present time, or now; we remember the past, which has already gone, and we look forward to future events which will eventually become the present, then afterwards the past. We use *tenses* in ordinary language, expressly to make these very distinctions.

But in natural science the only significant distinction seems to be whether one event occurs *before* or *after* another (at the same point of space). The concept of 'now' plays no part in this. In place of Newton's view that 'absolute, true and mathematical time or duration flows evenly and equally from its own nature and independent of anything external'—a notion of which Newton in fact made no use—modern physics substitutes the view of Weyl (1949) that 'the objective world simply *is*, it does not *happen*'. In the words of Gold 'one can regard a description of the physical world as merely a map of the world-lines of all the particles . . . having done this, there is nothing left out . . . there is no hint in this description of anything being pushed along the time coordinate . . . physics is the discussion of the repetitive patterns in the great pattern'.

But is not physics trying to be *too* objective in forming this strange picture? The world map of a spacetime pattern goes far beyond what we actually experience of the world and indeed it implies a 'godlike' view of a world laid out in space and time, as seen from 'outside time'. Ought we not to recognise our human limitations and retreat from this grand spacetime view to our actual intersubjective view, in which we experience the world a bit at a time?

We face an impasse. The objective view presumes an eternal vision of time itself, beyond our experience or understanding. The transient view is only too human and subjective. Those supporting the godlike view can admire its elimination of human existential limitations from the notion of time. Those opposing it can criticise it for precisely the same reason, for divorcing itself from the only world we know.

The problem poses in acute form the general dichotomy between the objective and subjective points of view. We have no place for 'now' in our scientific heads, yet in our human hearts we have unshakeable certainty of its reality. It raises an even greater issue, for we are aware of 'now' through our *consciousness*. The close coupling of mind to brain, for which there is much scientific evidence, makes it likely that our mental experiences are related to particular physical features or processes in the brain. Yet the brain is a biophysical system and therefore probably not fundamentally different from other physical systems, such as computers, in its obedience to physical laws. Hence we must either suppose that the feature of time which our minds recognise as 'now' must have some general physical basis; or we must accept a fundamental gulf between the mind and brain, i.e. that there really is a 'ghost' which is aware of 'now', living in a 'machine' which does not recognise 'now'.

Conclusion

What matters is not whether science is objective. It could not possibly be so, in any philosophically ideal sense of the term, since it is a human creation. What matters is that it is objective in spirit; i.e. that it strives for objectivity as a necessary aspect of its search for truth. In striving thus, it has largely rid itself of those obvious subjectivities that rule most human affairs; and the deeper subjectivities which it is now exposing are of great interest as starting-points for yet more penetrating explorations of the strange world we inhabit.

References

Feynman, R. P. (1963) *The Feynman Lectures on Physics*, **1** (London: Addison-Wesley).
Gold, T. (1974) in *Modern Developments in Thermodynamics*, ed. B. Gal-Or (New York: Wiley).
Medawar, P. B. (1967) *The Art of the Soluble* (London: Methuen).
Snow, C. P. (1959) *The Two Cultures*, The Rede Lecture (London: Cambridge U.P.).
Weyl, H. (1949) *Philosophy of Mathematics and Natural Science* (Princeton: Princeton U.P.).
Ziman, J. (1968) *Public Knowledge: The Social Dimension of Science* (London: Cambridge U.P.).

Otto R. Frisch

Otto R. Frisch, O.B.E., F.R.S., was Jacksonian Professor of Natural Philosophy, University of Cambridge, 1947-72, and is now Professor Emeritus. He is best known as the physicist who collaborated with Lise Meitner in 1939 to produce the first definite identification and explanation of the phenomenon of 'nuclear fission', a phrase which he himself coined.

He has carried out research in many parts of the world, including Berlin, Copenhagen, Oxford, Los Alamos, Harwell and Cambridge, and is the author of many publications on atomic and nuclear physics.

You can prove anything with statistics

Why is it that so many people have so little confidence in statistics? Why do they quote snide remarks like 'there are three kinds of lies: ordinary lies, damned lies and statistics' or words like the ones that head this essay? After all, according to the *Pocket Oxford Dictionary* (1961) statistics are simply 'numerical facts systematically collected on a subject'; an innocent enough pursuit, collecting numerical facts systematically. But a sceptic may doubt whether the facts have been collected carefully and honestly; facts are often hard to check, and suspicion is easily aroused if they appear to support some politically or emotionally loaded conclusion. Moreover, the process of drawing the conclusion from the numerical facts is usually not spelled out and employs techniques with which people are not familiar.

Actually the statement 'You can prove anything with statistics' contains two lies, not just one. In the first place you can never 'prove' anything with statistics, not as you can prove a theorem in mathematics. At best you can use statistics to give support to a statement; perhaps enough to dispel any reasonable doubt. Secondly—and that is more important—you cannot prove 'anything' with statistics. Some statements are just not true, and statistical evidence will not support them unless it is faked or misinterpreted, either through ignorance or on purpose.

Let me quote you an example of misleading 'statistics' (a single number) which was pilloried in the Introduction to *Elementary Statistics* by Levy and Preidel (Nelson 1947). A society opposed to immunization stated publicly that 5000 children got diphtheria in spite of having been immunized against it. No doubt that bald statement achieved its purpose of persuading a number of parents that immunization was useless; yet it proved nothing of the kind. It failed to state what fraction of the immunized children those 5000 represent or how many of unprotected children caught diphtheria. When those figures were inspected it was found that in

172

1942 the fraction which got ill was about nine times as big among the non-immunized children! In other words, the relevant figures showed that immunization was far from useless: it reduced by a factor 9 the risk that a child would get diphtheria.

That was an extreme case of statistics misused by over-simplification, by quoting just one emotionally loaded figure. The other extreme is often found in economic statistics, used by politicians to demonstrate the effectiveness of their own actions and the failure of what their opponents attempted. Here the evidence is unvoidably so complex that it cannot be presented in full; the numbers quoted are chosen carefully so as to support the presenter's case. If people worry because there are 20,000 more unemployed than last month there will quickly be a government spokesman who points out that the figure includes a lot of school-leavers who will soon be absorbed in the labour market (or briefly, find jobs); that the world recession has slowed down the planned expansion of industry and that—allowing for these factors—the increase in unemployment is less than it was in the same month of the previous Opposition government. But, says the Opposition spokesman, we had a miners' strike on our hands, the state of world economy was worse than now, and the present rate of reabsorption into the labour market has been greatly overestimated. That kind of argument, laced with suitably selected bits of statistics, is really just propaganda and tends to give statistics a bad name.

Certainly, behind that propaganda there are serious statisticians hard at work, trying to extract what conclusions they can from a mass of figures, both numerical facts and mere estimates. They are doing their best, but if they were to give their honest opinion they would probably agree that no reliable conclusion can be reached.

Yet hard statistical facts are surely available, say, about traffic accidents. If an increase of 14% from one week to the next is reported I see no reason to doubt that the figure was correctly computed from the police records. But by itself it means nothing. It could mean an increase from 7000 to 8000 weekly accidents in the whole of England, clearly a matter of serious concern. Or it could be an increase from 7 to 8 accidents in a village, a mere matter of chance. Where do we draw the line? Should we worry about an increase from 70 to 80 in a town? Or from 700 to 800 in a county?

Clearly we cannot draw a sharp line between doubt and certainty; the best we can do is to estimate the odds. More than 200 years ago some

French mathematician got sufficiently interested in gambling to create a theory of probability which made it possible to calculate gambling odds. Of course all life is a gamble, and soon the theory was adapted by life insurers and later by atomic physicists who applied it to the random motions of gas molecules and to the random disintegration of radioactive atoms. With the vast numbers involved in those events, probability theory allowed them, for all practical purposes, to extract certainty from randomness.

Traffic accidents fortunately do not occur in such large numbers. If there are 70 a week, on average, the chance that there should be exactly 70 in a given week is quite small, about 1 in 15, and the chance that there should be 69 or 71 is almost the same. The chance of 80 accidents is smaller, about 1 in 60. But that is not what we want; if we are faced with 80 accidents we want to know the odds against as many as 80 happening by mere chance, that is, 80 or more. Those odds can be calculated and come out as about 1 in 9, or if you like, 9 against. Then were those extra 10 accidents a mere matter of chance?

But we have not answered the right question. We were not told that the average accident rate was 70 a week, but merely that 70 accidents happened in the previous week. Given just that fact, which leaves the average rate somewhat uncertain, we can compute that the chance of 80 or more accidents in the subsequent week is about 1 in 5 (not 1 in 9). Knowing less than we assumed about the average rate, we have less reason to think that the extra accidents were due to anything but chance.

You may wonder how those odds are calculated. Obviously there is no room here for a treatise on probability theory, and I don't want to burden you with mathematical formulae; but if you can bear with me for another page or so, here are some simple rules for calculating rough odds.

It all hangs on the concept of 'standard deviation'. The height of new recruits, even if they come from a homogeneous population, will usually deviate from the mean height; some will be taller, some shorter, and there is a simple mathematical procedure for calculating a standard deviation from the ones that are actually observed for a reasonable number of recruits. Together with the mean height it will tell the quartermaster how many uniforms of various sizes he ought to stock.

With traffic accidents it is reasonable to assume that they happen at random: that the risk of an accident is not affected by the ones that have happened before. That may not always be true, and I shall come back to that; let us assume randomness for the moment. Then we can use a beautiful theorem from the theory of probability: the standard deviation of the number of random events is the square root of their mean number. If, on average, we have 70 accidents a week, then the standard deviation from that number will be the square root of 70, the number which, multiplied with itself, gives 70. $\sqrt{70}$ is about 8.4 (since 8.4 times 8.4 = 70.56).

Now, quite generally, deviations are likely to be less than the standard deviation in about two-thirds of all cases; the remainder will be split equally between values above and those below these limits. So roughly in two weeks out of three we can expect between 62 and 78 accidents; weeks in which there are 79 or more accidents are about one in 6, and so are weeks with less than 62 accidents. Indeed you can do better than that: the little table below gives you the odds, Q, against a given deviation or more. All you need to do is to divide that deviation by the standard deviation, calling the result N, and then look up the corresponding Q in the table (round numbers calculated from Gauss' Error Function). The odds against 10 extra accidents above an average of 70 are the odds against $N = 10 \div 8.4$ = 1.2; under 1.2 you find Q = 9 as I said before.

N =	0.8	1	1.2	1.4	1.6	1.8	2	2.2	2.4	2.6	2.8	3	3.2	3.4	3.6
Q =	5	6	9	12	18	28	44	72	120	220	390	740	1450	3000	6300

Again we have answered the wrong question: we want to compare two weeks, with 70 and 80 accidents respectively. The rule is then to take for the standard deviation the square root of the *sum* of those two figures, $\sqrt{(70 + 80)} = 12.3$. The odds against 10 or more extra accidents, about 0.8 times the standard deviation, are about 5, again as quoted before.

What if the reported increase of 14% means a change from 700 to 800? Then we must compare $\sqrt{(700 + 800)} = 39$, the standard deviation, with the actual increase of 100, almost 2.6 times as much; the odds are about 200 against that increase being due to chance.

Of course there is a lot more to it, and a statistician might well sneer at the crude rules and approximate numbers I have given you. Don't be dismayed; they should serve you well enough. Who wants accurate odds? Only a bookmaker; and he offers odds, not based on the theory of random events but on the bets that have been laid. What I have told you should at least save you the embarrassment of a certain politician who was pressed by an interviewer to explain why in his constituency, during the week just after the breath test was introduced, motor accidents *increased*. The interviewer admitted that it was a small increase, but still a definite increase by 0.5%! (It would have taken 100,000 accidents to make an increase of 0.5% anything like 'definite'.)

Why do we assume that accidents happen at random? Because any evidence that they don't, any above-random increase in their number, indicates the need for action. Sometimes the cause is obvious; if it was fog, perhaps the speed limit during fog should be enforced more firmly; if a junction has become a danger spot due to increased traffic, perhaps more traffic lights should be installed, or even the junction rebuilt. On the other hand, a dramatic decrease in the accident rate may also be grounds for action, such as placing the local Chief Constable on the honours list.

Obviously when interpreting statistics one has to add a few grains of common sense to the data, and randomness cannot be assumed as a matter of course. If you count the number of vehicles damaged each week in collisions you will find that number to have a greater standard deviation than the square root of the mean; while collisions may happen at random they usually damage two vehicles, and more if a pile-up results. Nobody would expect the number of people killed annually in airplane crashes to behave randomly; one plane crash may kill a hundred people, so the fluctuations are much larger than random. On the other hand, if during an hour only six buses pass my house instead of the normal ten I can be sure that something is wrong; buses don't run at random but according to a timetable, more or less.

The weather is of course a splendid playground for statisticians. Dry and wet days do not follow each other at random; we all know that there are dry and wet periods, often lasting several days or more. The square-root law I have given you is useless here. But weather statistics carefully kept over many years are still very useful to insurance companies. If somebody wishes to be consoled by a sum of money if his fortnight's vacation is ruined by, say, more than ten days of rain, or if a hotel wishes to be insured against loss of revenue caused by bad weather, one can calculate the premium that will guarantee a reasonable profit margin to the insurance company. Later statistics which show the reliability of long-range weather forecasts to have been improved may allow the company to lower the premium, without more than a minute risk that the inevitable chance element will lead to bankruptcy. Insurance of any kind is unthinkable without statistics.

How much I trust the interpretation of statistics will depend on its plausibility, not just on the odds against having been deceived by a chance fluctuation. If I was told that the number of weekly traffic accidents varies with the phase of the moon I would be ready to believe it even if the odds are modest. No doubt moonless nights increase the risk of accidents; or if I am told it is the weeks around full moon that have more accidents . . . perhaps there are more careless, lovelorn drivers on the roads! Anyhow, a plausible explanation can be found. But if someone tells me that the phase of Titan (Saturn's largest moon) affects our accident rate I shall be very sceptical and ask for very strong statistical evidence. Even in the face of such evidence I would look for a different cause which happens to operate with a similar period; maybe the sexual cycle of some animal causes a variation in its tendency to run across the road and startle drivers. To me that would be a more plausible cause than the phase of Titan (though to one who believes in astrology it may be the other way round).

In my occasional conversations with parapsychologists I usually try to make them see that some of the phenomena they claim to observe (such as precognition, clairvoyance or telekinesis) are very hard to believe and need very strong statistical support if they are to convince a scientist. Some answer me that they don't care if scientists remain unconvinced of what they know to be true; our conversation then either ceases or moves to a different subject. Others present very convincing statistics but admit that some series of observations were left out because the subject 'had a bad day'. If one uses statistics in that manner—leaving out data because they don't fit—one can indeed 'prove' anything.

Weathermen, insurers and traffic engineers need statistics; agreed. But why should ordinary citizens bother with them? Because we sometimes have to take difficult decisions. For example, the government has been urging us to have our children immunized against whooping cough, an unpleasant disease which, however, rarely kills older children. But it kills babies, who can catch it from those older. Fewer babies will be killed by whooping cough if its general incidence is reduced by immunization of older children. Unfortunately, immunization can cause brain damage in a small fraction of the children. Should we take that small but frightening risk to protect our babies, present and future? How does that risk compare with the other hazards of infection and accidents we have to live with? If we have and plan no babies, should we consider our neighbours where our child plays, putting their babies at mortal risk when he gets whooping cough? How can we find a rational answer to such agonizing questions without the best available statistics of the relevant risks, honestly presented and clearly understood?

Let me say it again: the interpretation of statistics is often the only way, in a situation of imperfect knowledge, of reaching conclusions on which we can base decisions. Even when those decisions—whether to change an industrial process, to build a new bypass or introduce a new drug—are made by specialists it is desirable that the people affected should understand, as far as possible, how those decisions were arrived at, on the basis of the available evidence. Otherwise much effort can be wasted, either through indifference which lets ill-conceived projects go ahead, or through the actions of ill-informed protesters.

How to give people a better understanding of what statistics can and cannot do? In my view, there are two things to be done. In the first place, the media should be goaded into presenting numerical facts more completely. Statements like 'accidents went up by 14%' should not go unchallenged; you should write and ask for the actual number of accidents. With enough challenges of that kind, one may hope, the presentation of numerical facts by the media would gradually improve. More readers and listeners will be enabled to understand the figures presented to them, and that in turn might persuade them to take an interest in what they used to regard as mumbo-jumbo.

Secondly, there are the schools. I really think children ought to be taught about randomness quite early. A little innocent gambling may enliven those lessons and, incidentally, reduce the temptation late in life ('gambling? kid stuff; we did that in school'). It should teach the kids that even numbers are a matter of luck, to some degree. There are some who say that arithmetic need no longer be taught in these days of pocket calculators. I don't agree; we all learn to walk in case the car breaks down, and we had better learn to do sums in case the calculator runs out of juice. Only we are obsessed with accurate numbers, and the calculator with its 8 or 10 displayed decimals feeds that obsession. I admit, it gives one a thrill of power to compute, in a split second, that the square root of 65 is

8.062257748; but who on Earth (or elsewhere) needs such accuracy? Not even an astronaut, I suspect. Bankers—who may lose thousands through a stock exchange rumour—like their books kept to the nearest penny; why? I suppose it keeps accountants in their jobs and makes the job just a little tougher for embezzlers.

By all means let children learn how to do sums accurately, but don't let them be blinded by the spurious accuracy of the results. If a foot is taken as 305 millimetres, does a cubic foot really contain 28,372,625 cubic millimetres? Only if the side of the cube has been measured to one part in a hundred million! Actually a foot is 304.8 mm; with that value a cubic foot equals 28,316,847 mm^3, and all but the first three figures have gone by the board .

Children ought to learn that figures are our servants, not our masters. In ordinary life we seldom need to know figures to better than one part in a thousand; it is mostly in science and engineering that the small difference between two large numbers occasionally matters, and then we need to know those numbers more accurately. For most uses the slide rule (now almost extinct) served us well enough. Let children learn how to get approximate results quickly (for instance, that there are 35 cubic feet to the cubic metre). Teach them how to work out rough averages, how to spot trends; teach them a little about the meaning of statistics.

Raymond A. Lyttleton

Raymond A. Lyttleton, MA, PhD, FRS, lately Professor of Theoretical Astronomy in the University of Cambridge, was educated at King Edward's School, Birmingham; Cambridge University, England; and Princeton University, New Jersey, USA. Honours received include the Hopkins Prize, Cambridge Philosophical Society, 1951; Gold Medal of the Royal Astronomical Society, 1959; and Royal Medal of the Royal Society, 1965.

His research interests are in astrophysics, cosmogony, physics, dynamics, and geophysics; his recreations are golf, motoring, and music.

The Gold Effect

My attention has been drawn by Professor T. Gold, F.R.S., to a remarkable arithmetical multiplicative effect that must almost always enter into the whole mechanism of how beliefs come to be entertained and eventually established and accepted. As with most good ideas, this one is so *obvious* (when pointed out) that it might seem scarcely worth emphasis. Yet I myself freely admit that I had never hitherto seen any reference to its influence, nor any recollection of even a suggestion hinting at it, until it was enunciated for my benefit by Professor Gold. It was then as if a curtain had suddenly been pulled aside to reveal the workings of a host of puzzling occurrences.

To explain. Suppose, in regard to an idea in some field of knowledge or activity, that a number M of people are concerned and interested by that idea. Diagrammatically, let the idea be represented by a point O on a line, and the *degree of non-acceptance*, of criticism, or of disbelief in the idea as proportional to the distance x from 0, in either direction along the line for simplicity. The attitude of any particular one of the M individuals to the idea can be used to classify him in a small range from x to x + dx of the line. Complete unqualified belief in the idea will place a person's representative point at 0, and strong disbelief far out towards $+\infty$ or $-\infty$. Next let it be supposed, as is very likely to happen, that for some reason a slight preponderance of the M people arrive at a state of near-belief in the matter, so that there occurs in the distribution of people with x a weak maximum at 0. A suitable well-known function adequately representing this for our purpose would be the gaussian exponential function $\exp(-x^2)$, with the scale of x sufficiently large to give a weak maximum at x = 0. Then the distribution of people by number in relation to the idea would be

$$M\,(\pi)^{-\frac{1}{2}} \exp(-x^2)\,dx\ ,$$

the factor $(\pi)^{-\frac{1}{2}}$ securing that of the number of people from $-\infty$ to $+\infty$ is

182

equal to M. It may be noted that there is nothing special to the argument (to be given) about this particular function, though it is convenient numerically for plotting curves, and any similar function or distribution-curve initially exhibiting the slight peak about $x = 0$ would do equally well theoretically and lead to results exactly similar to those that will be demonstrated.

Now if this represents the situation at a given stage, suppose that some action is decided upon in regard to the idea. For example, some or all of the M people may decide to hold a meeting to discuss the pros and cons of the idea. And let us further assume, for the present, that every effort is made to give all concerned equal opportunity to attend and to state their views and arguments. Perhaps attendance might need to be restricted in number, and names drawn out of a hat to effect this, but the attitudes and distribution of those attending would nevertheless automatically reflect the existing distribution. Thus there will be present more people favouring the idea than against it in equal ranges of x, and when all is said and done after the meeting, if the people are influenced by other than strictly scientific considerations, and the whole purpose of meetings (and of literature) is presumably to enable people to influence each other's opinions, the distribution in regard to the idea will now be in proportion with $\exp(-x^2)$ multiplied by $\exp(-x^2)$, that is to $\exp(-2x^2)$. The functions or curves will not be additive, for that would leave the distribution still proportional to $\exp(-x^2)$, and therefore unchanged: which would mean that the meeting would have had no effect whatever on the general attitude to the idea.

A following step might be to choose a 'representative' committee to get out a collected volume of papers to propagate and foster interest in the idea, and first select a list of contributors drawn from among the M people. Again there might be too many to invite all concerned, but even if the committee-members and invited authors were chosen entirely at random, the selections will have a distribution roughly but strongly proportional to the existing distribution, $\exp(-2x^2)$, and the totality of resulting articles will appear to show an increased consensus of agreement and acceptance of the original idea, now proportional to $\exp(-4x^2)$. And so it will go on, each and every step taken will be directly influenced by the currently existing distribution, and lead to greater and greater concentration of the peak at 0. For instance, if papers come to a journal relying on some refereeing procedure prior to publication, the selection of referees will obviously be influenced by the existing distribution. Without any ulterior motive, unless all concerned are from the outset influenced simply and solely by scientific considerations (which would require M to be very small indeed), after n such operations, the distribution of attitudes will have become proportional to something like $\exp(-n^2x^2)$. In order that numbers total up to M (which by now might not be the same as the originally interested M) the distribution function will be

$$M\,(\pi)^{-\frac{1}{2}}\,n\,\exp(-n^2x^2)\,dx\ ,$$

and the peak at the origin x = 0 will have become n-times as strong as at first. As time goes on and n gets larger, the distribution concentrates more and more round the idea having the initial slight advantage, there are fewer and fewer outliers, and an appearance of almost complete certainty of the correctness of the idea can come about purely through this multiplicative numerical effect. Of course in practice it does not work ideally with the uniform smoothness assumed here to simplify the discussion, but the tendency for an initial weak maximum to become enhanced more and more of its own accord will always be present, unless none other than purely scientific considerations are ever brought to bear, which as aforesaid would be almost impossible to suppose.

This then is what may be termed *The Gold Effect*, after its discoverer. In essence, it is that, even if only random moves and selections are made in regard to an idea initially supported by a slight majority, then there will develop an increasing concentration of people believing in the idea, when in fact it may be no more than an arithmetically brought-about illusion of truth, a simulacrum without scientific basis—a lie in truth.

The diagrams shown opposite illustrate the progress of the Gold Effect by means of a succession of gaussian curves of increasing (negative) index, as explained above. The area under each curve is the same, and in suitable units would be equal to the total number of people concerned.

Up to this point, the operation of the Gold Effect has been described in terms of its simply taking its natural course, but unfortunately it has to be recognised that in reality other influences come to bear that cause the effect to proceed more swiftly and certainly than if left to occur at its own rate. Few of those engaged in science are godlike supermen free from all weakness and above the conflict, as it were; indeed, there is no reason to suppose that scientists as a class, whatever their opinions of themselves,

Geometrical Illustration of the Gold Effect

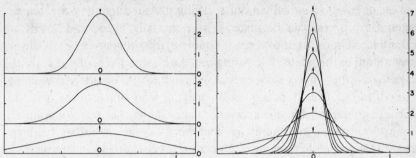

At left are shown separately curves of $n \exp(-n^2x^2)$ for $n = 1$, 2, and 3, the total area under each curve being the same and corresponding to the number of people concerned.

At right are shown superposed seven successive equal-area curves demonstrating the tendency for concentration more and more round the origin 0 as n steadily increases.

The ultimate state would be a so-called delta-function, attaining to the infinite at 0 with a host of true-believers and zero non-believers. This is the 'ideal' always being striven for by obscurantists bent on a search for certainty and the annihilation of all dissent.

(The exponential function has been used for numerical convenience in drawing the curves, but there is nothing essential to the argument about it. Any function or curve possessing initially a weak maximum at 0, or a series of such similar functions would lead in the same way to greater and greater concentration round 0 of the distribution.)

have been born free of any modicum of human frailty to make them morally superior to any other group of people. Scientists can often be seen to be unduly proud of their work, usually in inverse proportion to its worth, and as with ordinary unthinking mortals become so attached to their ideas as to be incapable of being adequately critical of them. Then again, although theories may be propagated that have no scientific validity, by far the majority of people are unable to perceive this through lack of analytical capacity and of understanding of the nature of knowledge. Witness the enormous popularity and widespread acceptance of works by such as Velikovsky and of claims to possession of occult powers. All beliefs in whatever realms are *theories* at some level, but even in science many 'theories' receive currency and are kept in countenance that do no more than asseverate verbally that postulated processes, having no basis in observation, experiment, or theory, will operate in a preconceived manner, with the support of a farrago of so-called 'facts', usually selectively selected, all wrapped in a cocoon of high-sounding words allegedly proving the theory, words that amount to little more than a fairy-story by scientific standards. It has never been demonstrated that by rearranging a set of existing labels, which is what words are, and augmenting them by new *ad hoc* ones, often undefined but specially invented for the occasion, any scientific progress can be made. These specially introduced words are often placed in inverted commas (or quote-marks), a practice nearly always a symptom of the bogus, suggesting to the uninstructed reader that for the *cognoscenti* they have some peculiarly significant (unstated) meaning, though in fact usually of a question-begging kind suited to the occasion. Modern literature, by all its vast verbiage, shows that many working in science are under the impression that words alone can suffice, with the result that verbal theories abound on all sides claiming to represent scientific explanations of things. So mesmeric is the effect of words, that these specially introduced terms gradually come, through continued repetitive use, to seem in themselves to be explanations of phenomena.

The reader may well be asking 'What can all this be to do with the Gold Effect?' Well, in the first place it is that verbal theories or explanations or rationalisations are far more readily producible and assimilable by others than are truly scientific theories, by which is meant theories based on admissible hypotheses sufficiently worked out experimentally if possible and in mathematical form to show the inter-relation of phenomena, and above all to enable verifiable predictions to be made. But how much easier to talk one's way through a problem and claim to have arrived at marvellously detailed definitive results—'the world was created on the 22nd October 4004 B.C. at 6 o'clock in the evening'*—rather than take the trouble first to study a problem and then analyse it in physical and mathematical terms. The lunar theory, for example, which concerns a closely definable problem, involves a group of second-order non-linear differential equations whose solution depends on complex-function theory, on contact-transformations, on infinite determinants, advanced computing techniques, and suchlike, before successful predictions can be made, yet nowadays the solutions of far more intricate problems for which the relevant equations have not yet even been set up are claimed to be known and abundantly established. The scientific approach, by its essentially esoteric nature, leaves the vast majority uninformed, whereas the all-embracing declamatory verbal method gives them the impression and illusion that they are comprehending real science. Compare the vast outpourings

*The writer has been unable to discover if this was 6 p.m. Greenwich Mean Time in Britain, or 6 p.m. Eastern Standard Time in the U.S.

nowadays on what is termed continental-drift in popular writings, which is just the sort of 'theory' to appeal to the unskilled reader devoid of analytical capacity, with the number (if any) of articles describing the successes of the lunar theory. The former is no more than wishy-washy verbal speculation claiming inescapably established but non-existent results, and capable of predicting nothing, whereas the latter is a recondite scientific theory, but of negligible sales-value commercially, which enables predictions of meticulous precision to be made. Only when proposed solutions to problems are put in mathematical form is there provided a worthwhile basis for discussion, but there exists little appreciation of the resulting need for mathematical skill, the greater the better, for the simple reason that most of those occupied with science and in organising science are themselves without any such capacity, and think mere words enough. Persons engaged in such subjects as astronomy and physics, yet devoid of such skill, are about as useful to the advancement of science as an ice-hockey player that could not skate.

Verifiable predictions can seldom if ever be made by means of verbal theories, for they offer no structured formalism that could be manipulated for the purpose. But this is not appreciated by those without understanding of the nature of knowledge, who naively think they are dealing directly with the mechanical properties of an independent external world, and many of whom like to claim that everything should be capable of explanation in elementary terms intelligible at their own mental level. That this is so implies that well over ninety per cent of the members of almost any society, scientific societies included, can readily be taken in by purely verbal or even bogus theories. Thus it comes about that such theories very readily get into publication as seeming to be more intelligible than genuine theories and requiring less effort and experience for their 'understanding'. The authors of such 'works', being of that same mental calibre themselves, will be proudly pleased by the large number of adherents their handiwork attracts, despite the fact that most of these may be quite unqualified to hold any worthwhile opinion. The proponents can turn their backs on the comparative few that could competently criticise and expose the deficiencies of the work, and continue to address themselves to the nursery. With the Gold Effect distribution thriving much as a servo-mechanism, editors will almost invariably receive favourable comment from readers and referees of bogus or semi-bogus work, and, devoid of scientific capacity

188 *The Gold Effect*

themselves, welcome it for inclusion in their journals and publications as more likely to please the majority, which is often their main concern rather than the advancement of science. The printed word makes powerful impact on many minds, and if something is read in a supposedly reputable journal, perhaps written by a person occupying high position, the innocent-minded, unversed in the subject, will read it quite uncritically with the eye of faith, absorb it at their own level, and pass it on as gospel to others.

> It was just after this adventure that we encountered a continent of im-
> mense extent and of prodigious solidity, but which, nevertheless, was
> supported entirely upon the back of a sky-blue cow that had no fewer
> than four-hundred horns.
> '*That*, now, I believe,' said the king, 'because I have read something
> of the kind before in a book.'
>
> *Edgar Allan Poe*

The gregarious instinct will also tend to draw together people that enter-tain the same 'beliefs', and the desire not to feel outside the accepted official group is so strong with most people that they are willing to adopt views quite unacceptable scientifically, instead of always forming their own independent opinions on the basis of purely scientific considerations, not on the opinions of others and on the numerical strength of professed adherents. All such factors can be seen to accelerate the Gold Effect. Very soon an idea may rise to the always-dubious status of what is termed 'generally accepted', and as a result of the all-round pleasure-associations thereby produced will come to seem to its proponents and supporters, blind to its defects, as constituting well-established truth. There will form of its own accord a psychological club, not with rigorously defined rules and membership, devoted to defending the idea by all possible means, while those not accepting the creed, however valid their reasons, will be beyond the pale, outside the club, and regarded by the in-group as for some inexplicable reason mentally deranged. The club mainly deal with them by accusations of prejudice and other abusive personal attacks rang-ing all the way from patronising high-sounding seeming analyses, describ-ing them as hypercritical paranoiacs at one extreme down to being mere nit-pickers, sanguinary imbeciles, or simply supercostive at the other, to give just a few examples. Editors will publish such abuse without cavil since it generally corresponds to their own opinions of the critics whom they regard as a nuisance casting a shadow on their power and glory.

But regrettably matters are not left even to just these simple additional tendencies, and further direct steps are always being taken to see that every difficulty is placed in the way of anything the least critical of the current club-theory. By now this will have developed well on its way to becoming something akin to a religion with a following of devout believers, and as with all religions dissenters are not to be tolerated. The theory has become hallowed, self-evident in its own unassailable correctness, and its adherents feel it their natural and proper right, and indeed duty, to defend it against irresponsible and malicious attack, as they see criticism to be, by any and every means within their power, however improper, so long as they judge they can get away with it. One would have thought that feeling so certain of the correctness of their views, and being so numerous in holding them, there would be little need to be concerned about a few transparently moronic critical malcontents, yet curiously enough the existence of a refractory few that do not assent to the creed and instead point out (non-existent) defects seems to disturb them mightily and cause breakdowns in their observation of the amenities of polite discussion. This could just possibly be taken as suggesting that perhaps after all they are not quite as sure of their precious theory as they would like to have people think. There might be some hope in the situation if they frankly admitted what they are up to, but instead they consider themselves to be acting with judicial calm in the best interests of science and society.

If a rival theory should by any chance be advocated, then this will be handled by sycophantic editors and secretaries in a manner pleasing to those they see as the safely established tribal leaders and their flock, while the advocate in the course of the processes required for the rejection of his work will, as aforesaid, be subjected to such degree of comminatory invective as seems appropriate to the occasion. Scientific considerations will not come into it. On the other hand, any paper seeming to support the official theory, or the opinions of those in positions of power, or any paper that is critical of a rival theory, will be eagerly and uncritically snatched at, perfunctorily refereed within the club, if at all, and rushed into print. When such papers turn out to be erroneous, as they frequently do through their hastiness of preparation and their authors' ignorant anxiety to come to the desired preconceived conclusions, the machinery of the 'system' then shifts rapidly into reverse, and any attempt to expose the mistakes, however flagrant these may be, is grimly suppressed by the responsible (?)

society. The reaction of such authors, when their shoddy workmanship is called in question and exposed, is not to act scientifically, seek elucidation and insist on correcting their errors, but to tar-and-feather the critic. It would be a rare and unwelcome accident if by some mischance there should get appointed an editor or secretary prepared to carry out his duties to science properly rather than always being primarily committed to the club-interests and ever anxious to show up well in the eyes of the tribal chiefs and any others holding power—'Constrained by assumptions that uncannily fit their superiors' preconceived ideas'—as Zuckerman so delicately described it. Any papers showing up defects in official theory, which usually consists mainly of these, will be carefully steered to referees expected to be hostile, if necessary with a covering letter alerting them to the need for an adverse report. Every circumstance of sharp-practice, chicanery, and legerdemain will be resorted to, according to the strength of the attack, in order to protect official theory from exposure as erroneous, and ward off the enemy at the gate. Any such paper can be sent to a succession of referees, with favourable reports if any just ignored, until are obtained an adequate number of convenient reports, written always with more or less insolence and offensiveness, and then these sent off to the critical author with feigned regret that the paper must as a result be rejected. Sometimes nothing more than rejection itself may be communicated, with no reason or report given if it is deemed unsafe or too risky to do so. Or again, an awkward communication can simply be not-received, or somehow get lost, or just no action taken. These sorts of manoeuvres give the Gold Effect more impetus, as is the intention, and in the eyes of the intellectually unwashed, who are largely ignorant of what goes on behind the scenes, the defended theory comes to resemble more and more the milk of truth, injurious though the swallowing of it may be. Henry W. Shaw put their situation something like, 'It ain't what a man don't know as makes him a fool, it's what he does know as ain't so'. Hoyle at one time made light of such shenanigans as 'noise in the system', but what is to become of any particular area of science if its activities and policy amount to such an extent to 'noise' that no worthwhile coherent signal emerges, which is what is happening in some subjects today. One wonders if Hoyle would continue to maintain that it is mere noise in the system after his own later special experiences of the club in action.

It would be impossible if only for reasons of space to discuss here more than a few of the numerous devices that result in amplification of the Gold Effect. For young people entering science, the need to publish is nowadays forced upon them by appointing-bodies and administrators, many of whom could not understand a scientific paper if the wind blew one into their hands, and are thus a ready prey to partial and cunning referees who appeal to them on their own mental level. The majority of such people, not being scientists, can only go by impressions, and can be influenced more by the quantity of material published than by the quality, if any, of its content. In some institutions it is policy that an annual amount of publication is actually required if promotion is to be considered, thereby allowing no fallow periods of thoughtful preparation for assaults on deep problems, but instead encouraging snippety superficial verbal papers. Clearly the necessary publication can be much more readily achieved by going in for papers favourable to the existing club-views, rather than by confronting them head-on by pointing out manifest blunders in these treasured beliefs, for new additions to the sect, proclaiming their allegiance by worthless papers, sometimes worse than worthless, are always welcomed with open arms to the greater numerical backing of the glorious creed of the day.

Then again, anything that people have become used to—here the club-theory, which is published everywhere and anywhere on all sides, from so-called learned journals down to the popular press, over and over again to achieve acceptance by mere dogmatic repetition—seems right and proper, and arouses no criticism, whereas any deviation or contradiction of the normal and usual seems wrong, and immediately provokes criticism. Almost everything people have heard and read seems to accord with the by-now official generally accepted theory; they become more or less hypnotised with it, and do not like to be emotionally disturbed by new ideas, which are always inflammatory and 'rouse the passions' as the French put it. Committees can be quietly and effectively stacked by the club-leaders, and with the Gold Effect distribution already prevailing, this will tend to happen of its own accord, though even with this climate care is taken not to let it operate just on its own when a helping hand can be given by attention to the details of the election-process, which is a topic worthy of an essay in itself. Then, once in power, the club-committee can flout such rules as may exist, suitably change them, and drop any that seem not in their interest or so found to work out. Everything connected with publication will be kept floating, covered by a few vague generalities, rather than by carefully defined rigid rules as to procedure. No attempt is made to draw up such rules to be applied impartially to all papers, for the simple reason that this would not be in the interests of the club, who wish to be free to make up the rules as they go along to suit the occasion. They regard this as freedom to be jealously guarded, when in fact it is a form of anarchy.

Even in the realm of sport, to take a very low-level activity, the need for such rules is not only fully recognised, but failure to observe them can even mean complete ostracism or dismissal from the game. Science, unlike popular games, is not played in full and open view of an understanding and appreciative audience frankly recognising their own limitations as performers, and never can be so played because its subtlety takes it beyond the comprehension not only of people in general but even of other scientists if outside their own special fields. Thus science and its organisation are vulnerable to 'ways-and-means' whereby cunning can provide a dark sanctuary in which lack of desiderated qualities can be concealed from all but a few. What would we think of a golfer, knowing the vast majority of would-be spectators are 'blind' and unacquainted with the rules, who wrote down 4 on his card when his actual score was 6 or more, who trod his opponent's ball into the ground or even appropriated it, who persuaded his caddy to cheat for him, who got the 'club' to handpick the referee to ensure everything is decided the 'right' way, with the hole to be cut only after the balls are on the green, and the rules adjusted when any unforeseen emergency arises, plus a host of other dodges. By such means, it is possible today to be a 'scientific champion'—of sorts. The writer was recently at a tennis championship, and no fewer than 16 people were actively engaged to secure the observance of the rules. In tennis, golf, cricket, and numerous other *mere games,* the rules are meticulously drawn up beforehand, impartially disposed to all concerned, to the interest and high standing of the several activities. Why cannot something like this be done for science, for which millions of the taxpayers' money are lavishly handed out, instead of continuing in a spirit of utter anarchy with no stated rules. At best there are a few vague conventions, but even these are broken if their observance should seem to conflict with the general interests of the club.

One of the most marked anti-scientific tendencies of 'establishments' is their tenacious adherence to outdated or even totally incorrect theories, as the history of ideas right down the ages shows, then also to the perennial pecking away at the dry bones of some completely exhausted valueless subject, and to the hanging on to obsolete routines and procedures that no longer serve any worthwhile purpose. Even among scientists there are many that unconsciously resent any prospect of resolution of long-standing time-honoured problems, for they have come to nurture their pleasure-mechanisms from the related ideas they have grown up with, and deep down do not really want to see these overthrown, even though it is plain (to some) that the problems remain in obvious confusion as a result of them. They seem able to extract a kind of perverted joy from the confused state, which is susceptible of interpretation as implying an impenetrable profundity that lends a certain glory to their subject. As Bagehot has truly said: 'One of the greatest pains to human nature is the pain of a new idea.'

Also let not be forgotten the position that most people occupying posts today in science (it would scarcely do to use the term 'scientists') find themselves in: they have struggled through formal postulant-exams at some modest level, perhaps been allowed to go on to 'do research' under some amiable supervisor, who not only practically writes a thesis for him but often examines him on it into the bargain, and then manages when jobs are in bountiful supply to find a 'scientific' post, and 'become lost in a gloom of uninspired research'. His grasp and attitude towards his subject are about on a level with a 24-handicap golfer's ability to break par on a championship course, and he has about as much real aptitude and zeal for genuine scientific research as a turtle has for pole-vaulting. United by bonds of mutual worthlessness, such people actually set about minimising any important advances: they will club together for the purpose and write books of the style 'One Hundred against Einstein', with the aim of persuading the gullible public that it is they and they alone that are the real scientists doing the important work. Some of these specimens may, at great personal sacrifice of course, never mind the denying of posterity the fruits of their intellect, give up research for a career of administration, and thus swell the ranks of those unqualified to make decisions about science that nevertheless make it their business to make decisions about science, such as the appointing of safe incompetents to high office and the handing out of huge sums of public money for entirely worthless activities. Naturally enough, being *ipso facto* failed scientists, they are an easy prey for the energetic con-men of science whose expertise lies, not in real science, but in securing cash for pseudo-science, which they succeed in doing by appealing to the administrators on the latter's own mental level where they meet them on equal terms.

The history of science is replete with instances where contributions displeasing to the establishment have been rejected, repulsed, and contradicted out of hand, to the accompaniment of vituperative personal attack on the authors, sometimes even on their physical well-being, the more valuable the work the greater the degree of obloquy extended to them, as if the magnitude of the potential threat were instinctively appreciated even though the work itself is not consciously understood. All this is nothing new and peculiar to the present day, as is shown by the following considered opinion from no less a person than Lord Rayleigh, who in discussing the notorious example of the rejection in 1845 of Waterston's paper on the kinetic theory of gases (which, Rayleigh himself saw to it, was published in 1892 a decade after Waterston's death and the threat safely past) delivered himself as follows:

> "The history of this paper suggests that highly speculative investigations, especially by an unknown author* are best brought before the world through some other channel than a scientific society, which naturally hesitates to admit into its printed records matter of uncertain value. Perhaps one may go further, and say that a young author who believes himself capable of great things would usually do well to secure favourable recognition of the scientific world by work whose scope is limited, and whose value is easily judged, before embarking upon higher flights."

Although this highly questionable if not ludicrous judgement naively gives the whole show away, one can see what Rayleigh was tactfully trying to say: that it is best for an intending scientist to commence operations by toadying to the establishment, allowing them to be wise in their own conceit, the whiles keeping to himself any researches of importance that might possibly advance science: in other words, adopt a wordly wise sycophantic course of personal advancement first and flash the genius later—something no true scientist of the smallest integrity could bring himself to do. But Rayleigh, whatever the situation may have been like then, would have great difficulty today in excusing such conduct of learned societies by 'hesitation to admit into their records *matter of uncertain*

*All authors are *unknown* till they become *known*.

value'. No such uncertainty attaches to a great deal of modern printed records when useless publication is in full swing with trivial, unoriginal, repetitive, erroneous, plagiarised, and bogus papers, couched in semi-literate style, have no difficulty in securing publication if only they are from an acceptable source and no serious threat to the establishment. Even many of those papers falling outside these categories are little more than innocuous routine material that does not disturb people even should any by chance take the trouble to read them.

On taking an opportunity to enquire of an experienced statistician whether there were any data on the average number of readers per paper published in science, the writer was answered in the affirmative and told that the figure was 0.6. Astonishment banished any presence of mind to ask for the source, but after some recovery, upon recounting the episode to a colleague a few days later, he wanted a breakdown of the figure, and asked, 'Does that include the referee?' Upon some reflection, it would seem it probably does, for there is 'reading' and 'reading', and it would be difficult to suppose that some present-day papers can have been critically read or refereed at all. One of the problems here is that refereeing is still an entirely honorary task, a state of affairs largely carried over from an age when science was more or less a dilettant occupation of gentlemen not always driven to unseemly hurry. But to carry out the task properly and satisfactorily sometimes takes not only a great deal of time and trouble, not to mention knowledge of the subject, but above all integrity. Nowadays many referees evidently prefer to be guided by policy rather than by the merits or demerits of the paper itself, a course so much simpler in every way and requiring far less expenditure of time and effort. A quite farcical feature of the process is that the moment a good club-member is selected as referee, he becomes in the eyes of his appointers a kind of omniscient demigod to whom all has been revealed *a priori*, and credence is attached to any wildly assertive claims he may make without his being required to supply the slightest element of justification. He is permitted off-the-cuff to contradict conclusions carefully established, or without serious reflection differ from opinions reached by the author after perhaps years of thoughtful study. These often transparently erroneous assertions will then be made the basis for action and decision even if, as may be the case, the author has far more ability in the subject than the referee and those relying upon him. Of course all this is perfectly understandable once the general situation is appreciated, for it is recognised that he will only be acting in the best interests of the club and of their subject whatever he may claim, and accordingly his word honoured without question.

The trouble lies in that our so-called learned societies, together with their antiquated procedures, are a century out of date, if not more; and their structures and machinery quite inadequate for the real needs of present-day science. When one considers the millions upon millions of the tax-payers' moneys that are now made available, with a high proportion largely wasted on ill-conceived worthless projects, and on time-servers engaged on so-called routine-research, it is obviously absurdly short-sighted to leave the management of the production of the end-product, which is the publication of results for general dissemination, in entirely irresponsible hands answerable to no one beyond their immediate coterie for their conduct, or in some cases hands concerned only with commercial success. Unrestrained censorship goes on in all directions, but the system is widely regarded as one of freedom when it is really no better than anarchic suppression to keep in countenance manifest rubbish claimed to represent scientific research. When the great Rutherford had under his direction probably the most able team of scientists ever assembled in one building, his annual budget for equipment was £100, though admittedly when their scientific achievements and celebrity penetrated to every corner of the globe, the Cambridge authorities, with complete disregard for the solvency of their university, did increase this to £200. Long before that stage, Rutherford had called his staff together and told them, 'We have no money, so we've got to think', and that was the secret of their success. Nowadays the formula is, 'We can get tons of money, so we needn't think', and that is the reason for their lack of success and for their need for unofficial rings to defend their positions. The great Norbert Wiener saw the writing large on the wall thirty years ago when he protested, 'We are raising young men that will not look at any scientific project that does not have millions of money invested in it. We are for the first time finding a scientific career well paid and attractive to our best young go-getters. But the trouble is that scientific work of the first quality is seldom done by the go-getters, and that the dilution of the intellectual milieu makes it progressively harder for the individual worker with any ideas to get a hearing. The degradation of the position of the scientist as an independent worker and thinker to that of moral irresponsibility has proceeded even more rapidly and devastatingly than I had expected.' And the process continues apace.

The present organisers of science are oblivious to the extent to which they are imbued with the sacrifice-complex, of which they have probably never heard, or if they have only associate it with feathered tribesmen in remote jungles. (It is possible to suffer from a complaint not yet diagnosed officially.) Their unrecognised belief is that if only they spend enough money and set up enough people in jobs, the solutions to problems will emerge of their own accord. But mother-nature happens not to be a girl of the mink-and-diamonds variety, and lavishment of money and display of pompous fussy activity will seldom induce her to reveal her well-kept secrets: if anything, the contrary. Not being of superficial temperament, she prefers genuine admiration, dedication, and devotion for her own sake, rather than sail-trimming opportunism aimed at currying favour by augmentation of the Gold Effect. In chocolate-factories, the employees are allowed to eat as much chocolate as they like: the result is that after a few weeks they could never be persuaded to eat chocolate again as long as they live. In science-factories, people are set up with every facility to do research: leisure to study, offices, secretaries, telephones, machines, libraries, and so on: and the result is that after a few weeks nothing could ever induce them to do any real research. The present-day situation, the causes of which are too extensive to analyse fully here, is much as if the objective of winning the olympic high-jump were gone about by rounding up thousands of self-alleged athletes that can with difficulty clear three-foot-six, whereas the scientific procedure (which is in fact the one adopted in athletics) is to seek out the few that can clear six-feet naturally without training, and then provide them with the right conditions in which to develop into champions. The rest could only get in the way and interfere, and unless such interference is effectively prevented, things develop to 'a state of chassis', to use O'Casey's phrase, and progress becomes impossible. Analogous happenings characterise some branches of science today, but they are not discernible by the great majority, to whom any branch of science must remain a closed book. Although it is always freely admitted that gross irregularities of oppression, repression, and suppression characterised earlier times, it is one of the illusions of each generation that no such conduct any longer occurs and is altogether a thing of the past. A central defect, prevalent far beyond the scientific realm, is refusal to permit any feedback or enquiry with a view to identifying sources of mistakes to see how they happened in order to avoid their repetition in the future.

It would be idle to suggest that the influence of the Gold Effect is to be found only in science, where in fact it may be least. Quite obviously it is the explanation of all localised religions: these begin with an extensive equipment of verbal theory, every word of which is claimed to be literally 'true', whatever that may mean, but which gradually gets modified and eroded away until eventually nothing more can be claimed than that the meaning is allegorical, though just of what is not made clear. Socratic scientific discussion remains strictly prohibited, but nevertheless large numbers continue to take part within the hush of hallowed walls, transported ecstatically it seems by mere procedures and rituals, which are all that may survive. In wartime, the Gold Effect is to be seen on all sides pushed to its utmost limits, and men are thereby conditioned and coerced to lay down their lives for hypothetical causes that few if any could offer the ghost of an acceptable explanation for, if their lives depended on it. In a brief essay such as this, it would be impossible to elaborate on the details of the manifestations of the Gold Effect.

The first step in regard to the effect would seem to be for scientists to move towards a new standard of conduct by recognition of its operation within their own realms, much as medical men may be alerted to a newly recognised disease, and henceforth take every possible step to prevent the harmful results of its spreading. At first impulse, probably many would be inclined to deny strongly that any such injurious influence permeates science at all, never mind being helped along as suggested in the foregoing pages by cunning artifices, but if they do they would be quietly ignoring the whole history of ideas back to time immemorial. But claim what they may, the Gold Effect has been and *is* at work blindly but remorselessly all the time, whether aided or not, and the main object of this essay is to draw attention to it in the hope that, unlike the satellites of Jupiter, people will not refuse to recognise what may well come to rank as one of the most important discoveries of our age.

Arthur Koestler

Arthur Koestler, CBE 1972, CLit 1974, FRSI, FRAS, was born in Hungary in 1905. From 1926 to 1931 he was Foreign Correspondent in the Middle East, Paris and Berlin, and has since travelled widely. His many publications include *The Gladiators*, 1939; *Darkness at Noon*, 1940; *Arrival and Departure*, 1943; *Insight and Outlook*, 1948; *The Age of Longing*, 1950; *The Trail of the Dinosaur*, 1955; *The Sleepwalkers*, 1959; *The Ghost in the Machine*, 1967; *The Case of the Midwife Toad*, 1971; and *The Roots of Coincidence*, 1972. His hobbies are canoeing, chess and good wine.

Nothing but . . . ?

I became convinced a long time ago that the citadel of orthodoxy which the sciences of life built in the first half of our century is crumbling. I also discovered that many of my academic friends shared this belief, but were less outspoken (or ill-mannered) about it. Proverbs ix, 1 says that the House of Wisdom rests on seven pillars (but unfortunately does not name them). The citadel of science, too, rests on a number of impressive pillars, but some of them are beginning to show cracks and turn out to be hollow, or reveal themselves as monumental superstitions. The most important among them I have called* 'the four pillars of unwisdom'. They represent the doctrines:

(a) that biological evolution is the result of *nothing but* random mutations preserved by natural selection;

(b) that mental evolution is the result of *nothing but* random tries preserved by reinforcements;

(c) that all organisms, including man, are *nothing but* passive automata, controlled by the environment, whose sole purpose in life is the reduction of tensions by adaptive responses;

(d) that the only scientific method worth that name is quantitative measurement; and, consequently, that complex phenomena must be reduced to simple elements accessible to such treatment, without undue worry whether the specific characteristics of a complex phenomenon, for instance man, may be lost in the process.

The common element in these four fallacies is the philosophy of Reductionism (or 'Nothing But-ism') which holds that all human activities can be reduced to (explained by) the 'elementary responses' displayed by

* *The Ghost in the Machine* (Hutchinson, 1967), p. 3.

lower animals (such as the psychologist's laboratory rat); and that these responses in turn can be reduced to elementary physico-chemical laws. This belief, derived from the mechanistic world-view of the last century which physics itself abandoned long ago, is still the orthodox attitude in the life sciences, from genetics to psychology.* By denying a place for values, meaning and purpose in the interplay of blind forces, the reductionist attitude has cast its shadow beyond the confines of science, affecting our whole cultural and even political climate.

*Cf. *Beyond Reductionism—New Perspectives in the Life Sciences*, ed. A. Koestler and J. R. Smythies (Hutchinson, 1969).

Sir Hermann Bondi

Sir Hermann Bondi, FRS 1959, KCB 1973, was born in Vienna in 1919. He came to England in 1937 to study mathematics at Trinity College, Cambridge (BA 1940). After war work on naval radars he returned to Cambridge as Fellow of Trinity College and University Lecturer until in 1954 he became Professor of Mathematics at King's College, London. His researches have been in cosmology, gravitation, relativity, etc. Since 1967 he has held posts in the public service, first as Director-General of the European Space Research Organization (1967-1971), then as Chief Scientific Advisor to the Ministry of Defence (1971-1977), and now as Chief Scientist, Department of Energy.

Religion is a good thing

My thesis will be to make clear why I regard this statement as a lying truth, why indeed I regard religion as a serious and habit forming evil.

I need hardly start with a list of quotations of the view, so widespread during the last fifty years at least, that belief in religion, indeed in *any* religion, is to be welcomed as a matter of public policy. I recall President Eisenhower speaking of all good Americans living by their religion, immediately assuring his listeners that he did not care which religion it was. This was as clear a statement as one could wish for of an uncritically accepted and frequently repeated attitude which if analysed is a horrifying mixture of paternalism and hypocrisy. For if the speaker seriously believes in one of the major (Western) religions then by definition he must view all believers in one of the rival ones to be in serious error and ought to care which it was they believed. If the speaker is not a serious believer then he prescribes for others something that he regards himself as having outgrown, presumably because he thinks they need a crutch that he can do without.

The nature of belief: It is important to come to a clear and viable definition of religion. 'Atheism', I may say in passing, has always seemed to me to be a meaningless term. For one cannot deny the existence of an undefined concept, god, in a general sense. If I am asked whether I am an atheist I can only respond by asking the questioner what he means by 'god' and only then can I take an attitude. For after all what can one say to a pantheist? If told that god is the universe (whatever that phrase may mean), am I to deny the existence of the universe?

I am too ignorant of Eastern religions to talk about them, but *revelation* seems to be a cornerstone of Western religions and of some other forms of belief. An event or process is thought to have given knowledge in a manner utterly certain and wholly different from our normal daily ways of acquiring it. Belief in the validity of such a revelation is something sufficiently precise so that one *can* disagree with it (and, to speak personally, I am very willing to declare myself an *anti-revelationist*, while uneasy about the term 'atheist'). Revelations may be purely personal (like those that Joan of Arc claimed had guided her), but more often are expressed in oral tradition or in written form in which they are open to study—such as in the case of the Bible.

An interesting and probably necessary part of belief in revelations is that they were originally only accessible to a small and select group. According to the Christian Gospels themselves, only a small minority of those present at the crucifixion were convinced by the reported 'miracles', while Jewish revelations are taken to be confined to 'the chosen people'. In the view of the faithful it is their possession, direct or indirect, of access to such revelations as they happen to believe in, that is of such benefit to them. Attitudes then vary from a purely personal belief that is regarded by the believer himself as a private matter and has no inordinate consequences for external behaviour, to an extreme desire to convert the rest of the world, if necessary with fire and sword. I can have no quarrel with people's purely private views, and if somebody, say, finds comfort in his grief through belief in a revealed life after death, but is otherwise unaffected in his behaviour, then I for one could not object.

But such purely private faith is the exception rather than the rule. Generally the state of mind of a believer in a revelation is the awful arrogance of saying '*I know*, and those who do not agree with my belief are wrong'. In no other field is such arrogance so widespread, in no other field do people feel so utterly certain of their 'knowledge'. It is to me quite disgusting that anybody should feel so superior, so selected and chosen against all the many who differ in their beliefs or unbeliefs. This would be bad enough, but so many believers do their best to propagate their faith, at the very least to their children but often also to others (and historically there are of course plenty of examples of doing this by force and ruthless brutality). The fact that stares one in the face is that people of the greatest sincerity and of all levels of intelligence differ and have always differed in their religious beliefs. Since at most one faith can be true, it follows that human beings are extremely liable to believe firmly and honestly in something untrue in the field of revealed religion. One would have expected this obvious fact to lead to some humility, to some thought that however deep one's faith, one may conceivably be mistaken. Nothing is further from the believer, any believer, than this elementary humility. All in his power (which nowadays in a developed country tends to be confined to his children) must have his faith rammed down their throats. In many cases children are indeed indoctrinated with the disgraceful thought that they belong to the one group with superior knowledge who alone have a private wire to the office of the Almighty, all others being less fortunate than they themselves. It is an easy step from this, taken all too frequently, to the believer feeling himself entitled, nay obliged, to do all in his power to convert others, or at least to enforce the particular prohibitions of his faith on others, fellow believers and the rest alike. Naturally how far this goes depends precisely on the amount of power wielded. Thus, after a long struggle the strength of the Church of Rome proved insufficient to continue the outlawing of divorce in Italy, but in Malta the prohibition on the importation of contraceptives remains. In the same manner throughout much of Israel the rearing of pigs is illegal, while in the stricter Muslim countries alcohol remains proscribed for all.

The powers of religious institutions have fortunately diminished in the Western world during the last few centuries through the long struggles of free thinkers and dissenters, and with it some at least of the characteristically religious cruelties have disappeared. In much of Christian Europe the godfearing used to burn old women suspected of being witches, an arduous duty they felt had been clearly put upon them by the Bible. The facts on witch burning are clear enough: First, faith made otherwise decent people commit acts of unspeakable horror, showing how ordinary and everyday feelings of human kindness and revulsion at cruelty can be and have been overruled by religious belief. Secondly, it exposes as utterly hollow the claim that religion sets an absolute and unchanging foundation for morality. The attitude of the Churches to witch burning has undergone a total and profound change from what was regarded as holy duty to revulsion and disbelief. Of course the earlier attitude is now viewed as having been caused by a mistranslation. That may well be so, but surely it is witness to the blindness of faith and to its totalitarianism, if a simple mistranslation could make people act thus. What have we in belief, exhortation, and enforcement today that may not be explained away one day as a mistranslation? It is at least plausible to speculate that the Christian adulation of virginity may turn out to be due to a faulty translation. The centuries of the Church's inhuman and anti-human exhortation in favour of virginity may then be seen for the awful perversion that they are, pressurising and indeed forcing people away from their freedom to work out their sexual lifestyles in their own way.

Religion sets no sure foundation of morality, indeed history proves that religious faith can pervert man's, alas very incomplete, friendliness and social consciousness to outrageous and horrific beastliness in the treatment of those of different beliefs. Christian genocide against Jews was less efficient than the Nazis, but this was due to the organisational incompetence of the Middle Ages, not to restraint. The treatment of the native populations of Latin America by the Christian invaders is one of the ghastly examples, but equally the wars of religion in Europe between groups of only modest doctrinal differences drenched the continent in blood. Of course it is also true that Christianity inspired and continues to inspire selfless and devoted service to fellow humans, but this can no more erase the stains on Christian history than the selflessness and devoted service of many of his supporters during the Hitler period can whitewash this awful dozen years. Wilberforce certainly was a major reformer and helped materially to advance the freeing of slaves, but surely this cannot excuse his persecution of prostitutes, let alone Christianity's earlier burning of heretics.

The fact is surely that a true believer regards the commands of his faith as an absolute, whether or not they agree with his (and his period's) moral preconceptions. No doubt much of what Moses or a Jesus or a Mohammed said sounds sweetness and light to us, but not only did they say a good deal else besides, but their teachings have more often than not been interpreted as justification for barbaric and inhuman attitudes and acts. We do not need to recall instances of physical cruelty which, thanks to the waning power of religion, are largely in the past, but can look at the common and undisguised contempt for women enshrined in the three great Western religions, the basis for the cruel, inhuman and wasteful sexism still so rampant. This was the basis for all faiths to have been so slow to appreciate the humanizing and liberating effect of easier contraception, with the Roman Catholic Church still unable to reconcile itself to it.

Yet with all these well-established facts of inherent religious viciousness (to give another example, the Jewish faith asks a family to mourn for a member who has left the faith as though he had died) there is still the thought that religion is a 'good thing' to be supported by the state. An instance of the absurdity this leads to is shown in Northern Ireland. It is surely true that the troubles of this unhappy province are due to the fact that there are two culturally somewhat different and very separate communities there. To say that the troubles are not religious in origin may well be true, but for what reason other than religion would anyone have regarded it as decent or tolerable that the children of the two communities went to separate schools?

Separatism in the schooling of children on any grounds other than religion is viewed as something to be deplored and perhaps outlawed, but nowhere is this separatism more vicious in its effects than in Ulster. Yet there is no feeling of outrage at this divisive arrangement, where children either go to state schools (where by custom more than half the governors of each school are protestant clergymen) or to catholic schools. The majority indeed takes pride in the generous state support for the catholic schools, but only gradually is there beginning to be a feeling that this divisiveness makes a truly foul system, accepted and supported because it is religious, and religion is thought to be 'a good thing'. Yet the Northern Irish situation is totally in line with what religion has always done: dividing people into mutually hostile groups and setting them against each other, each sure that they have the knowledge and the support of the Almighty. Yet whether it is Hindus and Moslems in India, or Christian crusaders* slaughtering Moslems and Jews indiscriminately in conquered Jerusalem, or support for separate schooling preventing community contact in Northern Ireland, religion always shows the same cruel and bloodstained face of giving a group a feeling of moral superiority over others of differing views, and making them feel justified in committing vicious and violent acts whenever they have the power to do so.

Why then with all the clear evidence demonstrating the divisive and bloodstained nature of religion, is there this feeling of support for it? Nowadays mainly I think because of the impression that religion acts as a brake on criminality. How does this impression arise? Because, and only because, we regard some of the ethical teachings of the major religions as

---

* The absurdity of prevalent attitudes is evidenced by the use of the word 'crusader' as a term of honour when surely crusaders were nothing but a disgusting gang of self-opinionated vicious invaders and slaughterers robbing and murdering whoever they met, including Greek Orthodox Christians.

supporting common standards of morality. However, one does not need to
be steeped in psychology to know that the responses of human beings to
exhortations and even to threats of punishment is unpredictable and
indeed irregular. Hard evidence that believers are less likely to be
criminals than non-believers does not exist. What evidence there is points
in the opposite direction. To quote from just one authority:

There are fewer criminals where atheists abound than where, under equal conditions, either
Catholics or Protestants dominate. This fact may proceed from their greater degree of
education, the more so as in Europe atheists are especially numerous among the more highly
educated.

(Lombroso, *Crime its causes and remedies*, Heinemann, 1911)

Since all statistics tend to be equally barren for those who want to show
that religion is good for avoiding delinquency, to base a public policy of
support for religion on any idea that it reduces criminality is working on
the basis of entirely unsupported biased thinking.

Let me give another example: a woman falls down in the street and a
man passing by helps her to get up again. Can we deduce from this that the
helpful passer-by belonged to any particular religion or any religion at all?
No, because being helpful is the ordinary normal human behaviour that
we all share, and has nothing to do with religion. But if we see the
abnormal behaviour of the passer-by not helping, then we might well
suspect the ugliness of religion to be at work. Perhaps he is a Protestant
and she a Catholic in an area of local tension or he is a high caste Hindu
and she an untouchable, or he an Orthodox Jew fearing she might be in the
'unclean' state after menstruation. Ordinary decency is one of the
pleasanter facts of life, deviation from it sometimes has the most ordinary
of causes (e.g. the passer-by may have been too absorbed in his own
thoughts to notice, or in too much of a hurry), but equally may stem from
belief in some *super human, and therefore inhuman* revelation.

Of course religion is a very common human trait, but this does not mean
that it should be supported. A capacity for envy is probably an even more
widespread human trait, but is not considered thereby to qualify for
support by public opinion or by the state. In fact envy has done the human
race far less harm than has religion.

What then should be the public attitude to religion? Private religion is
surely the personal prerogative of each of us, and must not only be
permitted, but its freedom must be assured. Anybody has a right to his

views and his beliefs, provided he does not permit these to obtrude on his public stance so he does not attempt to coerce others in any way. For a Catholic woman not to have an abortion is her perfect and undeniable right, but it is intolerable for her, because of her own religious beliefs, to attempt to limit the right of others to have one.

Thus religion should be firmly confined to the private domain. Toleration, that great achievement of non-religious thinking, is now so much accepted that in the civilized world it is impossible for the great religions to resist it, much though it must hurt the faithful to stand by and let what to them is falsehood be spread. Toleration in this the Jeffersonian sense is deeply enshrined in the Constitution (though not necessarily in the social practice) of the United States of America. Thus religion has been largely kept out of schools there. Unhappily the widespread acceptance of the 'lying truth' that religion is a good thing is still delaying the complete success of this unifying and healing principle of tolerance.

Nicholas Mosley

Nicholas Mosley was born in 1923. He has written eight novels, two biographies, a travel book and a book about religion. Films have been made from his novels *Accident* and *Impossible Object*. He wrote the book and the script for the film *The Assassination of Trotsky*. His latest work of fiction, *Catastrophe Practice*, is being published in June 1979.

Human beings desire happiness

A lifetime of happiness! No man alive could bear it.
It would be hell on earth.
                    Bernard Shaw: *Man and Superman*

It was Aristotle who formulated the idea that human beings desired happiness. He argued in the logical way of the Greeks, without paying too much attention to experience, that there must be some aim to human life and that this, as a matter of definition, should be called happiness. 'Happiness, then, is something final and self-sufficient, and is the end of action.' (Ethics. 1.7.) From this point on, of course, the word and the idea could be hedged around by as many qualifications as anyone liked. Aristotle argued that perhaps no man could properly be called happy until he was dead: but then, according to logic, what a man would properly desire was to be dead. Logic and definitions took precedence over experience; and people were saddled with the idea that happiness was what they desired even if what for the most part they seemed to achieve was being miserable.

Later ages have not always been so obsessed by the need for definitions as were the Greeks: but the idea that as a matter of common sense human beings desire happiness has remained. It has become such a truism that when a self-conscious merchant of paradoxes such as Bernard Shaw said that if human beings ever got a lifetime of happiness they would find it hell on earth, the remark could be taken as just one of those witticisms by which platitudes are stood on their heads. It is only if one gives oneself time to think that one sees what Bernard Shaw means. Human beings think they desire happiness, but its achievement would bore them to death. So how can it sensibly be said that this is what they desire? The predicament is one of confusion rather than of failure. Another commonplace saying is that heaven would be boring: all those pious angels with their harps! For entertainment, one would have to go to hell. But then—what is meant by happiness? and heaven? There is such confusion here that it is not surprising that human beings seem to get so little of what they say they want.

It seems to me that both sorts of truism are wrong—both that human beings desire happiness, and that if they got it it would be hell. I think these sorts of truism are maintained in order to protect a slothful *status quo*. What I think is true is that human beings do not particularly desire happiness but that it can be won by skill and hard work: and that if it were achieved, it would be a very pleasant state on earth.

What present-day human beings desire, it seems to me, is a condition in which they can be reassured as to their status and identity by a feeling of being superior to other people and by being able to complain: they like being one up on the people around them, and being resentful of anyone they think is trying to be one up on them. In this state people know just where they are: but it is a state not of happiness, but of power. It is also a condition of constant anxiety. A state of happiness is an absolution from anxiety; a feeling of being at one with other people; a conviction that in spite of the sorrows of the world, there is nothing of which to complain.

It is easy to pile up evidence that power is what people desire rather than happiness: for the most part nowadays in the Western world power takes the form of the possession of money. Most people would agree that large amounts of money do not bring happiness: there are popular songs and sayings to this effect: but few people surely would be eager to choose, if they had the magic choice, happiness rather than money. They might choose money and say that they believed that money would bring happiness: but to choose happiness knowing that it would not bring money—that would be a hard choice! People are aware of what very rich men are like—Howard Hughes, for example, for years trapped and bemused in a hotel bedroom. Yet how eagerly human beings desire to become like Howard Hughes! And how few people wish to become like present-day saints, however palpable their happiness. A trapped millionaire knows exactly where he is; and can tell other people what to do with themselves. A saint is at the mercy, as it were, of whatever wind blows; and he can tell other people little of what to do except to try to do as they like.

Few psychoanalysts would suggest that human beings desire happiness. Freud described how people were torn between rival impulses towards sexuality and self-preservation: the peace that a person might hope to achieve was a precarious balance between the two. Jung described men as having to maintain themselves between competing archetypal forces that might destroy them: some sort of resolution might be achieved by skill, but the demand for skill was constant. In all this sort of understanding there is no suggestion that happiness is what people naturally desire: happiness is something constructed by intelligence and artistry out of the dangerous forces of impulses.

There are very few works of European literature—or indeed so far as I know of any literature—that are about happiness. What people like to read and to be reassured by are stories about characters even more tragic or sadly comic than they feel they are themselves. Lasting works of literature are for the most part to do with people who come to a dim end: and even when they seem to succeed—in getting married, for instance, at the very end of a book—there is usually the hint of what poor fools they are, for soon their bubble of happiness will burst and they will be seen as silly as the older married couples around them. There is a sort of sub-literature of wish-fulfilment of course in which it is suggested that happiness might last: but this is acceptable only if it is deliberately in the form of dreams. For representations of reality what human beings require is that their own resentments should be reassured by the inabilities of others. This is what the ancient Greeks required from their tragedies, and it is what audiences require from the Theatre of Absurdity and the Theatre of Cruelty of the present day. Almost the only works of literature that might be said to be truly about happiness are to do not with human beings but with animals—*Winnie the Pooh*, or *The Wind in the Willows*.

It seems to me that at the heart of all this preference for sadness is just the idea that human beings *should* desire happiness, and so when they do not, or when they do not get it, there is some guilt at the apparent failure and even satisfaction in the guilt; because what an impossible idea it was anyway that human beings should desire happiness! There is even the idea that if the achievement of happiness is so obviously a dream, then there is nothing better for human beings to do than to give up: and perhaps this is what human beings really want: for as Freud noted, another basic drive in human nature is the desire for release from tension and for death.

So long as it is assumed that a state of happiness should be natural, then no start can be made on the hard graft towards achieving it. Skill and effort can only be applied when it is known that they are required.

In his play, *Man and Superman*, from which the quotation at the beginning of this essay was taken, Bernard Shaw argues something about all this; especially in the long scene in the third act when Don Juan is in hell. Shaw demonstrates the propensity of human beings for hopelessness: but the argument, as so often in Shaw, is done with a view to charming the audience—to sending it away, however shocked, comfortably shocked—for what it will have been reassured by is that it is an audience of progressive ladies and gentlemen, just like the author. Perhaps Shaw had to keep everything he said as a bit of a joke; how else would he have got an audience to listen to him? But one of the themes of *Man and Superman* is just this—that human beings in their present state of evolution are not ready for anything so subtle and serious as happiness: what they like to be reassured by are expressions of common despair and resentment—even if these can be made out to be a bit of a joke. Shaw suggested that before there could be any true embracing of happiness a new type of human being would have to evolve—a type of man as different from present man, in some respects, as present man is different from the apes. Shaw used the word Superman deliberately in honour of Nietzsche: but he does not elaborate much about Nietzsche in his play. The way in which Nietzsche's idea of the Superman has come to be misunderstood is that of the Superman being some sort of political élitist (what a subject here for a Lying Truth!) whereas in fact Nietzsche wrote in praise of someone who overcame not other people, but himself. The things that a man, in order to reach a higher state of evolution, would have to overcome in himself, were just those things which, in the present state of humanity, seem to be his ruling obsessions—the desires for dominance, for resentment, for wary self-protection—what Nietzsche called the Will to Power. The Will to Power was just what the Superman would have to overcome in order to achieve—though Nietzsche did not exclusively use the word—happiness. But the question remained: if the propensity of present-day human beings was towards primitive attitudes such as dominance and resentment, how was it that any work for the Superman could be encouraged?

One reason why people find it so difficult to face the idea that what human beings desire is not happiness, is perhaps the thought that, if this

state of affairs is indeed true—if it is man's desire for power and resentment that is innate—then there may be very little that he can do about this,
for no amount of effort can change his inborn character. Once there was
God: if a person desired change, and felt that change was not within his
scope, then he could pray to God to change him. After the so-called death
of God there was a period in which it was thought that a man might pull
himself up by his own boots: then there was Darwin, who seemed to suggest that although a man might indeed change his environment, what was
innate in him he would not change. This could only change as a result of a
chance mutation, and consequent natural selection. Thus a man, so far as
his basic propensities went, was at the mercy of chance: and a chance such
as to bring about change could be expected to happen only once in hundreds of thousands of years—and then most likely not to the species'
advantage. So what was there left for a man to do about his lack of propensity for happiness other than to ignore it; or to pretend it was something
different, by making jokes about it?

Recently, however, there seems to have been a change in the views held
by some scientists—

(One of the basic characteristics of most scientists, may it be said in
parenthesis, seems to be to have a strong dislike of sentences written by
laymen beginning 'Recently however there seems to have been a change in
the views held by some scientists . . .'. Scientists are quick to say that they
are being misrepresented; that laymen do not understand their mysteries;
that an attempt to translate their jargon into intelligible language is
misconceived and dangerous. But these scientists, it seems to me, are exhibiting just those present-day propensities for resentment and will-to-
power that should be challenged; and so—)

Recently there seems to have been a change in the views held by some
scientists; since although it is still held as undoubtedly true that innate
propensities cannot be directly affected by what has been learned, yet after
all there may be some way of being able to talk as if characteristics acquired
by effort might be passed on: for it seems there may be so many myriad
chance mutations already in existence within an organism—in existence as
potentials though latent and unexpressed—that some dispensation of circumstance might encourage some of these potentials to flourish which
hitherto have not grown; and in this sense what might be passed on might
be in a man's control. A man's ability to control his circumstances, that is,

might affect which innate result of chance is brought to the fore. So that if a few human beings wish to acquire a built-in propensity for happiness, then there is in fact some point in their practising happiness with skill and application; in the hope that in time this skill might become habitual; might even be passed on—that which previously had been innate but stifled becoming innate and expressed. Genetic propensities are like seeds; some may be dormant for a million years; but if there is a certain cultivation they might grow. But nothing new can grow—indeed there is little sense in the idea of cultivation—so long as it is assumed that men have no need of skills. The prerequisite for happiness is the realisation that happiness is not something easily desired: but it is something that can be created if its creation is what is desired.

Peter Walker

Rt. Hon. Peter Walker, PC 1970, MBE 1960, Conservative Member of Parliament for Worcester since 1961, was born in 1932. He was PPS to Leader of House of Commons, 1963-64; Opposition Front Bench Spokesman on Finance and Economics, 1964-66; on Transport, 1966-68; on Local Government, Housing and Land, 1968-70; Minister of Housing and Local Government, 1970; Secretary of State for the Environment, 1970-72; Trade and Industry, 1972-74; Opposition Spokesman on Trade, Industry and Consumer Affairs, 1974. In 1977 he published *The Ascent of Britain*.

Charity begins at home

Charity begins at home. It is a nasty phrase normally used by nasty people.

Over the years whenever I have pleaded the case for doing more to solve the problems of the West Indian immigrants in Britain, or whenever I have expressed the importance of assisting in the newly developed countries of Africa and Asia, I have always been guaranteed a stream of abusive and bitter letters containing the words 'charity begins at home'. Whenever I have spoken at meetings where race relations have been one of the topics or when one has talked about the inner city problems to meetings in prosperous suburbs nearly always a thin-lipped and chippy person has stood up at question time and used the magic phrase 'charity begins at home'.

The users of this phrase really mean that charity ends at home—ends, in fact, in their own home where, judging by the appearance of the people who love the phrase, they dispel very little charity even in their own homes. I would not be surprised if a large percentage of the wife beaters and baby batterers are people who constantly indulge in preaching the total immoral gospel that charity begins at home.

It therefore reflects an attitude of mind based upon selfishness, an attitude of mind that is disruptive of progressive and reforming policies.

It is a phrase that leads to ignoring such problems as race relations, the problems of gipsies, the plight of the inner cities, and the need to bring a fairer re-distribution of wealth throughout the country.

It also reflects an attitude which demands economic policies that add prosperity to the strong and do nothing for the weak.

The element of selfishness that is inherent in the use of the doctrine that charity begins at home results in the individual who has no desire to recognise the appalling living conditions and problems of other members of the human race.

Is it not remarkable that so many of our population can live in prosperous suburbs in our major urban conurbations without giving any thought to those localities in the conurbation in which they themselves live where poverty, slum housing, crime and unemployment combine to create a living hell?

Is it not remarkable that many can work in comfortable office blocks without ever observing or recognising the noisy, dirty and dark conditions in which fellow-citizens work day after day in factories or in mines?

It is my desire to eliminate the attitudes epitomised by charity begins at home and to replace it with an attitude of mind that recognises that in a modern world charity, to have any meaning, must be universal.

Modern communications have meant that the media in all of its forms can convey to us the harsh realities of the world in which we live. We can now immediately see on our television screens the floods in India, earthquakes in South America, and poverty and injustice world-wide. Modern communications have brought to the have-nots of the world a recognition of the degree to which they are deprived, and to a lesser extent they have brought to the haves of the world the degree to which they are privileged. In the post-war period alone the enlightened and progressive have come to recognise that divisions based upon race, religion or geographical location must be lessened and not widened if this world is going to be a tolerable place in which to live.

If we are to achieve a recognition that charity needs to be universal we must strive to obtain a wider freedom. Freedom in the fullest meaning of that word includes the freedom from the humiliation and restraints of poverty; freedom from unfair discrimination; freedom from arduous toil; freedom from the debilitating effects of slum housing.

It means not just prosperity sufficient to provide the basic necessities of food, clothing and shelter, but also prosperity sufficient to enable the individual to lead a fuller life, and be able to take advantage of the multitude of benefits and pleasures that the world provides.

It means a concern for the quality of life so that progress is measured not just in GNP or motor cars but in new parks, leisure centres, artistic endeavour—the joy of living.

It means a society in which education is given a new priority and a new role—a perpetual process throughout life and not simply limited to the 5 to 22-year-old.

It means a society thriving on diversity but undivided by class, race, regional disparities or generation gaps.

Laissez-faire capitalism in the 19th century was very much based upon the principle that charity begins at home and that society would only succeed on the basis of each individual developing his abilities and talents in disregard of the needs of others. It was out of the calamitous effects of these policies that both Disraeli and Karl Marx recognised that two nations were emerging, one rich and one poor, both becoming increasingly hostile to each other. Marx advocated that the poor nation should bring about a revolution and establish a dictatorship of the proletariat. Disraeli advocated social reform and methods to re-distribute wealth so as to turn the two nations into one. We should rejoice that in Britain we took the Disraeli road and not that of Marx. For there is little doubt that the quality of life for the majority of our people and the availability of freedom far exceeds anything achieved by those nations that took the Marxist route. The fact is, however, that after a century of such reforms in far too many spheres of our national life there are still two nations and not one.

We have two nations within our major cities—the poverty and the unemployment of the inner city area in contrast to the prosperity of many of the suburbs.

We have two nations in housing where every town and city is divided between the owner-occupied estates and the council house estates.

The spirit of two nations still permeates the factory floor. Indeed 'them and us' attitudes have increased rather than decreased in recent years.

We still have two nations in the geographical sense with the prosperity of the South-East in sharp contrast to the high unemployment of the North.

We have two nations—one coloured and one white—in many of our urban conurbations where the coloured community has greater unemployment, worse housing conditions and lower educational standards.

And it is this divisiveness, this two-nations spirit, which is threatening law and order in so many of our towns and cities.

The charity begins at home brigade are having a field-day in industrial relations. The worst of the trade union leaders have an approach that is purely based upon obtaining the biggest increase for their members irrespective of the damage it does to the future prospects of the firm, to the inflationary prospects of the nation and to the unemployment of others. Bad employers pursue charity begins at home policies so as to give the minimum to those they employ irrespective of the efforts and productive skills displayed by them. It is for this reason that it is essential if capitalism is to survive in a modern world we must have positive programmes that substantially extend participation in the fullest sense of the word.

We should produce positive programmes in which there is a greater spread of capital, and profit sharing becomes a reality in its various forms for the majority of those working in firms and corporations whose activities are based upon the profit motive.

The man who transformed post-war France from decline to revival, President de Gaulle, wrote in his autobiography: 'I have been convinced that modern mechanised society lacks a human incentive to safeguard its equilibrium. A social system which reduces the worker—however respectably paid—to the level of a tool or a cog is, in my opinion, at variance with the nature of our species and indeed with the spirit of sound productivity. Notwithstanding the undoubted benefits which capitalism produces not only for the few but for the community as a whole, the fact remains that it carries within itself the seeds of a gigantic and perennial dissatisfaction. I believed that it was incumbent upon our civilisation to construct a new one which would regulate human relations in such a way that everyone would have a direct share in the proceeds of the concern for which he worked, and would enjoy the dignity of being personally responsible for the progress of the collective enterprise on which his own future depended. Would this not be tantamount to the transposition on to the economic plane of what the rights and duties of the citizen represent in the political sphere?'

De Gaulle introduced profit-sharing schemes. Prior to his departure from office he desperately wanted to introduce employee participation and he reflected: 'It was an attempt to throw the door wide open to participation in France, an attempt which was to rouse against me the determined opposition of all the vested interests, economic, social, political and journalistic, whether Marxist, liberal or diehard. This coalition, by persuading the majority of the people solemnly to repudiate de Gaulle, was to shatter there and then the possibility of reform at the same time as it shattered my power. Nevertheless, beyond all the ordeals and obstacles, and perhaps beyond the grave, that which is legitimate may one day be legalised, that which is rightful may in the end be proved right.' I hope the Tory Party will reflect upon these wise and thoughtful aspirations of a great political leader.

Advances in technology mean that even if it was acceptable employment would probably be only available to perhaps 70% or 80%. A society in which 80% were employed and 20% were unemployed would be a society destroyed by friction and divisiveness.

We must become dedicated to the importance of full employment. There is a crying need for vision in employment. We have lived in a society in which the main objective has been to provide work to human beings from the age of 16 to 65. I can remember the post-war sensation when union leaders demanded the five-day week. That has now been attained. But we no longer have a generation leaving school which will be satisfied by a guarantee that they will be able to work in an unattractive factory, or a mine or even an office for fifty of the remaining fifty-five years of their lives.

We must see to it that capitalism uses technology in such a way that future generations are not obliged to spend a great part of their working hours doing work of little mental or spiritual satisfaction.

We verge on the lunatic in our approach to economic affairs. We have machines that can replace much of the unsatisfying, dirty and unrewarding work previously carried out by men; we have machines that can produce at greater speed and greater efficiency than in any previous era; we have machines whose parts can be renewed and whose performance can and will be constantly improved. We should rejoice and create a society in which the machine works 24 hours a day 7 days a week 52 weeks a year whilst man toils less and has available to him the time for leisure and pursuits more congenial to human happiness.

Instead we place every restrictive practice upon the machine in order that man may continue a pattern of life heavily committed to unnecessary toil and, for many, unnecessary poverty.

Unique in history we have the circumstances in which we can create Athens without the slaves. The machine, the computer and the microprocessor are available as the willing, effective and unquestioning slaves. Only the folly of man prevents us from taking advantage of this unprecedented opportunity.

If charity begins at home there are quite a number of households in Britain that charity has yet to reach.

On average one household in six has someone on social security
One household in nine has no inside toilet

One household in ten has a family in which there is only one parent

One household in eleven has no bathroom for themselves

One household in eleven has someone unemployed

One household in fifteen has no hot water tap

One household in twenty-three has someone who is physically or mentally handicapped

One household in thirty is coloured

One household in fifty has the head of the household who has never been able to work

One can add to these statistics the large number of households that have someone in prison or in borstal, someone in a hospital or mental institution, some relative now confined for the rest of their life to a geriatric ward, some member of the family who has already had one, if not several, bouts of mental illness.

We have a desperate need to eradicate the decades of neglect of the facilities for the mentally ill and the geriatric patient. Britain's mental hospitals and geriatric facilities remain appallingly poor. The occupants of both are inevitably inarticulate. We need some loud political voices, believers in the concept of universal charity not limited charity, to speak up for them and their relatives.

In their hostility to the coloured population in Britain the National Front are perpetual users of the charity begins at home slogan. It is vital for Britain, and perhaps on a wider scale for Europe, to succeed in creating harmonious race relations amongst all British citizens. At present due to the lack of a genuine charitable approach to this problem in Britain we are failing. We are particularly failing as far as the 120,000 households of West Indian descent are concerned.

When I enjoyed the privilege of being Secretary of State for the Environment I was deeply concerned that there were concentrated in a number of our inner city areas a coloured population suffering from considerable multi-deprivation. A combination of bad housing, bad education and racial prejudice meant that they were destined to be the unemployed and the perpetual poor. The true facts were not available and to obtain the facts was one of the purposes of my instigating the three Inner City Studies in Liverpool, Birmingham and London—all three in districts with a substantial immigrant population.

Although during my period as Secretary of State for Trade and Industry there was relative full employment it was clear from my observations as the Head of that Department that our coloured minority was not enjoying anything like the opportunities that were available to the country as a whole.

The reality of their bad housing, bad education and high unemployment is of such dimensions that unless tackled effectively and quickly it will bring to Britain the crime, the bitterness and the resentfulness that has been such a tragic feature of those American cities that equally failed to identify the aspirations, hopes and deep disappointments of their coloured population.

Birmingham and London possess the main concentrations of West Indians. Our first and second biggest cities are therefore threatened unless we succeed in taking effective and imaginative action.

A very high proportion of the West Indian population are young children and teenagers. Alas, the proportion of one parent West Indian families is half as much again as the proportion of our population as a whole. With this background housing is, of course, fundamental.

I remember the horror with which, within a few weeks of becoming a Minister, I talked to one West Indian family—husband, wife and four children—who were living in one room in Brixton without a single window to that room. I was determined to see that such conditions ended. They have not. They are getting worse.

If you are a West Indian there is six times the chance that you will be sharing accommodation with another family than if you are not West Indian. West Indians have two-thirds again more people per room than the population as a whole. The proportion of West Indian families living in what is officially described as overcrowded conditions is ten-fold the proportion of the country as a whole.

In London it has been shown that not only have the West Indians obtained about half of the proportion of council houses that their population warrants, but they have also been allocated housing in what tend to be the worst and oldest estates. In the enquiries I have made it is certain that their lack of articulation has resulted in them obtaining but a small proportion of the rent allowances and rent rebates to which they are entitled. Nor are they aware of the statutory rights that are available to them in the sphere of housing. Of all groups in our country there can be none who are suffering from more overcrowded conditions and who are deprived of what we consider to be the basic standards of housing. Of the late teenagers in certain districts I believe there are as many as one in five who could now be defined as homeless.

Being concentrated as they are in our worst inner city areas the majority of West Indian children are in old schools. The turnover of teachers is massive. You will find few teachers in any of the schools in which they are concentrated who have been there for five years. Some of the children have as many as three or four different teachers in one year.

A high proportion of West Indian children are leaving school with totally inadequate standards of literacy and numeracy to the deep disappointment of their parents.

It is not surprising that with the fast turnover of teachers and the fact that 74% of West Indian women of working age are out at work that the truancy rate is of massive proportions and in many cases the teachers are relieved when some of their more difficult pupils are absent. Far too many young West Indians from the age of 12 and 13 onwards are leaving school to join the homeless and the unemployed, living on cash earnings and sometimes on crime.

As yet these increasing groups of unemployed and homeless teenagers have not been mobilised for political or criminal purposes on any scale; but if they are the effects could be massive in both London and Birmingham— effects that have only previously been seen in the worst inner city areas of America.

The 1971 survey showed that of the West Indian unemployed only two-thirds registered. From the enquiries I have recently made in both Birmingham and London I believe this is still the position, particularly amongst teenagers. The boy who has played truant from school tends not to sign on for unemployment.

From 1974 to 1976 unemployment in Britain doubled but for the West Indians it nearly quadrupled. In some districts you will find over half of the West Indian teenagers without a job and those with a job have had to make three times as many applications for a job as their white counterparts of identical educational achievement.

The history of cities has shown that irrespective of being black or white, high unemployment among teenagers has always meant a massive increase in crime. The present crime rate amongst West Indians has increased dramatically. We are in danger of losing a substantial proportion of a whole generation of young West Indians to prisons, borstals and psychiatric units. We are bound to pay a heavy price if a generation of young people is lost in this way. The reality of the West Indian young is that they are frequently badly educated. They have little motivation; no skills; they are homeless; they are devoid of guidance and more and more devoid of hope. In such conditions they are increasingly becoming positively hostile to the white population and particularly to white authority.

Of 120,000 West Indian households I believe that two-thirds of them are either badly housed or are suffering from unemployment and the majority of them have a much lower standard of literacy and numeracy than the nation as a whole. There are probably, therefore, 80,000 West Indian households in urgent need of a change for the better if they are to have anything like the equality of opportunity that the rest of the country enjoys.

We have districts in which in every street there are West Indian families in overcrowded and deplorable housing conditions. Every other teenager is unemployed or playing truant from school; there are low incomes and numerous one-parent families; and above all, no hope. This situation must be ended.

To fail will not just mean the continuation of the misery of large numbers of the coloured population in Britain. To fail will bring increasing misery for the white indigenous population living in our cities. For to fail will mean an increase in crime. Failure will bring increased burdens on the social services. Failure will mean deteriorating industrial relations. To fail when the task is relatively so small will show a nation incapable of tackling a problem, the details of which are known and the solutions for which are readily available.

Successive governments have operated in Britain general improvement areas, the priority neighbourhood schemes, the housing action areas, the educational priority areas, the urban aid programme, the job creation programme, the youth employment scheme and the community industry scheme. And yet the help is not reaching this group of people who need it most. During the operation of all of these schemes their unemployment has increased, their housing conditions have got worse, the crime rate has soared to new heights, and we are making no substantial break-through as far as education is concerned.

There is no doubt that with determination, within five years we can by positive action bring an end to the misery for this population and bring them somewhere near to an equality of opportunity with the rest of the nation as a whole.

It is no use talking of lack of racial discrimination in this country if a lack of positive action means that the worst housing, the worst jobs—or no jobs—tend to be concentrated upon one community.

There is no reason why with an imaginative five-year programme positively managed that at the end of that five years the housing, educational training and the job opportunity standards of the West Indians should not be at least equal to those of the rest of the population. Eventually this action will have to be taken. The question is will it be done after racial relations have deteriorated still further, hatred has been built up in the hearts of the West Indian community, hostility has been created by the white community's resentment of the crime and the property damage that will have been attributed to the coloured community? Britain has a size of problem that is manageable. Britain does have the resources to manage it. Let us therefore begin our campaign to see that charity is universal in these 80,000 West Indian households where the situation is desperate. For to succeed in these homes would be a success that would set an example to the world as a whole.

The inward and selfish attitude expressed in the cry of 'charity begins at home' is an attitude that fails to recognise that society is held together only by the moral bond of mutual obligation. Destroy this and society disintegrates in anarchy. The most fundamental of all mutual obligation is the obligation to guarantee to even the humblest the means to live and enjoy a decent life. In my vision of society that is an ethical postulate inherent in the very fact of society. It is not enough that the fruits of society go to the successful even if there is equality of opportunity. In my vision everyone has the right to a decent quality of life. We can, in fact, move towards a new Athens without the slaves, provided we recognise that charity has universal application.

E. W. F. Tomlin

E. W. F. Tomlin has written a number of books on philosophical and literary subjects. He has held professorships in both the USA and France. He is a C.B.E., and a Fellow of the Royal Society of Literature.

Novelty is the chief aim in Art

1

Before the advent of urban industrial society, most communities were organised on traditional lines. That is to say, their implicit aim was *to conform to the past*, to follow 'the way of the ancestors'. The role of the patriarchs, elders, or guardians was to watch over traditional standards and to interpret them afresh in each generation. But the overseers remained the servants of tradition, not its masters. Perhaps the extreme form of such worship of tradition was to be found in the ancient Chinese civilization. Indeed, the character signifying 'religion' in Chinese was composed of three signs—'to beat', 'child', and 'to imitate': in other words, to impose a rigorous *paideia* so that the child should be brought to conform to the ideals of his forebears.

Not that change was excluded. But if changes were introduced, they were made for the sake of upholding or asserting a *purer* or more purified tradition. There was reformation or renewal (*aggiornamento*) rather than revolution or convulsion. The spiritual reorientation brought about by the Pharoah Ikhnaton in about 1350 BC was initiated for the sake of affirming a more exalted form of monotheism. The great movement of spiritual renewal which occurred throughout the civilized world in the 6th century BC must have been for the sake of purifying a tradition which had become affected with superstition. With the advent of Christianity there had been another great movement of spiritual renewal. Finally, Mohammed, the 'seal of the saints', conceived his mission as a reformation, the assertion of a more refined spirituality, a reaction against the theology of those who 'joined God with gods'. Until the advent of modern social messianism, all the great spiritual innovators were preoccupied with the preservation of traditional values.

In the so-called primordial cultures, art, using that word in the widest sense, was an offshoot and by-product of religion, and therefore the artist worked within a tradition from which he strayed at his peril. In the field of literature in particular, certain works came to be regarded as *classics*, i.e. works in a class by themselves. In Sumeria, there was the *Epic of Gilgamesh*; in Greece, Homer; in China, a series of standard works that were recognized, up to the 20th century, as an essential equipment of the *literati* and even of the civil servants, whose knowledge of the classics was tested in examinations.

In 16th- and 17th-century Europe, a change began slowly to come about. This was due to an inevitable combination of causes: the circulation of printed books, the discovery of new lands and peoples, and, no doubt as a result, considerable religious turmoil. Even so, the major religious reformers, like their predecessors in the primordial cultures, were seeking, at least at the outset, not to overthrow the tradition but to purify it. And both the Renaissance and the Counter-Reformation saw a fresh efflorescence of religious art.

The *Sturm und Drang* of this epoch of Renaissance, Reformation, and Counter-Reformation gave rise to a new form of controversy. The traditional mediaeval 'disputation', while simulating 'free discussion', was in fact conducted according to a rigid set of rules, and it was so designed as to issue in the reaffirmation of orthodoxy. The rejection by the reformers of the Catholic Scholastic system did away with this essentially *dialectical* form of discussion in favour of a polemical or *eristic* one. Hence the bitterness of the religious controversies of the 16th and 17th centuries, in which discussion often gave way to diatribe. Combining elements of the old disputation and the new eristic were the famous debates between the Ancients and the Moderns. These consisted of arguments concerning the merits of modern and classical literature, but at heart they were occupied with two diverging *Weltanschauungen*. In France, Boileau and Racine argued in favour of the Ancients and Perrault in favour of the Moderns. In England, the Ancients were defended by Sir William Temple and the Moderns by William Wotton; but it was Swift's defence of the Ancients in his *Battle of the Books* (1704) that constituted the most famous contribution.

That the debate between the Ancients and the Moderns should have flourished chiefly at the end of the 17th and the beginning of the 18th centuries was understandable, because the European intelligentsia of that time was persuaded that, having emerged from the epoch of superstition, it was on the threshold of a new kind of culture, guided by reason, whose reign

should be everlasting. This was the view of many members of the Royal
Society. And although what arose in fact was something rather different—
the Romantic Revival—this movement itself claimed to be a return to a
form of rationality: for 'common speech' and 'common sentiment', being a
manifestation of reason at the natural level, were held to be the norm from
which the intellectual world had strayed. The work of Rousseau, especially
his educational manifesto, *Emile* (1762), was permeated with the idea of
natural reason as the light whereby man should live. The Bergsonian view
of life as 'a gushing forth of novelties' was far distant. Contrary to
prevailing belief today, no educational theory was less permissive than that
of Rousseau. In his view, to 'follow nature' was the reverse of engaging in a
free-for-all.

After the Reformation, Europe's great watershed was undoubtedly the
French Revolution. True, there was a moment in the Revolution when
Reason, as the manifestation of the Supreme Being, seemed—to
Robespierre at least—about to triumph in human affairs, which must have
stirred him to melancholy reflections when he in turn was being driven to
the scaffold. For except for limited secular achievements (the introduction
of the metric system, etc.), the triumph of reason was shortlived, and the
Revolution began to devour its offspring, rationality included. Never
before had there been so complete a rupture with the past; after the Terror,
communal life was no longer the same. Moreover, the reverberations of the
Revolution threw out circles of influence far beyond the borders of France.
Henceforth it was possible to be a 'revolutionary', a professional subverter
of established ideas and conventions, an advocate of novelty *for its own sake.*

One conspicuous type of revolutionary that emerged in the decades
following the Revolution was that of the artist as a figure existing in his
own right and dedicated to an ideal of art that was *sui generis.* This was
somehow regarded as signalizing the liberation of art, its final escape from
the tyranny of religious dogma. If the artist was thus thrown upon the
mercy of society, and if he starved in a garret, such martyrdom was the
consequence of society's ignorance and ingratitude. There grew up the
conception of the artist as the misunderstood or unheeded prophet, the
rejected messianic figure, almost the social outcast, but at the same time
the harbinger of a new dispensation and a new freedom.

In English Literature, the most complete example of the artist in this
new role—the role of liberator and revolutionary—was Shelley: poet,

propagandist, reformer, and the adored of women; for it was womankind who, for a variety of reasons, rallied most enthusiastically to the artist in this new role. As to that role, Shelley himself defined it magniloquently in his *Ode to the West Wind*:

> Drive my dead thoughts over the universe
> Like withered leaves to quicken a new birth;
> And, by the incantation of this verse,
> Scatter, as from an unextinguished hearth
> Ashes and sparks, my words among mankind!
> Be through my lips to unawakened earth
> The trumpet of a prophecy! . . .

This clarion call was something altogether new. Nobody had spoken quite like that before. The poet had addressed himself histrionically *as poet*, from Ronsard to Shakespeare, but not as mystic leader and transformer of the social order. In German literature, indeed, a figure not unlike Shelley was the young and almost contemporary genius who took the name of Novalis. To him, as to so many later aspirants, life was to be 'lived' poetry; the poet and the mystic were essentially one; and the Woman, exemplified for Novalis in the person of Sophie von Kühn, became the incarnation of the Muse.

As the 19th century progressed, and with it a great increase in readership, the novel took over what poetry had initiated, until another change came with the arrival of the movement extolling Art for Art's Sake. This served to revive the figure of the artist as an isolated and independent priest of culture; but by this time it was becoming clear that the Art which had existed *sui generis* was being steadily evacuated of content. 'As for living', said a character in Villiers de l'Isle Adam's *Axel's Castle* (1890), 'our servants will do that for us'. As for art, the pure artists might have said—and as Oscar Wilde did say—our concern with it is only so far as it is useless.

How did this sterilization of art come about? After all, the apostles of the Post Impressionist Movement maintained that they at last were producing *pure* art, and that all previous art was the product of impure emotion and bogus sentiment. This new aesthetic, though most clearly exemplified in the domain of the plastic arts, exerted great influence in other domains as well. Mallarmé attempted to produce 'pure poetry'; and similar attempts were made, first by the Surrealists and then by Gertrude Stein and her imitators, to produce 'pure prose', while in Dada there was 'pure dance' and 'pure drama'. Nor was the new dispensation confined to the aesthetic order. In so far as it had a metaphysical dimension, traditional philosophy was put into liquidation by the Vienna Circle; and although there followed a reaction against the pure gospel of Logical Positivism, the claim to have repudiated the tradition continued to be advanced by those who called themselves analytical philosophers. Several generations of students were told—and are still being told, judging from the syllabuses of several philosophical departments—that philosophy had nothing to do with 'the great problems', but only with clearing up 'linguistic confusions', etc.

What this amounted to was a deliberate repudiation of the tradition altogether. And the corollary of such repudiation was the exaltation of novelty as the primary aim of aesthetic and indeed intellectual activity. Diffused and indeterminate, this neophyliac attitude remains powerful. It has become an unconscious and implicitly-held doctrine, espoused by both practitioners and critics, and therefore easily imposed upon the public. It can be regarded as one of our chief contemporary fallacies.

2

The truth is that the attempt to achieve a pure art, a pure poetry etc., leads very soon to an empty art, an empty poetry—that is, in the case of poetry, a poetry that has passed over into music. The celebrated example of pure poetry put forward by the Abbé Brémond in his *Prière et Poésie* (1927), which made such a stir in France, namely the line of Racine 'La fille de Minos et de Pasiphaë',[1] is beautiful not for its sense but for its sound; and what is interesting in that connection is that the two principal words happen to be foreign names.[2] But the paradox that purity implies emptiness is more apparent than real. What the apostles of pure poetry were apparently aiming at was a *content* purged of everything extraneous to the poetic vision, and obedient to the conception of the poet as concerned solely with his art: that is to say, deprived of all didacticism, 'morals', etc. But if this purgation proceeds far enough, there is no pure aesthetic residue left. What serves for content—for there must be some content; it is impossible to be left with 'lettrisme'[3]—must be the nearest thing that can be pure, namely sensation. And that is what is usually to be found. The sensations are those least dependent on the human will, namely the erotic. That the stream of Surrealist prose, whether of André Breton or Louis Aragon, and the nonsense dialogue of Dadaist drama, not to mention the subject-matter of much 'non-representational' art, should be suffused with erotic themes is not an accident.

What is being isolated here for purposes of analysis is, needless to say, a tendency in our culture, but a tendency reflected in several domains at once. The search for novelty for its own sake is, if the paradox may be forgiven, nothing new. Its springs are to be found in Renaissance humanism, and one of its most vocal later apostles was Nietzsche, whose 'transvaluation of values' was an attempt to reach a condition 'beyond value': which was in effect not to usher in the Superman, as he supposed, but to escape from humanity altogether. Nietzsche's own tragic fate may have been bound up with his convictions: it is no derogation of a philosophy to suggest that it might have influenced and brought about the mental condition of its originator. The repudiation of values in much philosophy and implicit in much art today gives rise to a view of man very different from that reflected in the histrionic flourishes of Renaissance humanism ('What a piece of work is man! . . .'); for although the decline of traditional culture may be traced back to the Renaissance and even earlier, the overt signs of decadence took a long time to make themselves apparent. There are first and foremost the reductionist views of man with which the scientists enjoy teasing and bewildering the public: e.g. Professor H. O. Wilson's description of a human being as 'DNA's way of making more DNA'.[4] Such extreme views need not detain us. A highly respected philosopher, Susanne Langer, writing on art, declares that it reflects 'the life rhythms we share with all gnawing, hungering, moving and fearing creatures: the ultimate realities themselves, the central facts of our brief sentient existence'.[5] In other words, man is not a being committed to 'pursue virtue', as in Dante's world view, but simply a gnawing, hungering, fearing creature: in short, a predatory, mischievous animal, occupying a brief existence for no other purpose than to engage in more gnawing, hungering, etc. For these are the 'ultimate realities', the 'central facts'. And we have only to look at much sophisticated drama and fiction, from Jarry's *Ubu Roi* to the latest experiment in *cochonnerie*, to perceive this view of man reflected in what claims to be art. Even men of undoubted

artistic mastery may be found to devote their genius to the elemental level.
'It's not altogether stupid to attribute an obsession with horror to an artist
who has done so many paintings of the human scream', as a critic has said
of Francis Bacon.[6]

Since the artistic impulse is inherent in man, it cannot be totally suppressed, though it can be weakened by lack of stimulus. There are regions
of the world today, not necessarily confined to the totalitarian countries, in
which the artist and his public are spiritually and physically under-
nourished. Certainly, an instinctive activity which needs to seek its satisfaction in expressing the equivalent—or, in the case of some drama, the
reality—of grunts, screams, orgasmic wails, etc., is one that is suffering
from progressive inanition. Many critics and artists have lost sight of the
fact that 'the purpose of art to reflect the invisible world of spiritual
entities was taken for granted not only in religious but also in many
branches of secular art'.[7] What was taken for granted was of course
precisely the traditional view, which, as René Guénon insisted, implies a
suprasensible reality.[8]

3

The argument so far has sought to show that the search for novelty, or
rather the elevation of novelty into the be-all-and-end-all of art, has
resulted in artistic impoverishment; and also that such artistic impoverishment has been accompanied by, if it has not reflected, a view of man which
reduces him to an animal at once predatory and callow. Nor is it an accident that this view of man should so often find a place in modern works
concerned with the philosophy of art—Suzanne Langer's is an obvious
example.

In conclusion, the sense in which a work of art can legitimately be *new*
will be examined.

When a writer or artist—especially if he be young and at the outset of his
career—sits down and starts working, he may experience an exhilarating
feeling of limitless freedom and opportunity for creativity. Here is his
chance to be thoroughly modern and contemporary. This impression is
largely illusory. The writer has a limited vocabulary (i.e. his own language,
of which he will use only a portion); the artist and the composer have at
their disposal a restricted range of expression, and their occasional

recourse to accessory modes (as in tachist art) yields usually little of value. Moreover, the scope of every artist and writer is necessarily restricted and conditioned by the work of his predecessors. It is in architecture that the restrictions on modernity and contemporaneity are most obvious. 'At any historical period, and in any country, "contemporary" architectural style is displayed in the form of variations upon a basic ordinance, framed by the leaders of the craft and accepted by all its practitioners. Only in the variations in interpretation, as by detailing, may the architect display his originality. For without the acceptance of a basic ordinance, any architecture will dissolve into chaos, history will come to a halt, and development cease for lack of any organization relying upon continuity.'[9]

It may be argued that 'the acceptance of a basic ordinance' is necessary in architecture because architecture is after all a utilitarian art. Buildings are either to be lived in or to be used for work, meetings, or the performance of ritual, etc. But if we study the history of the arts, including literature, we observe that such basic ordinances are present throughout. Every artist, every composer, every poet writes within a particular art-form; he belongs to a school, even if he believes himself to be independent. Indeed, it is in the annual Salon des Indépendants in Paris that some of the most *derivative* painting is to be found. As Paul Valéry said: 'The most exalted figure is never "an original". With him what is really personal becomes as insignificant as possible.'[10] And T. S. Eliot, in his famous essay 'Tradition and Individual Talent', speaks of 'our tendency to insist, when we praise a poet, upon those aspects of his work in which he least resembles anyone else. In these aspects or parts of his work we pretend we find what is individual, what is the peculiar essence of the man. We dwell with satisfaction upon the poet's difference from his predecessors; we endeavour to find something that can be isolated in order to be enjoyed. Whereas if we approach a poet without this prejudice we shall often find that not only the best, but the most individual parts of his work may be those in which the dead poets, his ancestors, assert their immortality most vigorously'.

It is not impossible that, in writing this passage, Eliot had in mind a remark of Dante in the *De Vulgari Eloquentiâ* that 'the nearer we approach to the great poets, the more correct is the poetry we write'.[11]

Not novelty for its own sake, but *renewal* within the traditional or inherited modes of expression, thereby extending that tradition and that heritage, is what characterizes an authentic work of art. And this can be verified by studying not merely the art and literature of one's own country and of Europe, but the great oriental heritage, which, until the invasion of Western art, was traditional in a more exact sense than anything attained in the Occident. Whether this was due to the fact that the fount of oriental art was calligraphy, and that 'the ideogram is the only abstract art in which form and content complete each other',[12] is worth pondering.

References

1. *Phèdre*, Act 1, Scene 1.
2. For that same reason it is interesting to find a character in André Gide's *Faux Monnayeurs* (1926) declaring 'hémorrhoïdes' to be 'le plus beau mot de la langue française'.
3. The term invented by Isodore Isou, a Rumanian expatriate, in the Paris of the late 1940s.
4. *The Socio-Biology of Man* (1977).
5. *Philosophy in a New Key* (1942).
6. David Sylvester, *Interviews with Francis Bacon* (1975).
7. Sir Ernest Gombrich, *Symbolic Images* (1975).
8. It might be useful to cite an example of the creative inanition referred to. The following excerpt from a novel received respectfully by the critics, *Success* by Martin Amis (1978), is not untypical:

   'You'll have to excuse me for a moment.
      Mouth-fuck, bum-fuck, fist-fuck, prick-fuck. Ear-fuck, hair-fuck, nose-fuck, toe-fuck. It's all I think about when I'm in my room. Bed-fuck, floor-fuck, desk-fuck, sill-fuck, rug-fuck.
      And in the streets. Tarmac-fuck, lamppost-fuck, shop-front-fuck. Bike-fuck, car-fuck, bus-fuck. Rampart-fuck, railing-fuck, rubbish-fuck.
      Pen-fuck, clip-fuck, paper-fuck. (I'm at the office now.) Char-fuck, sec-fuck, temp-fuck. Salessheet-fuck, invoice-fuck, phone-fuck.
      And everywhere else. Land-fuck, sea-fuck, air-fuck, cloud-fuck. In all kinds of moods. Hate-fuck, rage-fuck, fun-fuck, sick-fuck, sad-fuck. In all kinds of contexts. Friend-fuck, kid-fuck, niece-fuck, aunt-fuck, gran-fuck. Fuck-fuck. I want to scream. . . .'

   An example of critical assessment: 'Every page of this novel displays a command of style' (George Bull, *New Fiction*, January 1978). It is not perhaps surprising that so resourceful an author, with his 'subtle insight into shifts of character' (*Ibid.*), should describe one of his personages as 'an incredibly old and fucked up man', and another as 'a cunning fuck'.
9. Hugh Braun, *Parish Churches: their Architectural Development in England* (1970).
10. *Introduction to the Method of Leonardo da Vinci* (1895).
11. See the edition of that essay, with an introduction by Ronald Duncan, 1973.
12. Fosco Maraini, *Meeting with Japan* (1959).

Index

241